D1431918

1/6/49 ℓ

3.83

DATE DUE

Sept '74	JUL 1 8 1986
OCT 15 71	OCT 1 0 1986
	NOV 7 1988
DEC 10 '71	DEC 1 4 1992
MAR 25 '74	
NOV 4 74	
MAY 19 75	
MAY 19 '75	
SEP 06	
MAR 2 4 1980	
MAY 1 8 1981	
MAY 1 8 1981	
DEC 1 3 1982	
FEB 1 8 1985	
APR 2 9 1985	
OCT 12 198	
FEB 0 1 1988	

EPHESIAN STUDIES

LESSONS IN
FAITH AND WALK

H. C. G. MOULE, D.D.

LONDON
PICKERING & INGLIS LTD.

Pickering & Inglis Ltd.

29 Ludgate Hill, London, E.C.4
229 Bothwell Street, Glasgow, C.2
59 Cross Street, Manchester, 2
105 Bold Street, Liverpool, 1
95 St. Mary Street, Cardiff
56 Grainger Street, Newcastle upon Tyne
29 George IV Bridge, Edinburgh, 1
Home Evangel, 418 Church Street, Toronto, 2

FIFTH IMPRESSION

OF THE SECOND EDITION

Made and Printed in Great Britain

PREFACE

THE present Volume completes a series of expository "Studies" upon the Epistles of St Paul known as the Epistles of the First Roman Imprisonment. As in dealing with the Epistles to Philippi, Colossæ, and Philemon, so with this to Ephesus, or more properly (as we shall see) to Asia, the author has sought, as his one aim, to exhibit something of the treasures of "edification, exhortation, and comfort," lodged for us by the Inspiring Master in the wonderful work of the inspired Servant. To this everything else has been subsidiary, alike the brief historical and critical introduction and the occasional grammatical discussions. The highest ambition of the interpreter has been to bring the reader into closer contact with the "Celestial Letter" itself, and with the mind and message of GOD in it.

May His mercy be pleased to make some use of the work for His ends in His Church.

CONTENTS

CHAPTER I

PAGE

INTRODUCTORY - - - - - - - 3

CHAPTER II

GREETING, AND PRAISE FOR DIVINE SALVATION (EPH. i. 1-14) - 23

CHAPTER III

THE APOSTLE'S PRAYER (EPH. i. 15-23) - - - - 43

CHAPTER IV

THE SALVATION OF THE EPHESIANS (EPH. ii. 1-10) - - - 65

CHAPTER V

ONCE REMOTE, NOW MADE NIGH (EPH. ii. 11-22) - - - 85

CHAPTER VI

A DIGRESSION: THE GOSPEL, AND ITS WORLD-WIDE SCOPE (EPH. iii.
1-13) - - - - - - - - - 105

vii.

CONTENTS

CHAPTER VII

PAGE

PRAYER FOR THE INDWELLING AND THE FULNESS (EPH. iii. 14-21) - 125

CHAPTER VIII

A RETROSPECT AND REVIEW - - - - - - 147

CHAPTER IX

HUMILITY, LOVE, HARMONY (EPH. iv. 1-7) - - - 169

CHAPTER X

DIVERSITY AND HARMONY OF GIFTS AND SERVICE (EPH. iv. 7-16) - 189

CHAPTER XI

THE OLD MAN AND THE NEW (EPH. iv. 17-24) - - - 209

CHAPTER XII

TOTAL ABSTINENCE FROM SINNING IN THE FORGIVEN LIFE (EPH. iv. 25-v. 2) - - - - - - - - 229

CHAPTER XIII

PAGE

THE WORKS OF DARKNESS AND THE FRUIT OF LIGHT (EPH. V. 3-14)   247

CHAPTER XIV

THE CHRISTIAN'S WATCHFULNESS, TEMPERANCE, AND SONG (EPH.V. 15-21)   -   -   -   -   -   -   -   -   265

CHAPTER XV

THE CHRISTIAN HOME; HUSBAND AND WIFE (EPH. V. 22)   -   -   281

CHAPTER XVI

THE CHRISTIAN HOME; PARENT AND CHILD, MASTER AND SERVANT (EPH. vi. 1-9)   -   -   -   -   -   -   -   299

CHAPTER XVII

THE CHRISTIAN HOME; CONCLUSION; THE SPIRITUAL CONFLICT (EPH. vi. 10-20)   -   -   -   -   -   -   317

CHAPTER XVIII

SALUTATION: BENEDICTION (EPH. vi. 21-24)   -   -   -   335

INTRODUCTORY

FAREWELL Pembroke Hall, of late myne owne Colledge, my cure and my charge. In thy Orchard (the wals, buts, and trees, if they could speake, would beare me witnes) I learned without booke almost all Paules epistles, yea, and I weene all the Canonicall epistles, saue only the Apocalyps. Of which study, although in time a great part did depart from me, yet the sweete smell thereof I trust I shall cary with me into heauen: for the profite thereof I thinke I haue felt in all my lyfe tyme euer after.

NICHOLAS RIDLEY, *Bishop and Martyr*, 1555.

CHAPTER I

O N a spring day of mingled shower and
sunshine, March 5th, 1897, I stepped for
the first time on the shore of Asia. Landing
at Smyrna, we travelled by rail, a large company,
from the port through a fine and fertile country,
to a roadside station bearing the name Aya
Salouk. At this place we left the train, and for
some hours traversed the neighbouring hills and
fields, making our way from fragment to fragment
of a vast scene of ruins. Here was a Byzantine
church, there a track, scarcely to be called a road,
bordered with Greek sarcophagi. On the western
side of a commanding hill in the midst of the
region was the grass-grown hollow of a Greek
theatre, the steps of the seats still traceable under
the vegetation, the structures of the stage a
confused mass of ruin. Sitting there a little
while alone, I looked over the landscape at my
feet as it stretched towards the Gulf of Smyrna

3

and the westering sun. A small river shone with its broken silver reaches along the middle of the scene, and noble hills bounded the broad vista, right and left; those on the right, northward, lying at a considerable distance. Not very far off upon the plain in that direction was visible, as I moved a little from the nook where I sat, a wide hollow in the general level, a sort of small sunken field, overgrown with thorn-bushes, and heaped with the confused wreckage of walls, columns, and steps. A few birds were singing near me; "the breezy whispers of the hill" were heard in tune with them; now and then a fellow-traveller's voice at a little distance was audible; otherwise the scene was one of beautiful but pathetic silence and repose, the quiet of a vast cemetery of the ancient days.

It was all that remains of Ephesus. Aya Salouk is *Hagios Theologos*, the Holy Divine, St John. The place where I sat was once the Theatre where for two long hours that dense throng stood shouting, "Great is Artemis of the Ephesians." And yonder hollow field, with its thorns and its stones, what is it? It is the site, determined at last, of the great Temple of Artemis herself, "the Ephesian Miracle," the world's wonder. where stood the adored image, grotesque and barbaric, of the prolific Nature-Power, and along with it the *Diopetes*, "the Thing fallen from Zeus," from Jupiter; whatever it was, meteoric stone or not. There "all Asia and the world" were wont to worship.

Many and heart-moving were the memories which arose during that walk, during that quiet session in the *cavea* of the Theatre. But the one commanding and inspiring memory was St Paul. Here was his well-known Ephesus. Here for the space of three complete years—a unique length of stationary work for him—he had lived and laboured, not as the apostolic missionary only but as the apostolic pastor. Here he had taken that critical and momentous step, the "separation" of the disciples from the Synagogue to a distinct place of teaching and no doubt of worship, "the school of one Tyrannus," the lecture-hall, we may suppose, of a friendly professor in what we may call the Ephesian University. Here he had laboured, watched, and wept, for both the community and individuals. Here he had met and influenced visitors from every part of the Asian Province, till his power for Christ was felt in every district, yes, even in the remote valley of the river Lycus, from which Laodicean, Hieropolitan, and Colossian citizens, finding their

way to the capital, had been found by Paul's
Lord and won to Him.   Here he had built up
the Church till its presbyters were a large group,
men of the Holy Spirit, and devotedly attached
to himself as father and leader (Acts xx.).
Yonder, where the sea shines under the declining
sun, he had, on a memorable occasion, summoned
them to meet him at Miletus, and they had
obeyed, travelling probably down the great ship-
canal which then connected the spacious inland
haven of the city with the distant coast.   And
in later years it was to this Ephesus that the
Missionary addressed, from Rome, the wonderful
Letter which we are about to study.

There I sat in 1897, with the Epistle to the
Ephesians in my hand.   That Epistle was written
not improbably in 63, eighteen hundred and thirty-
four years before.   Yet it was new that day; a
" fallen leaf that kept its green," its immortal
green ; aye, and not fallen either ; for its true
Author is not dead, though His servant who
wrote the Letter for Him sleepeth.   HE, and
therefore His Word, " liveth and abideth for
ever."

Solemn and inspiring is the contrast, in a case
like that of Ephesus, between the total decay of
the place and the everlasting youth and newness

of the Scripture. It has an indescribable pathos, and a heart-searching warning, from one point of view ; but it is full from another of " everlasting comfort, and good hope through grace."

So we approach the Epistle to the Ephesians, for a series of spiritual " Studies." The word " Studies" I half deprecate while I use it ; it may so easily seem to mean something quite other than what is offered here. It may suggest original research, critical discussion, minute en- quiry. As a fact I pretend only to provide the reader with a careful paraphrase or running ren- dering of the Epistle, accompanied with a simple development of its main spiritual and practical lessons. But after all I will not apologize for the word " Studies" in such a connexion. The purely spiritual use of the Holy Scriptures, if it is what it should be, calls as truly as any critical handling does for care, for reverent atten- tion, for the watchful while devout use of reason ; we may use the word " Study" for an attempt to read the Bible thus.

As we take up this wonderful writing, let us pause for a few moments to reflect upon the fact that it *is* an Epistle, a Letter. Has the reader ever appreciated the significance, the value, of the

2

fact that so large a mass of the New Testament is in Letter form? I cannot forbear quoting on this subject. Its importance is well presented in that masterly book, Canon T. D. Bernard's Bampton Lectures, *The Progress of Doctrine in the New Testament*; a full extract will prove none too long. The passage is introduced by an enquiry into the place and function of the apostolic Epistles ("the Apostle," as the Fathers often call them collectively) in the plan of Revelation. Attention is drawn to the evidence given by our Lord's words, and by the nature of the case, to the divine *intention* that the Apostles should develope and complete the personal teaching of their Master; were it otherwise we should (provably) have to face the riddle of a delivery of doctrine by Christ which assumed, which promised, a sequel and completion, but never received it. Accordingly we are right to read the Epistles with the same reverent confidence which we bring to the Gospels and their Discourses; they are equally, and with a profound purpose, the message of the King.

Canon Bernard now proceeds[1]:

"The Lord recognized this necessity He met it by the living voice of His Apostles; and

---

[1] Lect. vi., p. 135, ed. 1873.

their Epistles remain as the permanent record of this part of their work. They are the voice of the Spirit, speaking within the Church to those who are themselves within it, certifying to them the true interpretations and applications of the principles of thought and life which as believers in Jesus they have received. . . . The *form* in which this teaching is given to us is very significant. 'The epistolary form,' says Bengel, 'is a pre-eminence of the Scriptures of the New Testament as compared with those of the Old.' It is a suggestive remark, reminding us of that open communication and equal participation of revealed truth which is the prerogative of the later above the former dispensation; indicating too that the teacher and the taught are placed on one common level in the fellowship of truth. The Prophets delivered *oracles to the people*, but the Apostles wrote *letters to the brethren*, letters characterised by all that fulness of unreserved explanation, and that play of various feeling, which are proper to that form of intercourse. It is in its nature a more familiar communication between those who are, or should be, equals. That character may less obviously force upon us the sense, that the light which is thrown on all subjects is that of a divine inspiration; but this is only the natural effect of the greater fulness of that light; for so the moonbeams fix the eye upon themselves, as they burst through the rifts of rolling clouds, catching the edges of objects, and falling on patches of the landscape; while under the settled brightness of the genial and universal day, it is not so much the light that we think of as the varied scene which it shews.

" But the fact that the teaching of the Apostles is represented by their *letters*, is a peculiarity, not only in comparison with the teaching of the Prophets, but with ancient teaching in general, which is perpetuated either in regular treatises or conversations preserved in writing. The form adopted in the New Testament combines the advantages of the treatise and the conversation. The letter may treat important subjects with accuracy and fulness, but it will do so in immediate connection with actual life. It is written to meet an occasion. It is addressed to particular states of mind. It breathes the heart of the writer. In these respects it suits well with a period of instruction in which the Word of God is to be given to men, not so much in the way of information as in the way ot *education*; or in other words, in which the truth is to be

delivered, not abstractedly, but with a close relation to the condition of mind of its recipients.

"Thus it is delivered in the Epistles. Christ
has been received ; Christian life has been
commenced ; Christian communities have been
formed ; and men's minds have been at work
on the great principles which they have embraced. Some of these principles in one place,
and others of them in another, have been im-
perfectly grasped, or positively perverted, or
practically misapplied, so as to call for explanation or correction ; or else they have been both
apprehended and applied so worthily, that the
teacher . . . feels able to open out the mysteries
of God. . . . These conditions of mind were not
individual accidents. Rome, Corinth, Galatia,
Ephesus, supplied examples of different tendencies of the human mind in connection with the
principles of the Gospel—tendencies which would
ever recur, and on which it was requisite for the
future guidance of the Church that the Word of
God should pronounce. It did pronounce in the
most effectual way, by those letters which are
addressed by the commissioners of Christ, not to
possible but to actual cases, with that largeness
of view which belongs to spectators at a certain
distance from the scene, and with that closeness

of application which personal acquaintance dictates
and personal affection inspires."

A little below, Canon Bernard speaks of the
method of apostolic teaching, as in perfect harmony with this its *form*. "It is a method of
companionship rather than of dictation.   The
writer does not announce a series of revelations,
or arrest the enquiries which he encounters in
men's hearts by the unanswerable formula, ' Thus
saith the Lord.' He . . . utters his own convictions, he pours forth his own experience, he
appeals to others to 'judge what he says,' and
commends his words 'to their conscience in the
sight of God.' He confutes by argument rather
than by authority. . . . Such a method necessarily
creates a multitude of occasions for hesitation or
objection; and it has been proposed to meet
these difficulties by the principle that we are
bound to accept the conclusions as matters of
revelation, but not to assent to the validity of
the arguments or the applicability of the quotations. The more we enter into the spirit of the
particular passages which have been thought to
require that qualification, the more we feel that
it can only have seemed necessary, from a want
of real and deep harmony with the mind of
Scripture."

The extract is long; my temptation was to make it longer, so valuable is the whole context. What has been quoted will be felt, I think, to be altogether to the point as we address ourselves to the study not only of an Epistle but of this Epistle; so rich in revelations of the very *arcana* of the Gospel, yet conveying them in a form so entirely full of the personality and sympathies of the writer, and with such close and tender application to the realities of human life.

But let us actually take up the Epistle.

It is not my business here to conduct the reader at length through the question of its *genuineness and authenticity*. It will be enough to remind ourselves of a few outstanding facts in this connexion. We note that the early external evidence to the Pauline authorship is abundant and absolutely unanimous. Irenæus, the learned and careful theologian of the second century, expressly and repeatedly cites the Epistle, and as St Paul's. In the patristic literature as a whole, perhaps no book of the New Testament is more largely quoted. If the external evidence is inadequate, then we certainly have no adequate evidence that Virgil wrote the Georgics, or Horace the

Odes, or Augustine the Confessions. And to this let us confidently add the internal evidence. " Ephesians," says the late Dr Hort, a severely critical student of such a problem, "bears the impress of St Paul's wonderful mind." " No one but St Paul *could* have been the writer," says the late Dean Howson, a man who, if any man of our time, had made himself personally acquainted with St Paul. His words will bear inspection, bold as they are. For what is the problem to be solved, supposing St Paul not to be author? It is, how to find room within the required limits for another personality strong and illuminated enough to produce the Epistle, and at the same time low enough in moral perception to be willing to pass it off as St Paul's. It was written, it was reverenced as Scripture, long before Irenæus wrote; this leaves no broad margin for the supposed date of the " great Unknown." And it sounds the depths and climbs without an effort the heights of Christian idea; the " Unknown " was " great " indeed, great in thought, great in spiritual insight. And it not only bears the name Paul in its first sentence; it elaborately interweaves his life and his affections with its whole texture; it means, beyond a doubt, to pass for his. The human heart protests against the theory that fabrication, personation, in such a context, is credible for a moment.

Renan may presume to call the Epistle *une épître banale*, a third-rate composition.[1] The criticism, read in the light first of the Epistle itself, then of the verdict of all Christendom, can only convict the subtle literary critic of a spiritual paralysis which fatally affects even literary insight where the theme is spiritual.

A greater than Renan, Samuel Taylor Coleridge, subtlest of critics, and at the same time both philosopher and Christian, in a single brief sentence pronounces the Epistle to be "one of the divinest compositions of man."[2] A true testimony, yet after all how inadequate! "A divine composition of man" is a phrase perfectly justifiable in theory, as used of a book of Scripture. Yet it rings somewhat out of tune; for the words might be used to describe a work of sanctified genius which yet made no pretence to be an oracle of God; and if there is a writing which implicitly claims to be that or nothing, it is the Epistle to the Ephesians. But Coleridge meant the phrase soundly, and we may take it

---

[1] *Saint Paul*, p. xviii.
[2] *Table Talk*, p. 82, ed. 1852.

so, as one witness among many to that supreme
quality in the Epistle which is an evidence to
its origin weightier than even all the quotations
of the Fathers. We have in it the *ipsissima
verba* of the Chosen Vessel. We receive it,
delivered at our doors, as a Letter about
Christ's glory from the man whom He expressly
moulded, conquered and commissioned, to tell
us of Himself and His salvation.

Another question, altogether lower in its importance, but of peculiar interest, attaches to
the Epistle. Is it, after all, *an Epistle to the
Ephesians*? The reader of only the Authorized
Version will be surprised by the question. Is
not the Epistle entitled, *To the Ephesians*?
Does not the first sentence direct it *to the
saints which are at Ephesus*? It is so; but
the margin of the Revised Version informs us
that in that first sentence "some very ancient
authorities omit *at Ephesus*." The "authorities"
referred to are, among manuscripts, three important copies, the Vatican, the Sinaitic, and
another.[1] But these "authorities," considerable
as they are, take us up no further, at furthest,
than early in the fourth century, and their
weight could not possibly of itself counteract

---

[1] The "cursive" copy known as "67 of St Paul."

that of the whole catalogue of other ancient transcripts. What gives it an importance not its own is that certain of the Fathers, and among them Tertullian, whose activity began in the second century, give clear indications that they were aware of a problem attaching to these words. It is certain that Origen in the third century, and Basil in the fourth, and Epiphanius and Jerome in the fourth and fifth, knew of many copies of the Epistle, (Basil calls them "the older copies,") in which the first verse ran, "to the saints *which are*, and to the faithful in Christ Jesus." Origen, characteristically, sees a mystery in the phrase, and thinks that the Apostle is intimating the vital connexion of believers with the I AM; joined to Him, they become "those that ARE."

Archbishop Ussher in the seventeenth century, and Bishop Lightfoot in our own, have offered a solution of this phenomenon which appears to combine all the facts, or almost all. Ussher[1] suggested that the Epistle was indeed "to the Ephesians," but that it was not intended for them alone. "In some ancient copies," he writes, "this Epistle was addressed in general terms, . . . 'To the saints who are . . . and

[1] *Annales N. Testamenti*, under the year of the world 4068

to the faithful in Christ Jesus.' As if the letter
had been sent first to Ephesus, as the chief
metropolis of Asia; to be transmitted thence
to the other Churches of the same province,
the name of each being inserted in its instance."[1]

Lightfoot[2] adopts this conjecture of Ussher's,
only emphasizing the probability that many
copies would carry in their address the words
"at Ephesus,"[3] and that in copies made from
specimens where a blank was left after the word
"are," that blank would easily disappear.

If I may quote words of my own,[4] in which
a summing up of the case has been attempted:
"Something more than I find in Bishop Lightfoot's remarks seems to be needed to account for
the practically universal tradition of the *Ephesian
destination* of the Epistle. May not this be
somewhat as follows? St Paul did indeed mean
the Epistle for Asia ultimately. But the very
close connexion[5] between Ephesus and the

---

[1] I may be permitted to refer to my edition of Ephesians
(*Cambridge Bible*), and to my *Grace and Truth*, pp. 26-33.

[2] See his *Biblical Essays*, § x.

[3] May we not think it very likely that the original document
itself, dictated by St Paul, would do so? We may add that
copies for the public use of the Church would be more likely to
be taken from the *metropolitan* specimens than from others.

[4] *Grace and Truth*, p. 32.

[5] It was as a fact singularly close

Province led him to address it in the first instance to Ephesus. But it was to Ephesus not as the mission station but as the provincial capital; the trustee for the outlying missions. For them transcripts would of course be made, at Ephesus; and in many of these, if not all, the ἐν Ἐφέσῳ would be omitted, perhaps without any substitute; the blank might be supplied at each place tacitly."

It is obvious to remark, in support of Ussher's theory, that the Epistle is singularly devoid of allusions to persons and circumstances in the place to which it is addressed; and this although Ephesus had been, as we have already remembered, the scene of a work, more perhaps than any other in St Paul's life, pastoral and particular.

If we may return for a moment to our point of view on the ruined steps of the Ephesian Theatre, and open the Epistle there once more, we must not only scan the Ephesian plain to call up memories of the first readers of the Epistle; we must climb behind the *cavea* to the top of Mount Prion, and survey the vast horizon, even to the snowy top of the Phrygian Olympus, and think of the copies which were sped by faithful hands to Smyrna, to Sardis, to Philadelphia, to Pergamus, to Thyatira, and, not least, to Laodicea, the queen of the valley of the Lycus, thence to be sent on to Hierapolis and to old Colossæ in its glen.[1]

But now, it comes even unto us. That blank space shall be filled in by us with the name nearest to ourselves ; the land, the church, the town, the home, which to us makes life to be what it is. And the message sent, from the Roman prison immediately, from the heaven of heavens ultimately, shall be read as by those who know that what it says of Christ, of the Church, of grace, of holiness, of glory, is addressed *to us* by Paul, and countersigned *to us* by our Lord Jesus Christ.

---

[1] See Col. iv. 16. It is more than probable that " the letter from Laodicea " means, the copy of " Ephesians " sent there, to be passed on to the minor stations of the district.

GREETING, AND PRAISE FOR DIVINE SALVATION

DARK with excess of bright Thy skirts appear,
Yet dazzle heaven, that brightest Seraphim
Approach not, but with both wings veil their eyes.

MILTON

CHAPTER II

GREETING, AND PRAISE FOR DIVINE SALVATION

EPHESIANS i. 1-14

THE Epistle has been completed in the lodging of St Paul at Rome ; it has been carried safely over sea and land, till it has travelled up from the Ægæan shore, by the long ship-canal, and found its way to Ephesian hands.

We recollect that it has travelled not alone. Two other apostolic messages go by the same bearers ; a letter to the outlying mission-church of Colossæ, on some special dangers just now present there and at Laodicea, and a shorter missive, a note rather than a letter, for an individual Colossian, Philemon ; it commends to him his slave Onesimus, once a runaway and perhaps a thief besides, now "begotten" to the new life

3   23

in the miracle of a true conversion, and returning at all costs to duty.

Our reasons for the assertion that these three memorable Letters were carried by the same hands and at the same time are as simple as interesting. The Epistles to the Ephesians and Colossians are near akin in respect of subject-matter; the most rapid inspection shews this. Closer examination tells us that the connexion extends to phraseology as well, in a degree which makes it quite certain morally that they not only passed through the same mind but passed through it and from it at about the same time. Let the reader take the two Epistles, and compare (as a few examples out of many) the following passages: Eph. i. 22 with Col. i. 18; Eph. iv. 16 with Col. ii. 19; Eph. ii. 1 with Col. ii. 13; Eph. i. 7 with Col. i. 14; Eph. iv. 22-24 with Col. iii. 9, 10; Eph. v. 16 with Col. iv. 5; Eph. v. 19 with Col. iii. 16. On a more extended scale, let him compare the *domestic* paragraphs of the two Epistles, Eph. v. 22 to vi. 9 with Col. iii. 18 to iv. 1. Then let him note that the one friend or follower named by St Paul in Ephesians is Tychicus (vi. 21), and that this name appears also in Colossians (iv. 7), in a sentence of close verbal

similarity. Taking both Epistles as the genuine
utterances of St Paul, we may say with absolute
confidence that they belong to the same moment
of his ministry, and were meant for recipients
intimately connected with one another. Then
we turn to the letter to Philemon, and we find
abundant evidence for a close relation between
it and the letter to the Colossians. Philemon
indeed is not called a Colossian, nor does his
name occur in the Colossian Epistle. But
Onesimus (the name of his slave) is "one of
the Colossians" (iv. 9). And Archippus, who
in the private letter is named in close connexion
with Philemon (ver. 2), receives in Colossians
(for who can doubt the identity of the person,
looking at the whole context?) a solemn charge
(iv. 17). And when St Paul enumerates the other
friends around him as he dictates, and sends
their greetings, we find the same names in both
Epistles; Epaphras, Aristarchus, Marcus, Lucas,
Demas; only one such name, "Jesus, who is
called Justus" (Col. iv. 11), fails to occur in
the two documents alike. We are left without
a reasonable doubt; the letters to Philemon
and to the Colossians were sent together, and
together accompanied that which we know as
the Epistle to the Ephesians.

"To the Ephesians," we may be tolerably sure, it was in the first instance delivered, whatever its after-destination may have been.[1] To them first it would be read aloud; see Col. iv. 16 for such a "reading in the church," in the assembly of the disciples. Perhaps in the "school of Tyrannus," perhaps in some large private room furnished by a leading disciple, the reader gave to the listening throng of saints, sentence by sentence, uttered for that first time in ears representing universal Christendom, this glorious oracle of God through His chosen Vessel. Can we not almost see the scene, and catch the accent and the cadence, and watch the audience—perhaps the very large audience— with their eager faces, and many a look and perhaps many an exclamation of wonder and worship, as that scroll is slowly opened and, column by column, poured into their ears and hearts?

Let us take our seat beside them, for we are of the same family, and let us listen too, as those who have never heard before.

Ver. 1. **Paul, apostle of Christ Jesus,[2] envoy of Him who**

---

[1] See above, p. 17.

[2] This is the best attested order here, not "Jesus Christ." It is peculiar to St Paul.

is first the Hope of Israel and then of the world, **through
God's will,** commissioned by nothing less than His fiat,
to the holy ones who live at **Ephesus and faithful in Christ
Jesus;** the men and women separated from sin to God
(ἁγίοις) and living the life of saving reliance (πιστοῖς) in
their union with (ἐν) His Son ; persons thus wonderfully
enabled for that twofold life which is lived " in Ephesus,"
Ver. 2. externally, " in Christ Jesus," spiritually. **Grace
to you and peace,** free and benignant divine favour, and
its fair resultants of reconciliation with the Holy One
and inward rest through His presence in the heart, **from
God our Father and from the Lord Jesus Christ.** For
such is Jesus Christ, that though He was known,
amply *within living memory*, as dwelling with men in
Palestinian villages and towns, spending human life and
dying human death in uttermost literal experience, **yet,
as** truly as the Eternal Father, He, " this same Jesus,"
is the Giver of spiritual gifts to every recipient soul
of man.

Such **is** the Salutation ; and perhaps the
Reader pauses for a moment in the assembly.
Now for the message:

Ver. 3. Blessed, praised with worshipping love, be the
God and Father of our Lord Jesus Christ; HE " who
inhabiteth eternity," " dwelling in the light unapproach-
able," unknown and unknowable in His " perfection,"
but knowable, and known, and near, and dear, in *this*
respect, that our risen Lord called Him, in human

hearing (John xx. 17), "My Father and your Father, My God and your God"[1]; He who blessed us (for *the Blessed* loves *to bless*, with an act of blessing "which divinely effects the good it speaks") in, with a purpose expressed in, all spiritual benediction; spiritual, as shed from Him who "is Spirit" (John iv. 2) upon the inmost spirit of His creatures, for their spiritual birth, and life, and glory; in the celestial regions, in Christ. Yes, He blessed us as He sate there, upon the throne of love, viewing us sinners as also there, above all earthly place, before all human time; for we were represented there already "in" our blessed Head, in foreseen union with Him. Wonderful benediction! but it is only in correspondence and harmony with its occasion, which itself was an act of immeasurable and uncaused love.

Ver. 4. For it took place according as He chose us out, from fallen humanity, in Him, in Christ; chose us, selected us, His followers, His company who believe and love; chose us "not according to our works"; for reasons infinitely good, but hidden wholly in Himself; before the world's foundation, aye, before this universe in its most aboriginal beginning began to be. So sovereign, so sublime, so immeasurably antecedent to ourselves, was that decree for our salvation; so ante-mundane in date, so supra-mundane in sphere and scope. And what was to be its issue? That we should be holy and blameless before His face in love; given,

---

[1] Note that this infinitely precious designation of Him occurs also verbatim 2 Cor. i. 3, 1 Pet. i. 3.

by His love, a perfect "standing" in His presence, welcomed there in faultless title as His very own.[1]

This "choosing out" is to be described, from another side, as a destination beforehand; a definite divine intention of privilege and blessing antecedent to the very being of its objects. For He chose us out, Ver. 5. marking us out beforehand (προορίσας), writing down as it were our names for that happy future,[2] to an adoption, an instatement into the position of sons (υἱοθεσία), through Jesus Christ, unto Himself; for it is "through" the Son that we reach sonship, and so come to be related "unto" the Father in that wonderful

---

[1] I venture, though not without hesitation, to recommend this interpretation of the words εἶναι . . . ἐν ἀγάπῃ. It is obviously possible to explain them not of the *position* but rather of the *condition* of the saints, as that condition will be finally perfected by grace. But the context seems to plead rather for the other reference; the emphasis of the context is upon our welcome to all the love of the Father just because of our most mercifully given *union with the Son*. See further, note here in the *Cambridge Bible*.

[2] The Latin versions of the New Testament give the words *prædestinare*, *prædestinatio*, for προορίζειν, προόρισις. By an accident of language, "destiny" (*destinatio*) has come to be connected in thought with blind, impersonal, mechanical *fate*. And nothing can be further than that idea from the προόρισις of infinite love and wisdom (quite as much as of infinite power). Hence, for ordinary purposes, the word *predestination* is to be used sparingly, and with explanation; "foreordain," "mark out beforehand," are better phrases for practical use. But this is not to sweep away the mystery of the thing; it is only to remind us that the mystery, "dark with excess of bright," a sovereign "choosing," "ordaining," and "blessing," of us unworthy sinners, in Christ, is in the hands of personal and infinitely trustworthy Love.

position ; His very own, to belong to Him, to know Him, to serve Him, " to glorify Him, and to enjoy Him fully for ever."

And how came all this to be? What are we that thus, in an eternity above all time, we were seen, and loved, and blessed, after this celestial sort? " Even so, Father, for so it seemed good in Thy sight." It was according to, conditioned and caused by, the good pleasure, the royal and benignant resolve, of His will— that ultimate mystery and glory, that secret of good behind all good, the Will of God. And so its issue was and is to be good indeed, with a good unattainable

Ver. 6. by any lower cause ; unto the praise of the glory of His grace; so that He may receive from His adoring creatures the " praise " due to His " glory," His own manifested CHARACTER, manifested in this form of entrancing beauty, His " grace." It is that grace in regard to which [1] He accepted us in His (τῷ) Beloved One [2]; making us one with Him, as limb is one with head, as bride with bridegroom, and so giving us real part and lot in Christ's own welcome to the Father's heart.

Thrice blessed by us be the Εὐλογητός, the " Blessed," who thus loved, and chose, and welcomed.   Thrice

---

[1] Ἧς stands by " attraction " for ἥν.   See again below, ver. 8.

[2] Read, ἧς ἐχαρίτωσεν ἡμᾶς, κ.τ.λ.   I venture to retain the A.V. rendering for ἐχαρίτωσεν.   It is indeed rather a paraphrase than a rendering, but the context seems to justify it.   " Made us recipients of grace " would properly render ἐχαρίτωσεν ἡμᾶς.   But the context tends to suggest the " grace " specially of *acceptance*; God's love expressing itself specially in a paternal *welcome*.

blessed be the Ἠγαπημένος, the "Beloved," who gave Himself in that deep eternity to be not only the Deliverer of us sinners, but our Head, articulating us into Himself, identifying Himself with us for ever.

And now we are not to forget that by the Blessed Father and the Beloved Son this boundless gift given to us was not wrought by a *mere* edict, however omnipotent. It was a matter not of power only, nor even only of love, but of law too; it must harmonize the holiness of Him who "is consuming fire" with the tenderness of the same God, who "is love." So now the majestic sentences, like Him of whom they speak, "come down from heaven," and take us from the Throne to the mortal Cross. There was no other way, no easier way, to make actual the eternal blessing, uttered "before the world's foundation." Were we to be justified, and sanctified, and glorified? Then must the Father, constrained by His own holiness, "not spare His own Son, but deliver Him over for us all" (Rom. viii. 32). And the Son, under the same constraint, infinitely free of all other compulsion, but compelled by the fact that love, to be divine, must be holy, must not spare Himself—"becoming obedient, even to the length of death" (Phil. ii. 8). So, in Him

Ver. 7. we have our (τήν) redemption; we possess (ἔχομεν) in happy certainty our position as His rescued ones, rescued by His ransom paid for us; through His blood, for that was the price; "without blood-shedding, no remission" (Heb. ix. 22); without inflicted death, no peace with broken law. "Remission" it was indeed;

the remission, the forgiveness, the wonderful amnesty, of our trespasses; according to, in the plan and on the immense scale of, the wealth of His grace, "not grudgingly," but with a "cheerful giving" correspondent to the boundless resource of His free favour.

Did the Father so purpose and so provide? He also took merciful care in due time to reveal. This Ver. 8. grace, this loving favour He made overflow (ἐπερίσσευσεν) to us, from the deep well of His love, in all wisdom and intelligence; that is, He let it shew itself "in" our being by Him enabled to understand His purpose, to feel His heart of mercy, to approve and to concur with His redeeming plan, as men "made wise unto salvation." He "made His Ver. 9. grace overflow" thus, when He made known (γνωρίσας) to us, in His Son, and in the Gospel of His Son, the secret (μυστήριον) of His will; that bright secret, meant not for the darkness but the light, the hidden treasure which is in fact Jesus Christ; according to, true to the plan of, His good pleasure, His gracious resolve, which He proposed to Himself in Him (ἐν αὐτῷ), that is to say, in His Son. For the Son was its place and sphere; it moved and worked "in" the Son; it was to take effect wholly through Him, and to do so by bringing us into union with Him. Aye, and the whole process has regard to a consummation which will indeed take effect "in" Him. It looks forward, Ver. 10. with a view to the stewardship of the fulness of the seasons. The Son is the great "Steward" of the Father's house; the keys of all its life and history

are in His hands.   And His "management" will at
length conduct the whole operation to a goal, placed
and dated by God's own prescient wisdom.   Then all
the "seasons" of the story of redemption will attain
their "fulness," will be fulfilled, accomplished, so that
the actual result shall correspond to the divine ideal.

What is that ideal?   It is the glorification of Christ
as the Head of all things; Centre, Ruler, Life, of
whatsoever He has blessed.   It is, **to sum up all things
in Christ as Head** (ἀνακεφαλαιώσασθαι . . εἰς Χριστόν),
the things in[1] **the heavens and the things on the earth**;
the angelic host above, (which also, as well as we, has
in some unknown way felt His gracious power,) and
us mortals here below, "redeemed from the earth";
chosen angels and chosen men; glorious concentric
Ver. 11.   circles around Him the vital Sun.[2]   **In whom
we were as a fact** (καί) **taken into the inheritance,** so as
to become "the Lord's portion" (Deut. xxxii. 9), not
only in purpose but in act; **foreordained** as we were,
to this happy position, **according to the purpose of Him
who is working everything**[3] **in us according to the counsel**

---

[1] Perhaps read τὰ ἐπὶ τοῖς οὐρανοῖς, lit. "*on* the heavens"; the
heavens regarded as a country "on" which walk the glorified.
Cp. the adjective ἐπουράνιος.

[2] It will be seen that I so far limit the τὰ πάντα as to refer
the words not to existence in its universality but to the "things"
which the context suggests.   In that light, the reference is not,
surely, to the universe at large.   Meanwhile Col. i. gives a
notable intimation of the fact that the Son of God *is* the "Head"
also of the whole created Cosmos.

[3] Τὰ πάντα ἐνεργοῦντος : τὰ πάντα is the πάντα in question, the

of His will; the "counsel" which is directed full upon
Ver. 12. that wonderful object—upon our being to the
praise of His glory, our being so saved and so transfigured
as to win adoring admiration for His Character seen in
our redemption; us, who had hoped, who had trusted,
beforehand in His (τῷ) Christ. The "*beforehand*" has
regard to His Second Coming, when we "shall appear
with Him in glory." *Then*, finally and fully, we shall
be the occasion for "the praise of His glory." And we
shall be what then we shall be, as having "relied in
advance," by faith, not sight, upon His promises, as
yet unfulfilled in their ultimate splendour.

Now the message comes closer to the immediate listeners, the saints of Ephesus. Hitherto
the Apostle has spoken *generally* of the redeemed. "We," "us," "our," have been as
inclusive as possible. Now the whole facts of
grace and glory are applied to the particular
instance:

Ver. 13. In whom, in Christ the Head, "in" Him by
covenant inclusion and by vital cohesion, you also are,[1]

---

all-things *of salvation*. Ἐνεργεῖν *suggests* by its form the rendering given above, the "inward" working of God in the soul
and in the Church. But usage forbids us to press this without
reserve.

[1] Ἐν ᾧ καὶ ὑμεῖς: the above rendering is grammatically safe,
and simplifies an otherwise complex construction. Still, in view
of St Paul's often complicated style (complicated by a boundless
fulness of matter) it *may* be well to explain the Greek as if he

having found entrance into Him on hearing (ἀκούσαντες) the message of the truth, the Good News of your salvation; in whom also, on believing, you were sealed with the Spirit of the Promise, the Holy One; the gifts and power of the Paraclete were made yours at once on your union with the Christ of God,[1] and their presence and their fruit "sealed" you as genuine subjects of salvation, and also as the actually purchased property of your Lord.

Ver. 14. Thanks be to God for that sealing Gift; for it (ὅ) is an earnest, an *arrhâbôn*,[2] a part-payment given as promise of the whole, a pledge, of our inheritance, our coming "weight of glory," pending (εἰς) the redemption, the final emancipation from the last relics of evil, of the Acquisition, the purchased Property of God, even us His saved ones; to the praise of His glory.

We may well pause here for a little while. The golden passage forms so closely linked a chain that I knew not how to break its continuity by closing our "study" earlier. But this gold

---

had intended to write, simply, "In whom you too, believing, were sealed"; but had then conceived the thought expressed in the clauses ἀκούσαντες . . . σωτηρίας ὑμῶν, and woven this in as he went. The general import, however, is but little affected by the doubt.

[1] Those gracious gifts may indeed need the believer's constantly advancing *use*, and his growing discovery of what they are. But in covenant provision they are *his at once* "in Christ."

[2] To this day in Palestine the word *arraboon* is used of such payments, e.g. in the hire of a conveyance.

from the celestial mines weighs heavy, with the weight of mercies, graces, glories unspeakable. Reverently let us lay it down here, and gaze upon it as it lies, and give thanks in worshipping wonder.

A few links in that chain, radiant even above the rest, we will as it were touch and handle for a moment.

i. We note the splendid title of the recipients of the letter. They are, "the saints," the saints who live in Ephesus. The word "saint" shines starry bright with associations of heaven; habitually, for ages, it has been used in the Church to denote the glorified. But the usage of Scripture tends rather to attach it to the pilgrims of the Lord, not yet at home. They already, if His indeed, are "the holy ones," οἱ ἅγιοι, His votaries, His devotees, for so we may fairly explain the word. True, they may too often live below what, in Christ, they are. But let not this pull down the glorious word, as if it were a mere pale synonym for "member of a community called Christian." Let it rather lift up the bearer of the title, to recollect its glory, and, in Christ, to *live* it.

ii. Let us recollect with humblest reverence the wonderful words of the Epistle, that is to say, of the Heavenly Spirit, about the sovereignty of grace. " Blessed in the celestial regions in Christ"; "chosen out in Him before the universe was founded"; "foreordained to adoption"; such are some of the phrases in which the believer is reminded that behind all his believing, and all his receiving, lies this glowing mystery, the "everlasting love." It is the infinite Free-Will of God, (even more sacred than the free-will of man ;) a purpose and a plan older than the oceans and the skies. Who does not know the awfulness of the shadows that lie close to this glory—the dread questionings of the mind over the election of God? But these shadows are cast, as shadows always are, by light. And the purpose of the light is, not to cast shadows but to guide our steps. Do we indeed believe on the Son of God? Have we indeed been " sealed with the Spirit of the Promise"? Then let us leave absolutely to the Lord *the unknown* of the matter; we shall not be disappointed when He lets us know more about it, another day. But let us boldly grasp for our strength and joy *the known* of the matter; the sovereign grace that lies behind the sinner's repentance, faith, hope, and love ; the covenant, the purpose, the counsel, the WILL.

iii. Lastly, let us adore and rejoice, as we
contemplate the Trinity of Eternal Love coming
forth here "for us men and for our salvation"
in the threefold action of grace. Behold the
FATHER, "God and Father of our Lord Jesus
Christ." He is no half-adverse Power, needing
the persuasions of a more benignant Son to draw
Him over to the side of mercy. He is the
Fountain of the whole redeeming work; blessing,
choosing, accepting, working all things in the
line of His own benignant will. Behold the
SON, the Beloved One. He gives Himself in
the past Eternity to be already our all-sufficient
Representative, so that we were dealt with even
there and then "in Him." He gives Himself,
"on earth abased," to death, to sanguinary death,
to shed the streaming blood of sacrifice, that
we might have a redemption as secure as it is
merciful, a "forgiveness of sins" quite as holy
as it is divinely generous. He lives to be the
"Head" of His people; their Source of life,
their Secret of power, their unifying Centre;
and the day is coming when that Headship will
be seen as the centre of a whole Universe of
holy life. Look again, and behold the SPIRIT!

Behold Him dwell in all the saints,
And seal the heirs of heaven.

He comes, the Promise of the Father. Contact, in humblest faith, with Christ implies reception of the Spirit, the Lord, the Life-giver, the Sanctifier. And He is the Pledge of a " glory to be revealed in us," before whose brightness not only "the sufferings of this present time" but its experiences of grace will so fade in the comparison that it will be as if they had scarcely been at all. " The purchased possession " of our God will be so emancipated then into the eternal freedom that it will be as if its "redemption" had but just been achieved.

Great and wonderful are the promises. It is undertaken for believing sinners that here they shall be, in the Beloved One, the very "sons of God," walking and pleasing Him. It is undertaken for them that hereafter, when their Lord's time shall come, they shall "appear with Him in glory," such a glory that "it doth not yet appear what they shall be." "How can these things be?" The effect is great; but the CAUSE is greater.

> Of FATHER, SON, and SPIRIT we
>   Extol the threefold care,
> Whose love, whose merit, and whose power,
>   Unite to lift us there.

4

Tout vient de Dieu, et l'homme n'en a pas moins quelque chose a faire. C'est au nom de ceux qui croient que l'Apôtre rend grâces. C'est ceux qui croient qui sont prédestinés, qui sont élus, qui sont bénis, qui sont reçus en grâce, qui sont faits héritiers, qui sont scellés du Saint-Esprit, qui sont réservés pour la rédemption finale. Lecteur, avez-vous cru ? En êtes-vous bien sûr ?

ADOLPHE MONOD

THE APOSTLE'S PRAYER

DIEU est bon et Dieu est puissant, il veut et il peut : deux petits articles, qui renferment tout ce qui peut consoler une âme. Heureux qui les croit *réellement*.

ADOLPHE MONOD

CHAPTER III

ST PAUL has led us up to the heavens for the facts of eternal redemption. He has led us down again to Asia for the certainty of the possession of its blessings by the converts there. But even so his thought cannot rest. Nothing can satisfy him short of the assurance that those converts are fully " possessing their possessions " (Obad. 17). His soul goes up for them in warm thanksgiving, but also in prayer, strong and importunate, that they may know, with a supernatural insight, where they are and what they have.

It must be so, the Gospel being what it is. The life eternal is " to know the only true God, and Jesus Christ whom He hath sent "

(John xvii. 3). They who have it are indeed to
"rest and be thankful," in respect of the Rock
beneath their feet; they are to taste, and to
evidence, the deep repose born of the discovery
of the Summum Bonum itself. But they are to
be thankful *and never to rest* in respect of the
realization of what they have discovered. "He
who says *Enough*," writes Augustine somewhere,
"is already a lost man." If the Christian man
is indeed one who has caught a genuine glimpse
of "the glory of God in the face of Jesus Christ"
(2 Cor. iv. 6), how can he *not* be sure that he has
still before him indefinitely greater discoveries
there, "from glory to glory"? His root is
settled, and for ever; he will never find a substitute for the Cross. But his branches will
extend themselves, and for ever, in that place of
root and rest, to receive more and more the
living powers of the light and air around, and
to bring forth more fruit and yet more for the
heavenly Planter.

Ver. 15. **On this account,** because so great and wonderful is your redemption, so heavenly in its origin,
so divine in its possibilities, so full, so present, **I also,**
I as well as others who love you and pray for you,
on hearing, as I have done, (it was no doubt through
Epaphras of Colossæ,) **of the faith,** the reliance, prevalent

among you (καθ' ὑμᾶς), in the Lord Jesus, resting *in* Him
as anchor rests in ground,[1] and of the love [2] which you
shew towards all the saints, all your fellow-believers
that love which is the sweet fruit of faith the living

Ver. 16. root; am incessantly giving thanks on your
behalf, making mention of you [3] on occasion of (ἐπὶ τῶν,
at the times of) my prayers, naming you before the
throne of grace, individually or collectively; asking
that you may *know* more, because you *have* much,
and have already learnt to use your wealth so well.

In another moment, he will be telling them
what are the terms and special directions of his
petition. Let us prepare ourselves to listen the
better by recollecting how beautifully characteristic of him is this line of address. In seven
of his Epistles besides this he speaks to the

---

[1] For the construction cp. Mark i. 15, πιστεύετε ἐν τῷ εὐαγγελίῳ,
and Jer. xii. 6 (Septuagint), μὴ πιστεύσῃς ἐν αὐτοῖς.

[2] Some very important MSS. (A B ℵ*) omit the words τὴν
ἀγάπην, and thus refer πίστιν to "the saints" as well as to the
Lord. But the external evidence for retention is strong. *All
the chief ancient versions* give the words, and so do the uncial
MSS. D₂ G₂, and the immense majority of "cursive" mss. And
it is surely very unlikely that St Paul, who writes, to the Colossians
(i. 4), τὴν πίστιν ὑμῶν ἐν Χρ. Ἰησοῦ καὶ τὴν ἀγάπην τὴν εἰς πάντας τοὺς
ἁγίους, should in this Epistle, perhaps on the same day, have
varied that natural phrase for one so difficult (giving two senses
of πίστις in one clause) as this. An early mistake of transcription
is the probable cause of the various reading here.

[3] The word ὑμῶν is probably to be omitted, but we must supply
it mentally.

recipients first about his glad thanksgivings, and then about the prayers which, as it were, spring out of them. Writing to Rome (i. 8), he "thanks his God through Jesus Christ for them all, that their faith is spoken of throughout the whole world," and "makes mention of them without ceasing in his prayers." To the Corinthians (1 Cor. i. 4) he writes how he "thanks God always on their behalf for the grace of God which is given them in Christ Jesus," and then prays that they may grow in the grace of holy unity of spirit. He "thanks God upon every remembrance of" the Philippians (i. 3), "always in every prayer for them all making request with joy." For the Colossians (i. 3) he "gives thanks to God and the Father of our Lord Jesus Christ, praying always for them, that they may be filled with the knowledge of His will." To the Thessalonians, earliest recipients of his Epistles, he writes repeatedly of his thanksgivings: "We give thanks to God always for you all, making mention of you in our prayers" (1 Thess. i. 2); "We thank God for you without ceasing" (1 Thess. ii. 13); "We are bound to thank God always for you, because your faith groweth exceedingly, and the love of you all towards each other aboundeth; wherefore also we pray always

for you . . . that the Name of our Lord Jesus
Christ may be glorified in you and you in Him"
(2 Thess. i. 3, 11, 12); "We are bound to give
thanks always to God for you, brethren beloved
of the Lord, because God hath from the beginning
chosen you to salvation through sanctification of
the Spirit and belief of the truth" (2 Thess. ii. 13).
For Philemon (4, 6) he "thanks God, making
mention of him always in his prayers . . . that
the communication of his faith may become
effectual" as a witness for his Redeemer. To
his beloved Timothy, writing under the shadow
of the end, he blends thanks and yearning into
one pathetic thought (2 Tim. i. 3): "I thank
God . . . that without ceasing I have remembrance of thee in my prayers night and day,
greatly desiring to see thee."

Everywhere we find the deep sympathy which
rejoices and is grateful over the attained and
present blessing. Everywhere also appears that
holy insight which cannot rest without the spiritual
progress and full consistency of those who call
out the thanksgivings. The Prayers of St Paul
have been made the subject of extended spiritual
treatises. The study of them can never be complete without the study also of their connexion
with his Thanksgivings.

But now, how does his soul go up in prayer for the richly-blest recipients of this Letter? He prays that they may have supernatural light shed upon the gold of their supernatural wealth :

Ver. 17. That the God of our Lord Jesus Christ, His GOD, inasmuch as He, the Son, took the created Nature to Him, and became Son of Man,[1] the Father of the glory, Origin of all that is meant by heavenly and holy glory, all divine holiness, might, majesty, beauty ; above all, the Father of HIM who is the true Shechinah, "the Lord of Glory," crucified and risen ; may give you, as His promised Gift, the Spirit[2] of wisdom and unveiling, the Holy One who imparts new insight and lifts the veil higher and higher from the fair face of the eternal Love, in full knowledge (ἐν ἐπιγνώσει) of Him, of this ever-blessed Father, "whom to know is to live."[3] For philosophy comes to man with the message, *Know*

---

[1] So that He not only cried "Eli, Eli," upon the Cross, but on one memorable occasion, at Sychar (John iv. 22), called Himself a *worshipper* : "We know what *we worship*." Yet He receives worship addressed to Himself with all the calm majesty of the supreme King (John xx. 29).

[2] Lit. "a spirit," πνεῦμα, not τὸ πνεῦμα : and so the Revised Version. But I venture to retain the Authorized Version. In the case of great and well-known words, such as Θεός, Κύριος, the article is often omitted as unneeded for definition. So, if I read aright, it often is with πνεῦμα.

[3] *Quem nosse vivere* ; the ancient original (in a prayer of cent. v.) of the beautiful phrase in the Morning Collect of the English Church, "in knowledge of whom standeth (consisteth) our eternal life."

thyself; the Gospel meets him also with the far more glorious and fruitful watchword, *Know thy God*.[1] Yes,

Ver. 18. may He grant you this, granting you illumination of the eyes of your heart,[2] that is of all your inner powers, alike of affection, thought and will, so that on the whole "inner man" shall shine the smile of "the Father of Glory"; with a view to your knowing, with a deep and developed insight and experience, what is the hope of His calling, the eternal prospect opened up when He effectually calls man to union with Himself in Christ[3]; and what is the wealth of the glory of His

---

[1] I quote from Adolphe Monod, in his excellent Commentary on the Epistle. He says (referring to Pascal in a note), "La philosophie, prennant nécessairement l'homme pour centre, lui a dit : Connais-toi; mais la Parole inspirée, pouvant seule partir de Dieu, a seule aussi pu dire : Connais Dieu ; et cette connaissance renferme, avec l'unique connaissance salutaire de nous-mêmes et de notre misère, celle de l'unique remède capable de la réparer."

[2] Πεφωτισμένους τοὺς ὀφθαλμούς : lit. "the eyes illuminated."— Read καρδίας certainly.—"Heart" in Scripture "includes intelligence without excluding affections."

[3] Κλῆσις : the word in the Epistles probably refers not only to the general benignant invitation of the Gospel but to the voice of grace as it mercifully—not forces but—*decides* the will for God. See particularly 1 Cor. i. 24, where the Apostle draws a marked distinction between the rejecting and hostile hearers of the Gospel and the κλητοί, who find Christ to be all in all. Archbishop Leighton, on 1 Pet. ii. 9, writes of the inner call : "It is an operative word, that effects what it bids. God calls man ; He works with him indeed as a reasonable creature ; but sure He likewise works as Himself, as an almighty Creator. His call . . . doth, in a way known to Himself, twine and wind the heart which way He pleaseth." So, "whom He *called*, them He justified, and . . . glorified" (Rom. viii. 28).

inheritance in the saints, the rich, boundless life destined, in the final state, for those whom " He hath chosen for His own inheritance" (Ps. xxxiii. 12), His " purchased possession," His "acquisition" (above, ver. 14); so that His property is, as it were, lodged "in" them; and

Ver. 19. what is the surpassing greatness of His power, in the whole process of salvation, both in sanctification now and beatification in eternity, that power which is put forth towards us, the believing ones, and so the recipients of a strength not our own. And what is the scale, the measure, of " the greatness of that power"? It is according to, to be calculated by, the working of the strength of His might, (for only such accumulations

Ver. 20. of phrase can indicate its energy,) which working He put forth in His (τῷ) Christ, "in" Him as its sublime Object, raising Him from the dead, and seating [1] Him on His right hand, as Sharer of His

Ver. 21. throne, in the heavenly regions; far above [2] every government, and authority, and power, and lordship, all ranks and orders of celestial greatness in "the mighty kingdoms angelical" [3]; aye, and every name that can be named (ὀνομαζομένου) with fame and awe, not

---

[1] Read καθίσας.

[2] Ὑπεράνω: the word *may* mean merely "above," by general usage. But St Paul's marked love for compounds with ὑπέρ, to energize ideas, makes it certain that "*far* above" is the right rendering here.

[3] I borrow the phrase from an isolated paragraph in S. T. Coleridge's *Omniana*: "*To Thee Cherubim and Seraphim continually do cry.* The mighty kingdoms angelical, like the thin clouds at dawn, receiving and hailing the first radiance,

only in the present Age but also in the coming, the Age
of the everlasting Life (Mark x. 30); so that in that
"world" also the exalted Christ of God will be "the
Prince of the Kings," not of earth only (Rev. i. 5) but

Ver. 22. of heaven; and all things, the whole created
universe, He did put under His feet, in that great "act
and deed" of exaltation. Its full realization awaits
indeed the hour of His final triumph, but in the fiat
of the Father it is already fact.

So this wonderful Risen One sits supreme on "the
throne of God *and of the Lamb*" (Rev. xxii. 1), Commander of the hosts of angelic loyalty, and Conqueror
of all the dark powers of rebellion, who are destined
for "His footstool." And now, what of man, what of
us believers, what of our company and body? The
Christ, thus related to the angelic Universe, has received
a mighty exaltation in regard of us and our salvation:
And Him,[1] Him and no other, He gave as Head, as at
once Chief to rule and Life-Centre to vivify, over all
things, infinitely above all other imaginable claimants
to Headship, for the Church, the human Company joined
and organized into communion by spiritual union with

Ver. 23. Him; that Church which is His Body, as He
is its Head; His Body, as animated by His life, and
the tangible vehicle and implement of His thought and

---

and singing and sounding forth their blessedness, increase the
rising joy in the heart of God, spread wide and utter forth the
joy arisen, and in innumerable finite glories interpret all they
can of infinite bliss."

[1] Αὐτόν is emphatic by position.

will; that Church which is the Fulness, the Fulfilment,
the Realization of the grace, power, and glory of Him,
this blessed Christ, who is richly filling[1] all things in all;
the Replenisher of all the capacities for blessing of all
His members.

"What shall we say then to these things?"
Perhaps the first and best response is the Amen of
holy silence. May I even suggest to the reader
(and to myself) that after the perusal of such a
passage we should on purpose be quiescent for
a time, not from thought altogether, but as much
as may be from discursive thought? Let us "sit
before the Lord," and be still and passive. These
sentences were written first and supremely to be
believed, received, and—in a worshipping and
serving life—lived out. Let us *hear* them, in a
hush of the soul, without haste, and without talk.

But in due time it *is* our part to examine and
to remark, "What shall we say then to these
things?"

i. First, assuredly, let us note and admire this
great phenomenon, the glory of the Christ of
God, who was dead, and is upon the throne.
Think of the paradox. The Apostle is speaking

---

[1] Πληρουμένου: the middle voice enriches and deepens the idea.

of a Personage of history, of recent, of almost
contemporary, history. He had once, at Jerusalem, met and conversed with a Galilean religious
teacher, " James, the Lord's brother " (Gal. i. 19).
That man was a member of the same family circle,
in a small town of Northern Palestine, with
" Jesus, which is called Christ." In the same
sense in which James was brother of Jesus, Jesus
was brother of James. It was notorious that
Jesus had been an inhabitant for several years
of such a district and such a town, and that He
was related to such and such people, men and
women, by ties of blood and ties of law. He had
worked with His hands, He had walked from
place to place like other men, and many could no
doubt accurately describe His look and manner
when He talked. At last He had died, under
circumstances profoundly impressive indeed, but
still such as were also matter of human procedure ;
circumstances which had called in the prosaic
authority of a Roman magistrate and the physical
force of Roman soldiers. Well, but to the writer
of this letter, while all these aspects of " Jesus, the
brother of James," are present to his mind, what
is this same Jesus on the other hand ? With quite
the same certainty, as a matter of quite equal
fact, He is now " seated at the right hand of "

Almighty God, on His very throne, "in the heavenly regions," "aloft above" all the ranks and orders of the powers of heaven. He is the ruling and life-giving "Head" of a vast multitude of human beings who absolutely belong to Him, and absolutely live by Him. They are His Body; they exist, collectively, to be His limbs and implements. They are "His Fulness," the *Pleroma* in which this sublime Person actualizes His will. He is their "Ful-filler"; all that is receptive of spiritual life and power in them, it is He who makes it and keeps it full.

He is such that He is the Source of all grace, and the Hope of all glory, for fallen man. Yet He was also "the brother of James." Paul knows all about Him in both characters.

God, the Son of God; Man, the Son of Man! It is the old truth of the Creed, old and eternal. But, that we may grasp it the more firmly and comprehensively, let us recollect it thus once more in its light as a fact of history. Look at it as it was to St Paul and to those first disciples. And, as you read the Apostle's words about Christ glorified, words glowing indeed, but absolutely sane and practical in manner, reflect upon the self-evidencing tone of the whole utterance. Here is either the very wildest delusion ever generated by a disturbed brain, or—the Incarnation of the Eternal Word. And it is not usual in history to find wild delusions, by their originators, or first victims, stated in terms of majestic tranquillity, and at the same time applied to the very highest and the most practically beneficial ends in human life.

"God manifest in Flesh" is fact.

ii. Then, "feeling the rock beneath our feet," assured yet again that we are not "following cleverly devised myths" (2 Pet. i. 16), we look up into heaven, where this wonderful "brother of James" is seated. The "region," to use that noble old word, is seen full of hosts and ranks of light around Him. "Thrones, Dominations, Princedoms, Virtues, Powers," behold them there.[1] It is indeed a scene of power; "His Angels, that excel in strength"; we trace their irresistible

---

[1] Surely the Apostle is here affirming, though passingly, the real existence of ἀρχαί, ἐξουσίαι, δυνάμεις, κυριότητες, and not merely taking up the terms of an unauthorized angelology to brush those terms away. In a passage like this, the glory of the Saviour may be said to *demand the reality* of the existences over which He is said to be supreme.

The majestic line of Milton quoted above has learning in it as well as poetry. It is based on the "Celestial Hierarchy," written under the name of "Dionysius the Areopagite," cent. v. or vi. "Dionysius" ranked the Orders, down from the highest, in three *Trines*; Seraphim, Cherubim, Thrones; Dominations, Virtues, Powers; Principalities, Archangels, Angels.

5

steps in many a scene of the story of Redemption.
But they are " all His servants."   " Angels and
authorities and powers are made subject unto
Him " ; with a subjection in which they find their
eternal law of liberty and joy.   What then is He,
so "far aloft above them "?   Is He not to us,
poor things on earth, " throned inaccessible " ?
Wonderful thought, it is so far from being thus
that *we* are here called in to make the crown
and climax of His prerogatives and glories.   For
what has the Apostle to tell us about Him as His
last and highest function " at the Right Hand " ?
It is that He is given to be Head above all
things—to the Church, to the Assembly, the
Community of *men*, men once " dead in trespasses
and sins," and still exposed to all the temptations
and all the sorrows of time, and still compelled to
cry, " Enter not into judgment with Thy servants,
O Lord."

Yes, this is here given as the final glory of the
infinitely exalted Christ.   Angels and archangels
are subject unto Him.   But believing men are
joined to Him, with a union such that He and
they, by this same messenger of His, are called
elsewhere (1 Cor. xii. 12) one " *Christ.*"

"What is man, that Thou art mindful of him ? "
(Ps. viii. 3).   In himself, he is the mere creature

of the sovereign will. Of himself, as he has ruined himself, he is a sinful wreck. But in the Christ of God, man is a being raised to the heavenly regions, living by the life of his Head, crowned with glory and honour. "And it doth not yet appear what he shall be."

iii. Lastly, in this passage we have men, these greatly favoured men, presented to us not individually but in community. The Christ is "given as Head to *the Church*." His "Body" is the Church. The Church is His *Pleroma*, His Plenitude, the sphere in which His blessed attributes are to be realized and displayed through the graces of His people.

It is a momentous word, Church, Ecclesia. Around it many a great controversy has been fought. Claims have been advanced in its name, as by the Roman power, but not by it only, which would make it as it were an almost substitute for the Lord. It has been presented as a vast organized republic, or oligarchy, or monarchy, worked and managed through an elaborate machinery of human officers. So given, the word Church has too often been the motto for repression and persecution. The individual conscience has been too often overawed and browbeaten because of it. Individual spiritual history, individual access to God, individual work and witness for Him, has again and again been discredited and hindered under the maxims of "corporate life," "Church life," and supposed necessary principles of Unity. It has come in many quarters to be assumed or asserted that a unity of order is a more important thing than a close adherence to scriptural conclusions about the individual's acceptance before God in Christ and spiritual conformity in life to Him. By an inevitable reaction the word Church has become to many Christians an unwelcome and distasteful word, hard and narrow, beclouded with ideas of officialism, I had almost said of bureaucratic tyranny.

In view of both the distortion and the reaction against it the Church doctrine of this Epistle is inestimably precious. The word Church occurs frequently. We have it here, in a connexion high as the heavens, and full of the very deepest spiritual suggestions. We have it below, iii. 10, where "the Church" is beheld as the scene in which, even now, "the governments and the authorities in the celestial regions" get informed of "the variegated wisdom of God, according to His purpose of the ages." We have it again iii 21, where "glory" is given to the

Eternal Father, "in the Church, in Christ Jesus,"
throughout eternity.   And in the fifth chapter
(23, 24, 25, 27, 29, 32) we have it set fully before
us as the Bride and Spouse of the Lord Himself.
He is the Church's Head, the Saviour of the
Body; it is subject to Him, with wifely reverence;
He loved it, He gave Himself for it, to hallow it,
to cleanse it "by the bathing of the water attended by an utterance," to present it to Himself
glorified, spotless, holy.   He nourishes it and
cherishes it.   He and His Spouse are one.

Here is on the one hand an Ecclesia which
is lifted for our view far above mere terrestrial
and visible limitations.   The one allusion to the
external is the reference to " the water," but even
this is at once connected so with the " utterance "
($\dot{\rho}\hat{\eta}\mu\alpha$) of the everlasting Covenant as to point us
straight through the ordinance to the heavenly
blessing which it seals.   The whole conception
soars in the high air of direct spiritual relations
between the Lord and a redeemed Company
whose units are all joined in an ineffable reality
of faith and love to Him, *and so* member to
member.   We may call it the Ideal Church.
We may call it the Invisible, in the sense of
invisibility which points to an Organism seen in
its true limits and relations by God alone.   But

however, it is a something which refuses to be
really identified with any one organization, or
aggregate of organizations, officered and tabulated
by human ministers.   It is related more nearly,
may we not say ? to heaven than to earth.   It is,
in its essence, with Christ where He is.   It is the
wonder of angels.   It is the sphere within which
glory is given to God as much in eternity (iii. 21)
as in time.   It (not parts of it, but it) is to be
presented to its Lord at last in the heavenly light.
Let us beware of lowering the radiant sublimity
of the conception by definitions of the Church
essentially conditioned by time.

Meantime, we have a correction here to any
mere individualism in Christian life on earth.
The individual's spiritual blessings are here
shewn to us as profoundly connected, for their
true development, with his recollection that he is
not an isolated entity but the limb of a Body, of
a Bride.   He is intended as truly to live not unto
himself but unto others as he is intended to live
unto the Lord.   And as regards *a true* place,
in our thought about the Church, for temperate
ideas of visible cohesion and order, we have a
deep suggestion here.   It lies in the words
which describe the Church as the Body and the
Plenitude of Christ.   For those words suggest

that the Church exists not only to enjoy mystic union with Him but to be of practical service to Him. And that thought, though it can *never* justify narrow definitions of the Church, must assuredly *always* bear towards all possible practical cohesion, with a view to co-operation, among its members.

To adjust with perfect logic the ideal of the Ecclesia, that is to say its ultimate truth, with a right understanding of the possible in organized and united Christian life, is, I hold, beyond our power. But the Church doctrine of our Epistle will be a safe and holy guide to us in the direction of adjustment.

HAIL, glorious HEAD of all Thine own,
  Our equal Source of peace and power;
Thou for our sins didst once atone,
  Thou art our Life of Life this hour.

Then, Lord, in strong communion still,
  O bind us faster, to be free,
Thou working out by us Thy will,
  We working out Thy will by Thee.

THE SALVATION OF THE EPHESIANS

La connaissance de Dieu sans celle de notre misere fait l'orgueil. La connaissance de notre misère sans celle de Jesus-Christ fait le désespoir. Mais la connaissance de Jésus-Christ nous exempte et de l'orgueil et du désespoir, parce que nous y trouvons Dieu, notre misère, et la voie unique de la réparer.

PASCAL.

CHAPTER IV

EPHESIANS ii. 1–10

OUR last Study was much occupied "concerning Christ and the Church." First the glory of the Lord, the Head, then the transcendent privileges of His true Body, "the blessed Company of all faithful people"—these were our lines of contemplation. We sought to follow the Apostle along them, not only to learn, but also to worship and to pray. For we found him addressing the Ephesians not as the lecturer or expositor, but as the evangelist whose soul burned with thanksgiving for the victories of grace among them, and who also, who *therefore*, prayed with intense supplication that they might realize yet more what they possessed in being joined in that Body to that Head.

He has by no means exhausted the theme. There is a great deal yet to be said about salvation in general, and the Ephesians' salvation in particular. Among other things, he has to dilate upon the *miracle of mercy* in the matter; the converts are to be reminded what they have been delivered from, as well as what they have been lifted into. They must be led to look down again into the pit, into the grave, from which grace called them out and set them free. So shall they be both the happier and the more secure, because the more humble, on the astonishing height to which that grace has borne them up, "seating them in the heavenly regions," where their Lord is set.

Thus we come to one of the great evangelic passages of the whole New Testament, deeply characteristic of the primeval Gospel in its essence. For never for a moment does the Gospel, in its eagle-flights into the sky of grace and glory, forget the wonder, the miracle, *the mercy*, of our having access to that sky at all. "Other Gospels, which are not other," may and often do ignore that side of things, till we hear little about the horror, guilt, and doom of man's sin, and the absolute gratuitousness of the grant of a rescue from it. We might almost think of

man, of "humanity," as they present him, rather
as of an unfortunate traveller upon some bye-
road of the universe, fallen among thieves, "more
sinned against than sinning," cruelly robbed and
maimed, with nothing to blame but his enemies
and his circumstances; so that the supreme King
stands in some sense obliged to redress him, and
to recover him, and to comfort him after his long
calamities.

Is not this, too often, not the language to be
sure but the spirit of what passes current as
Christian teaching? But it is not the Gospel
of the Lord and His Apostles. True, while they
ply no high-flown rhetoric about "the enthusiasm
of humanity," they do unfold in radiant colours
"the philanthropy of God our Saviour" (Tit.
iii. 4); the love of God for "the world" (John
iii. 16); the movement of the eternal Heart
towards the human Nature made in the divine
Image. But all this goes close along with the
unceasing recollection that that nature has itself
fallen by its own iniquity, and lies not only
wounded but guilty on the wayside. (Man is not
merely a sufferer; he is a runaway, a criminal,
a rebel, a conspirator.) Eternal Love regards
him. But eternal Law, lodged in the same Will
with eternal Love lays its arrest upon him, and

shews the death-warrant. And meanwhile, as part of the phenomenon of man's mysterious self-ruin, he lies there not only guilty and arrested, but alienated and resisting still. His destruction of himself expresses itself above all in this—that, in the Fall, he does not love God, he does not choose God. He "forsakes his own mercy." He lays the blame anywhere but on his own head. He loves himself best. Of himself, he is not contrite, penitent, submissive, believing. He is dead to his true life, which is to know God in His redeeming Son.

Let us ask for an entire sympathy with God's law against ourselves as guilty, and for just such a sight of ourselves, as self-alienated from love of the eternal Love, as shall make us feel *the mercy* of salvation. Only so, I dare to think, shall we ever fully respond to the real message of the New Testament. It is written (Acts v. 31) of our glorified Saviour that He is "exalted, to *give repentance* and remission of sins," not one gift only, but the two. And repentance means little if it does not mean the complete renunciation of the dream of self-wrought claims, and the recognition of salvation as wonderful mercy, from first to last.

I linger upon this side of truth, not as if I

could forget the glorious other side; what would life be without it? But I am sure that *this* side is what the Christian world is forgetting far and wide, while salvation is either taken all too indolently, (a very different thing from taking it simply,) or is practically put aside as what "humanity" can do without. In the course of my ministry I have known impressive examples to the point; one such is present to me at this hour. I have seen hearts actually resist and reject the most benignant offers made by Jesus Christ, in His character of Mediator and Advocate, because God *ought not* to need an Advocate for His unfortunate "children"; He *ought* to keep them safe, and bring them home. So it thought, that heart, a little while ago. But now, drawn by a grace divine indeed, it has come to see *itself*, in the light of an infinite Holiness; and lo, the perplexities and the resistance have fallen like leaves from the autumnal trees, and the "anxious enquirer" has asked that very old-fashioned question, What must I do to be saved? And the glory of Christ has shone upon the whole being, and repentance has kindled into joy unspeakable and full of glory.

Let us be sure of it, that species of joy is inseparably connected with "the broken and contrite heart." [Let the Church come to be strange to the experience of conviction of sin; it will come to be equally strange to that of "joy in God through our Lord Jesus Christ." Let the Gospel of "the enthusiasm of humanity" take the place of that of our ruin in sin, our redemption by Christ Jesus, and our regeneration by the Holy Ghost, and the "enthusiasm" will have very little in it of the victory which overcomes the world, and in which we go forth to bless the world by commending to it "the glory of God in the face of Jesus Christ."]

"Never was there a heresy, but it had something to do with an insufficient estimate of sin." And an insufficient estimate of the "thing which God hateth" is not only the parent of speculative error; it is the secret death of true spiritual joy.

So the Apostle is bent upon reminding the Ephesians of their past, and of the absolute mercy which had lifted them out of it into such a present, and for such a future.

"He teaches all the mercy, for he shews them all the sin."

Ver. 1. **And you He brought to life**[1] (from *His* viewpoint, it was when Christ rose again; from *yours*, it was

---

[1] The verb is supplied, as in A.V. and R.V., from ver. 5 below, where the wording is repeated nearly verbatim: ὄντας ἡμᾶς νεκροὺς . . . συνεζωοποίησε τῷ Χριστῷ.

when you believed on Him), being, as you then were, dead men, devoid of life spiritual and eternal, and wholly unable to generate it from within, in respect of your (τοῖς) trespasses and your sins (read ὑμῶν), your manifold forms of discord with the will of God, things which were at once the conditions and the results of that "death";

Ver. 2. in which sins once on a time you walked,[1] as on a path, as in a region, moving from thing to thing in the course of life, determined by (κατά) the course[2] of this world, this present order of human things,[3] aye, and by a dark personal power behind it and working through it, even by the ruler of the authority of the air,[4] or, in other words, of the spirit now at

---

[1] Περιεπατήσατε : the aorist gathers up the whole experience into a point of thought.

[2] Αἰών, "age" : the word is rendered "course" in A.V. and R.V., and it would be difficult to suggest a better English. We sometimes use "period" in nearly the same derived sense—a time *and its influences*.

[3] Such seems to be the meaning of κόσμος here. It certainly is not (as in e.g. John xi. 9, τὸ φῶς τοῦ κ. τούτου) the physical universe ; nor again merely mankind, but mankind as conditioned by sin, or rather this present sinful order of human life. So very often in N.T., notably in St John's First Epistle.

[4] "The great personal Evil Spirit, Satan ; whose existence, sparingly indicated in the O.T., is largely dwelt upon in the N.T. . . . For St Paul's recognition of [his existence], cp. Acts xiii. 10, xxvi. 18 ; Rom. xvi. 20 ; 1 Cor. v. 5, vii. 5 ; 2 Cor. ii. 11, xi. 14 ; 1 Thess. ii. 18 ; 2 Thess. ii. 9 ; 1 Tim. i. 20, iii. 6, 7, v. 15 ; 2 Tim. ii. 26, and below [in Eph.] iv. 27, vi. 11."—"*The authority of the air*" appears to mean the organized power of the world of unholy spirits, here indicated as having their abode not precisely on earth but about it. "We must seek a meaning of 'air' literal and local, rather than otherwise, looking at St Paul's usage elsewhere (e.g. 1 Thess. iv. 17). . . . On the whole we gather,

6

work,[1] as once it was at work in you, **in the sons of disobedience,** the human beings characterized by moral alienation from the will of God, and whose attitude therefore gives foothold and opportunity for the subtle "working" of His enemies and theirs.[2] As they are, so you were, nay, so *we* were; I the Jew, you the Greeks, were all alike in this, till grace found us out. As we look upon the pagans around us, we must say, with

Ver. 3. contrite memory, **Among whom we too all lived our life,**[3] **once on a time, in the desires of our flesh,** the bias and preferences of the self-life, whatever form they took, gross or subtle,[4] **doing the willings of the flesh**

---

as the revelation of this passage, that as earth is the abode of embodied spirits, mankind, so the airy envelope of earth is the abode, for the purposes of action on man, of the spirits of evil, which, if not bodiless, have not 'animal' bodies. . . . Observe our Lord's use of 'the *birds of the sky*' (Luke viii. 5) as the figure for the Tempter in the parable of the Sower." (Notes in the *Cambridge Bible*.)

[1] Τοῦ πνεύματος, κ.τ.λ. : this genitive puts the πνεῦμα in grammatical apposition not with "the ruler" (ἄρχοντα) but with the "authority" (ἐξουσίας). It is a startling phrase, perhaps best explained by taking it here to be a collective singular; the πνεῦμα is in fact the πνεύματα gathered into one idea, or regarded in the oneness of their malign influence.

[2] "*Sons* of disobedience": a familiar Hebraism; cp. 2 Pet. ii. 14, where the literal rendering is, "children of a curse"; and just below, ver. 3, τέκνα ὀργῆς. "Disobedience" renders ἀπείθεια better than "unbelief"; though the two ideas are, in spiritual experience, closely connected.

[3] Ἀνεστράφημεν: again an aorist, gathering a long experience into one idea.

[4] In St Paul, σάρξ "means human nature as conditioned by the Fall, or, to word it otherwise, either the state of the unregenerate being, in which state the sinful principle dominates, or the state of that element of the regenerate being in which the

and of the thoughts, the volitions of the fallen self,
whether coming out in concrete action or lurking in
unholy imaginations; and were by nature, not by
circumstance only, not by exterior accident and dis-
advantage, because of bad example or invitation only,
but by the inward wrongness of our own condition,
antecedent to the grace of God, children of wrath;
naturally, normally, exposed, as are also the rest of
men, to the moral displeasure of the eternal Holy One.[1]

Such was our position, as mysterious as
possible, but as much as possible a matter of
fact. Beings profoundly personal, conscious in
our depths of moral differences, able to say *I
will*, able to know *I ought*;—our will was in its
depths at discord with our duty; we preferred
darkness to light, we followed self-will rather
than the will of God. The manifestations of the
mischief were infinitely various. One person
plunged into bodily profligacy, another followed

principle, dislodged, as it were, from the centre, still lingers and
is felt; not dominant in the being, but present." (Note in the
Cambridge Bible.)

[1] "It has been suggested that 'children of wrath' may mean
no more than 'beings prone to violent anger,' or even to 'un-
governed impulse' generally. But the word 'wrath' is frequent
with St Paul, and in 13 out of the 20 places it unmistakably
means the divine wrath. . . . Add to this that this passage deals
with the deepest and most general facts, and thus it is unlikely
that any one special phase of sin would be instanced." (Note
in the *Cambridge Bible.*)

the star of knowledge, a third worshipped sen-
suous rather than sensual pleasure, a fourth set
himself aflame with religious zealotry. But the
root of the mischief was ultimately the same in
all. We chose ourselves rather than our God;
our will was sweeter to us than His law. And
this was "by nature." The disease was indeed
of the person, of the individual; but somehow
it lay deeper, it was in the state of *his nature*.
Here were no isolated accidents, under which
very many human wills were wrong with God.
There was a dark "law" in the phenomenon;
it was a universal case; *all* human wills were
wrong with Him. And so (how could it be
otherwise?) His holiness was displeased with us
all; we were "children of His wrath." No
tyrannic heat and violence lay in that awful
"wrath"; no blind jealousies and unregulated
inflictions surged out of that dark but immaculate
depth. It was the sinless aversion of Holiness
from sin. Yet none the less it was displeasure,
personal and incalculably formidable. And beneath its celestial frown we lay.[1]

---

[1] On the great mystery and great fact summed up in the
Christian doctrine of Original Sin, there are some pregnant remarks in the late Prof. J. B. Mozley's *Lectures and Theologica.
Papers* (§ ix., pp. 136, etc.). "Original sin is, fundamentally,
simply *universal* sin. . . . Nobody supposes that anything takes

What was to be done? Was the fate of man, his nature's self-inflicted fate, sealed and hopeless? No— because of God. "Thou hast destroyed thyself; but Ver. 4. in Me is thy help" (Hos. xiii. 9). But our (ὁ) God, being as He is, in *His* blessed state "by nature," wealthy in mercy, moved by nothing but Himself, because of His much love with which[1] He loved us, His Church to be, albeit our *condition* was repulsive to His holiness Ver. 5. in a degree to us inconceivable, aye (καί) when we were—as just now I said *you* were, but it was the same with me, with all—dead men in respect of our (τοῖς) trespasses, brought us to life along with His (τῷ) Christ, when the Head lived again for us, and then when we, believing, were made the Members of the Head; (yes, along with Christ, wholly because of His Sacrifice, His Victory, His Covenant; for never forget that not because of any claim on God but by grace, by a pure, free bounty of His goodness, you have been saved (σεσωσμένοι), brought into an actual rescue and safe-

---

place universally by chance; . . . we know there must be some law working in the case. . . . What we *call* the law is a secondary question." I may refer further to my small manual, *Outlines of Christian Doctrine* (pp. 173, etc.); and to Prof. Shedd's *Sermons to the Natural Man*, especially Nos. V. and XIV. Browning's lines are worthy of note :

> "I still, to suppose it" [the Christian faith] "true, for my part,
> See reasons and reasons ; this, to begin,
> 'Tis the faith that launched point-blank her dart
> At the head of a lie—taught Original Sin,
> The Corruption of Man's Heart."
> *Gold Hair, a Story of Pornic* (1864).

[1] Ἥν : the accusative takes the place of the dative, by "attraction" to ἀγάπην.

Ver. 6. keeping by union with your Lord [1] ;) and raised you from the grave along with Christ, bringing the new life out into manifestation, as when the living One stepped forth into the morning air in Joseph's Garden ; and seated us along with our Head [2] in the heavenly regions in Christ Jesus. For this glorious " *in* " must be recorded, to explain the wonderful " *with* " ; we are *beside* Him there upon His seat of victory and dominion, because we are embodied *in* Him, by the Spirit's power and in the bond of faith.

So astonishing is the revolution of our condition ; from wrath to a wealth of mercy ; from death in sin to resurrection-life ; from a walk among the sons of disobedience to a session with and in the Lord upon His heavenly throne, looking down from thence on our old miseries and on our terrible but now impotent adversaries.

And why was it all done? Assuredly, as we have seen, for pure love to us, but also so as to secure God's own glorification in His creatures' view for ever ; for

---

[1] " *Have been* saved" : so just below, ver. 8. Much more commonly our salvation is represented as a *process going on*, σώζεσθε, σωζόμενοι. But here the work of eternal mercy is, as it were, seen from the divine view-point, from which "that is a *fait accompli*" which from the human point of view is a thing in process." Or, to put it otherwise, the being already "has been saved" which is in the hands of an omnipotent and unfailing Saviour, though He has much yet to do with it while it is in His hands on the way to glory.

[2] It seems clearly best, in the context, to refer συνήγειρε, συνεκάθισε, to our union *with Christ* rather than *with one another*.

He, being what He is, cannot but work for the infinite

Ver. 7. End of His own glory: That He may demon-
strate in the ages that are coming on, in the long dispensations of the eternal Future, the overwhelming wealth
of His grace seen in kindness showered upon us in Christ
Jesus; "in Him," because on Him for ever descends
the Father's love, and so on all that is "found in
Him." For, solemnly to recite again that great formula

Ver. 8. of blessing, by His (τῇ) grace you have been
saved, by means of faith—by the reliance on His word
which makes the provision a possession; and even that,
the faith, the fact of your having come to trust Him,
is not of yourselves, not generated merely of your
unaided will; God's is the gift of salvation, in all its
parts, including the fact that "thy faith hath saved

Ver. 9. thee"[1]; it is not the resultant of (ἐξ) works, not
the outcome of your moral fitness and your moral efforts,
(for you were dealt with as "dead men in respect of
your trespasses";) so that no one may boast. Yes, the
process was divinely steered all along on purpose to keep
the saved ones off the quicksands of self-complacency,

---

[1] It is of course possible to refer the words "*and that, not of
yourselves*, etc.," not to the thought that we "have been saved
through faith," but to the more general statement that we have
been saved "*by grace*." This is the more possible, because
τοῦτο is neuter, and πίστις feminine; we might have expected
διὰ ταύτης if the reference were to "faith." Accordingly many
expositors, including Calvin, one of the wisest and most impartial
of all interpreters, do take "*and that*, etc.," to refer to the whole
previous thought of our grace-given salvation. Yet I still advocate the special reference to "faith"; and for the main
reason that καὶ τοῦτο is a phrase which always denotes some

as if either their strength or their insight were to thank
for their blessings ; they were to be landed on the firm
conviction that "all things are of God," and so to give
thanks, now and for ever, to "Him who worketh all
things in all" His people.

It shall be reiterated, it shall be summed up, once
Ver. 10. more : **For His making** ($\pi o i \eta \mu a$) **are we,** and
in no sense our own ; not in the least degree is our
regenerate state the issue of our unregenerate "works."
Our works, that are good works at all, are not the
condition up to our faith but the blessed consequent
upon it. For we, "His making," were constituted, placed
in a totally new state and order, **in Christ Jesus,** in and
by our union with Him, **with a view to** ($\epsilon \pi i$ with the
dative) **good works,** with them as the Maker's aim and
end, works which our (o) God prepared beforehand, long
before our resurrection out of spiritual death, for all
was ordered in His eternal purpose, **that in them we
may walk.**

The passage which we have just paraphrased
is, as we remembered above, one of the great
passages of all Scripture. The last three verses

marked additional element in the statement. Such an addition,
if I am right, can only be found here by bringing in the thought
that *even our believing* is "by grace." But for the grace of
God, opening our eyes, we should not see the infinite trust-
worthiness of Christ, and so be (not driven by force, but) *decided*
to trust Him. Thus explaining the clause, we must explain
$\tau o \hat{v} \tau o$ to refer not to the feminine noun $\pi i \sigma \tau \iota s$ precisely, but to
the fact of our exercising $\pi i \sigma \tau \iota s$.—For "faith" as a "gift," cp.
Phil. i. 29.

in particular stand in the front of those brief
pregnant oracles which, scattered over the Book
of God, seem given on purpose to put in its most
concentrated form the message of the GOSPEL.
From the age of the Reformation more particularly those sentences have been often on the lips
and in the hearts of believers. For the Reformation was above all things, in its true spiritual
aspect, the time of the re-discovery and of the
developed apprehension of the apostolic doctrine
of Gratuitous Salvation. Then at length, as never
before for ages,[1] the Church heard again the
glorious paradox of the Apostles, the *Evangelium*
indeed, the promise of life present and eternal to
"whosoever believeth on the Son," justification
complete and immediate because the Lord has
died and risen, and the sinner has "received
Him, believing on His Name." Then it was
announced far and wide in European Christendom
that such is Jesus Christ, and such His work for
us, that we are to find in Him a salvation not

---

[1] I refer of course to the public and prevalent teaching of the
Christian Churches. All along the centuries a bright stream can
be traced of personal, individual faith of the noblest evangelic
type. And in such writers as St Anselm and St Bernard utterances occur than which nothing could be more true to the
teaching of St Paul. But the medieval "Gospel" in its prevalent
form was a sorrowful distortion.

conveyed to us through our works, but given to us with sovereign simplicity for His sake, in order that now and therefore our works " may be done in God." And so a paragraph like this became inestimably precious, as a divine compendium. In its few lines, what did it not contain? A salvation present and, from the Lord's view-point, completed; σεσωσμένοι ἐστέ : a salvation whose every golden link, from eternal purpose to eternal glory, was "by grace; not of works, not of you"; a salvation conveyed to the saved one not by labours and through a process, but "through faith," through taking God at His word in Christ. In that salvation the saved one rests in the noble passiveness of the recollection that he is "God's making, constituted anew in Christ Jesus"; and then rises up in the blessed activity of one who knows what he possesses, and Who possesses him, and that before him now lies an ordered path of "good works"—the "next thing" of the will of God, and then the next, prepared for the traveller who is now prepared for it. To us, as to our fathers, and to our fathers' fathers, may Eph. ii. 8, 9, 10, be a watchword, a talisman, of truth, peace and joy, for rest, for labour, for life, for death, and for ever. For "the good works prepared for us

to walk in" are a path which runs unbroken
through the stream of death and up into the
hills of immortality; "His servants shall serve
Him, and they shall see His face."

Meantime our paragraph leads us to this lofty
and memorable close by steps which claim, each
of them, the Christian's deepest thought. The
wonder as well as the splendour of the true
Gospel is before us in them. Forget not, believing soul, thy original " death in respect of thy
trespasses." Thank God if the symptoms of it
were so restrained that the ill of it *for others*
was not what it might have been; but do not
forget that once, whatever the form and colour
of thy conduct, towards God thou wast dead.
Thy personality, thy consciousness, understanding,
will, affections, all were there, God's glorious
gifts; but thou didst not "know" (as He means
knowing) "the only true God, and Jesus Christ
whom He had sent"; and that, and that alone,
is "the life eternal" (John xvii. 3). Thou wast
dead, needing nothing less than a miracle of
resurrection. And an enemy sat at the door of
thy grave; "the Prince of the authority of the
air," the dread personal antagonist of Christ
and ruthless enemy of man; *a person*, however
much human speculation may (surely to *his* own

satisfaction) deny it, ridicule it, ignore it; and personally bent upon thy abiding spiritual death. And over that guarded sepulchre hung the cloud of the displeasure of the Eternal, His abomination of all things at discord with His holiness.

Remember this; ponder the extremity of the ruin. But then with new surprise, and with new assurance, remember that the mercy and the love are facts as certain, and as tangible, and all for thee. As a fact, thou art risen with thy risen Lord, and seated with Him where He sits, a monument of the "kindness" of His Father and thine. As a fact, by grace thou hast been saved. As a fact, thy feet are set upon the rock of the way of holiness, the path to glory. Remember, and rejoice.

ONCE REMOTE, NOW MADE NIGH

Tunsionibus, pressuris, expoliti lapides
Suis coaptantur locis; per manus artificis
Disponuntur permansuri sacris ædificiis.

Angulare Fundamentum Lapis Christus missus est,
Qui compage parietum in utroque nectitur,
Quem Syon sancta suscepit, in quo credens permanet.

From an Anonymous Poem, cent. viii. or ix.

CHAPTER V

ONCE REMOTE, NOW MADE NIGH

EPHESIANS ii. 11-22

Ver. 11. **Wherefore remember that once you, the Nations,** the Gentiles, members of the outside races,[1] **in the flesh,** as regards your physical descent and the absence of the physical sign of covenant, circumcision ; **called, as you were, and are, the Uncircumcision by that body which is called the Circumcision—only in the flesh, wrought** **Ver. 12.** **by hand**[2]—remember, I say, **that you were at**

---

[1] Hebrew, הַגּוֹיִם, *haggóyim.* "Rabbinic Judaism regarded them with feelings akin to those with which an old-fashioned high-caste Hindoo regards a European. . . . Meanwhile, these gross distortions had behind them the spiritual fact here given by St Paul, that 'the Gentiles,' before the Gospel, were on a *really* different level from Israel as to covenant with God in Christ. Pharisaism took a totally wrong line, but it started from a point of truth." (Note in the *Cambridge Bible.*)

[2] He means to suggest the fact that the contempt of the Pharisee for the Gentile shewed that the Pharisee was unspiritual, and so that his circumcision was not, what it ought to be, the seal of spiritual promises and blessings, but a thing valueless for those higher uses. It was *to him* a thing *merely physical.* Compare the close of Rom. ii.

that time, the time of your "death in trespasses and sins," separate from Christ, out of saving connexion with Israel's Messiah, the world's Saviour. Yes, the Pharisee was cruelly wrong in his spirit of scorn and indifference towards you; but he had just so much right in his wrong, that you *were* as yet isolated from actual contact with the Redeemer's promises and power; having been alienated (for you were fallen men, and manhood, in the fall, did alienate itself from all its true blessings) from the commonwealth, the spiritual State, of Israel, the people of God[1]; and strangers, "outlanders," to the covenants of the Promise, the many gracious compacts, as with Abraham, Moses, Levi, David, all connected with the great Promise of Redemption.

Such was your position in relation to Revelation and its blessings. And meanwhile as to your experience, as to the condition of your souls, you were conscious of no hope,[2] and Godless in the world; roving in the dark wilderness of sin and sorrow, without "the light of the knowledge of the glory of God in the face of Jesus Christ." Gods many, and lords many, you

---

[1] It is as if he would intimate that, ideally, MAN was the "chosen people," the original "Israel"; but that he fell, and then from his ruins was taken a minor chosen race, to bear the privileges from which the race as a whole had fallen. The peculiar phrase, "*having been alienated from*, etc.," seems to demand this; for "alienation" implies some sort of previous connexion.

[2] So I venture to render ἐλπίδα μὴ ἔχοντες. Μή, not οὐ, indicates here not only fact but consciousness. Not only was there actually no bright future for them, in their path of condemnation and sin; they *felt* hopeless. It was mournfully thus as a fact, as all

had; a pantheon with, perhaps, a vast and shadowy Somewhat at its back, as the supreme Power; but not GOD, not the Holy One, not the eternal Love.

Ver. 13. **But now, in the blessed actual state of the case,** as that eternal Love has ordered it, now, **in Christ Jesus,** in that living union with Him to which the Gospel has called you, **you, the once remote,** banished so far from the "commonwealth" of grace, **did become near,**[1] so near as to be embodied into the very life of the true Israel; **in the blood of our** (τοῦ) **Christ;** "in" it, as your sacrificial warrant and instrument; for He suffered to "sanctify His people with His own blood," the blood of death, of expiation, nay, of wonderful propitiation; and you now, believing in His Name, take place among His people, the people of His covenant.

Marvellous is this transition from far to near; but the reason is adequate for the effect. The blood has power indeed, because of HIM who shed it; **for HE** **Ver. 14.** **is our peace,** and nothing less than He. His ever-blessed Personality, giving essence and virtue to His atoning Work, is our reconciliation to God, for

---

readers of classical literature know. Even in the better regions of ancient pagan life and thought an awful uncertainty and misgiving is seen to underlie the anticipation of the future. An affecting illustration is to be found in the Lapidarian Gallery at Rome, where, on opposite sides, pagan and Christian epitaphs are arranged. The Christian mourner is full of peace and joy; the pagan lamentations are as from hearts "having no hope."

[1] "'Nigh' and 'far' were familiar terms with the Rabbis, in the sense of having or not having part in the covenant. . . . 'A woman came to Rabbi Eliezer, to be made a proselyte, saying to him, *Rabbi, make me nigh.*'" (Note in the *Cambridge Bible*.)

7

Jew and Gentile alike, and so it is our reconciliation
to one another. Pagan and Pharisee, we embrace each
other, for God has embraced us both in His dear Son,
who made both the things one thing, amalgamating in
Himself our several positions and relations, till all is
unified into one happy Community ; **and did take down
the parting-wall of the Fence,** (the Law, that great
bulwark between Israel and the Nations, dividing them—
till He fulfilled it, and so brought to an end its
Ver. 15. typical and separating enactments [1] ;)—**the personal enmity** between Jew and Gentile, **in His flesh,** in
the Manhood in which He bore His great reconciling
Suffering, **even the law of the commandments** couched **in
decrees,** in positive revealed edicts, **annulling.** Even so ;
He found us separated, race from race. And the
separation was intensified and emphasized by those
institutions which were, in part, *designed* to isolate Israel
from the world, till the fit time for the wider blessing.
And He " annulled " them, by fulfilling them, in His
sacrificial work ; thus at once reconciling man to God
and man to man. So did the Lord suffer, so did He
triumph, **in order that He might [2] create,** might sovereignly
constitute, **the two** parties, Israel and the Nations, **in
Himself,[3]** in the union of each with Him, **into one new**

---

[1] Perhaps the μεσότοιχον τοῦ φραγμοῦ is a phrase suggested by
the *Chêl*, the barrier in the Temple, dividing the Court of the
Gentiles from the rest. A fragment of the very *Chêl* of St Paul's
time is now in the Sultan's Museum at Constantinople.

[2] Lit. "that He *may*," ἵνα κτίσῃ. But it is a frequent idiom
in N.T. Greek to speak of a past purpose in present terms.

[3] Probably read, ἐν αὐτῷ, "in *Him*." But the reference in
either case is certainly to Christ Himself.

man, as it were one collective Personality, all being in
Him one Body ; making peace, as we have seen, between
man and man, as the glorious issue of the work whereby
He made peace between man and God.   For this
supreme blessing lay at the root of the matter.   He
Ver. 16.   suffered and overcame [1] in order that He might
also reconcile both the parties, in one body, to God, by
means of the Cross, killing the enmity in, by, it.   His
precious Death was borne in order to "reconcile to
God" Israel and the Nations alike ; that is to say, to
bring them penitent to a pardoning God, who accepts
the great atonement and welcomes the believing sinner.[2]
There they meet, in the divine forgiveness, procured by
the sacrifice of the Son, which was provided by the love
of the Father.   Meeting so, they come not only to God
but to one another, in a union unimaginable before.
The wounds of the Crucifixion, for those who have
become "one body" with the Crucified, have been the
death-wounds first of "the enmity" of the unpardoned
rebel towards his blessed King, and then, and so, of
"the enmity" of the unhumbled and unchanged human
heart towards fellow-men.

And when the work of Propitiation and Peace was

---

[1] The καί with which ver. 16 begins is omitted for the purposes
of the paraphrase, in which its meaning is however conveyed.

[2] Such assuredly is the true account of the meaning of "reconciliation," as the word is used in Scripture.   To reconcile man
to God means, primarily, not to persuade man to yield to God,
but to make it possible for God (if the words may be used with
reverence) to accept guilty man with peace.   I may refer to my
Outlines of Christian Doctrine, p. 79.

effected by the great Peace-Maker, He rose up to be
Ver. 17. the Messenger of His own blessings. And
coming, coming from the Cross and from the Tomb,
coming back from the Unseen " in the power of an
endless life," He preached, He "gospelled," peace, peace
with one another because of peace with God, peace to
you the remote, and peace [1] to the near, the believers of
the old Israel. Such was, in fact, the first word of
the Risen One to His gathered followers (John xx. 19),
" Peace be unto you." " God, having raised up His
Son Jesus, sent Him to bless " us (Acts iii. 26),
" preaching peace by Jesus Christ ; He is Lord of all "
(Acts x. 36). And peace it is indeed, for it means
nothing less than our entrance, hand in hand, into the
inmost presence of a welcoming, loving, rejoicing God.

Ver. 18. **Because by means of Him, this blessed Christ in
His atoning work, we have our ($\tau\acute{\eta}\nu$) introduction, both
parties of us (οἱ ἀμφότεροι), in one Spirit, unto the Father.**
There we are united indeed, fused into a wonderful
harmony and cohesion in that secret place of blessing.
" Both parties of us " are " in one Spirit " ; quickened,
animated, possessed, surrounded, by one " Holy Spirit
of promise." " Both " have one Lord to be their ground
of acceptance, and their Conductor into the inmost
chamber of the spiritual home. " Both " find one Father
there, welcoming and embracing all His people with
equal love, in the Name of His one Beloved. Wonderful
unification, deep and living as the heart of man, and
as the heart of God ; rooted in the Atonement, and

---

[1] Read εἰρήνην a second time.

made to live in us, and grow, and bear the fruits of Paradise, by the indwelling Spirit.

The holy fact, contemplated again, lifts the Apostle into a strain of loving joy. This " Pharisee, the son of a Pharisee," cannot rest without chanting to these Asians, these recent worshippers of Artemis and Cybele, the solemn triumph-song of their equal place with Israel Ver. 19. in God's present and eternal grace. **So then you are no longer,** as once you were, mere **strangers and aliens,** tolerated sojourners at best upon the territory of hope. **No, you are**[1] **fellow-citizens of the saints;** sharers with all who belong to God in all the privileges of His eternal City, enrolled now in the bright register of the heavenly Zion with Abraham, and Moses, and David, and Isaiah, with prophets, with apostles, and hereafter to " sit down with " them, in actual presence, within its starry walls; **and members of the family of God,** "children at home" with Him, by birth and by adoption too, as truly as "Israel His firstborn." All this you are, as having taken your stand upon the Gospel of Christ, Ver. 20. proclaimed to you by His messengers; **having been built upon the foundation of the apostles and prophets,** the "foundation" which consists of them, inasmuch as their doctrine is the basis of your faith, and so of your unity[2]; **the Cornerstone,** the great Stone in the angle of

---

[1] Read ἀλλ' ἐστέ.

[2] I explain "the prophets" here of the prophets not of the Old Testament but of the New. This seems to be best, in view of the use of the word below, iii. 5, iv. 11. It is plain that the Christian "prophet" occupied a place of impressive importance in the primitive Church, second to that of the apostle, but only,

the substructure, where the walls meet, their mighty
Bond and Unity,[1] being **Christ Jesus**[2] Himself; for all
the ranges of saving truth ever set before you by
Apostle or by Prophet meet in Him, and get all their
Ver. 21　significance and symmetry from Him; **in
whom,** in vital union with whom, in His work and
life, **all the building,**[3] getting in all its parts framed
together, drawing as it were closer within itself, into
a deeper solidity and coherence, as the union of each
saint and of all of them with their Lord developes,
is growing, with each new insertion into its living

---

apparently, in his not being necessarily "a witness of the Resurrection" and not taking a first place in government.—Meantime
the whole New Testament makes it clear that the prophets *of
the Old Testament* were, for our Lord and the Apostles, "evangelists before the time," giving oracles full of Christ.—"The
mention of [the N.T. prophets] here is in special point, because
public faith and doctrine is in question. The work of the
'prophets' had doubtless greatly contributed to the wide spread
of the truth of the free acceptance in Christ of *all* believers,
Gentiles with Jews. Observe that in Acts xv. 32 it is two
'*prophets*,' [Judas and Silas,] who 'exhort and confirm' (the
Greek word suggests precisely *settlement on a foundation*)
the Gentile believers at Antioch, in the very crisis of the conflict
between Pharisaic limits and the universality of the Gospel."
(Note in the *Cambridge Bible*.)

[1] Cp. Isa. xxviii. 16. The Septuagint rendering there is quoted
nearly verbatim in the parallel to this passage, 1 Pet. ii. 6, and
it runs, "I lay *among the foundations* of Sion a stone, etc."
St Peter's use of the words directs the thought not upon an *apex*
but upon a *basis*. And so it seems best to take it here.

[2] Read Χριστοῦ Ἰησοῦ.

[3] "R.V., '*each several building*,' as if the great Temple were
viewed for the moment in its multiplicity of porches, courts, and
towers; each connected with the great bond of the substructure.—
An interesting grammatical question arises over the reading

structure, into a holy sanctuary,[1] a place for the manifestation for ever of the eternal Presence; in the Lord,
the Lord Christ, who is the Secret, as we have seen,
of the coherence of the Sanctuary, and of its growth;

Ver. 22. in whom you also, you as well as all the saints
beside, are being built up together, to form (εἰς) a permanent abode (κατοικητήριον) of our (τοῦ) God, in the
Spirit,[2] by whose sacred power you have received the
life which makes you "living stones," and who now
permeates the whole structure with His combining
presence.

Again we pause, at the close of a long and
closely connected paragraph. Not often, even
in St Paul, even in this Epistle, do we find

here, and this rendering, and will occur again iii. 15:—does the
Greek phrase, in the best attested reading [πᾶσα οἰκοδομή, not
πᾶσα ἡ οἰκοδομή] *demand* the rendering of the R.V. as against
that of the A.V.? We incline to the reply that it does not. The
law of the definite article . . . is undoubtedly somewhat less
exact in the Greek of the Scriptures than in that of the classics.
And this leaves us free to use (with caution) the context to
decide problems which in the classics would be decided by pure
grammar. Such a case we take this to be; and the question to
ask is, Does the context favour the imagery of *detail* or that
of *total*? Surely the latter. The idea points to one great
building, getting completed within itself, rising to its ideal."
(Note in the *Cambridge Bible*.)

[1] Ναός, more limited and more sacred than ἱερόν. At Jerusalem
the whole precinct of the Temple-buildings was the ἱερόν, the
Holy House itself was the ναός.

[2] Ἐν πνεύματι: both A.V. and R.V. render this, "in (through,
A.V.) *the* Spirit"; surely rightly, in view of the prominence
through the whole Epistle of the work of the Holy Ghost.

clause springing out of clause, thought out of thought, in such extended succession. My paraphrase has here and there attempted to relieve attention by making a pause where the Greek barely indicates an occasion for it ; but even so the reader will have followed the thread with a sense of its close continuity throughout.

The comment now shall take a very simple line. Let us first reflect a little upon the splendid close of the paragraph, and then note some of the steps which have led up to it. This order of thought will have its message for us in the end.

i. What a climax is reached in ver. 22 ! Here is the eternal destiny of the true Church of God. It is not only that it is to be " saved in Christ for ever," ineffable as is the wonder of that fact. It is not only that it is " to enjoy God fully for ever," though that amazing prospect is so amply and definitely revealed. It is—to be a " holy Sanctuary," a Shrine, a divine Presence-Chamber ; "a permanent Habitation of God." In measure, the wonderful fact has already begun to be ; already HE " dwells in " His people, " and walks in them" (see 2 Cor. vi. 16) ; already, as we shall see later in this Epistle (iii. 17), the eternal Son resides in the very heart of the true member of the Church, by faith. But all this is as when

some building, planned already by the master in
its final glory, is slowly rising, and beginning to
shew, amidst fragments and dust, and the noise
of the workmen, some hints and outlines of what
it is to be ; the owner, the intending dweller in it,
walks in and out amidst the vast beginnings, and
perhaps rests and shelters himself under the un-
finished walls and roofs.   It will be otherwise when
the last stone is in place, and the last splendid
equipment of the chambers is completed, and
he receives his admiring friends in the banquet-
chamber, and shines out amidst the shining of
his palace, himself the central splendour of it in
all his dignity of wealth and welcome.   So it is
with the saints, and with their common life as
the Church of God.   Wonderful are the beginnings.   Amidst all the apparent confusions of the
field where the building is in progress, its form
and scale begin to shew themselves, across the
perspective of centuries and continents.   And
when the stones already in place are scrutinized,
it is found that each of them is a miniature of
the whole ; a shrine, a home of the presence of
the Lord, by faith.   But a day of inauguration is
drawing on when "we shall see greater things
than these."   Then the divine indwelling in each
" living stone " will be complete and ideal, " for

sinners there are saints indeed." And as for the community, it will cohere and be one thing with a unity and symmetry unimaginable now.

> There all the millions of His saints
> Shall in one song unite,
> And each the bliss of all shall view
> With infinite delight.

And the everlasting FATHER will perfectly reveal Himself, to all the watchers of all the regions of the eternal world, not anyhow but *thus*—in His glorified Church, in the Race, the Nature, once wrecked and ruined, but rebuilt into this splendour by His grace. In the Church of the Firstborn, in the Bride, the Lamb's Wife, the blessed Universe shall see for ever GOD present, GOD resident. A transfigured Creation shall be His temple-courts; a beatified human Church shall be His sanctuary. That sanctuary shall reflect without a flaw its Indweller's glory; our union and communion with Him shall be, in other words, perfect, absolute, ideal. And the crowning thought, for the soul which loves God, is this, that we shall be HIS Abode; HE shall somehow find His home, His shrine, His throne, in our happy congregated being.

" It doth not yet appear," no, not yet. It is coming. Every evangelization, every conversion, every spiritual union and combination now, is a contribution to that result. It is coming. But what will it be when it is come ? Then at length the desire of GOD will be fulfilled, and His eternal joy will be felt through all the once " groaning and travailing creation." Then, and therefore, will be at length fulfilled the innermost desire of every one of His true children ; they shall all consciously contribute to the existence of what He has planned and, in the mystery of His ways, has waited for—a perfect " sanctuary," a perfect " habitation," for Him the blessed King. " Built on the Son, in the Spirit, for the Father," and finished to the last stone with the skill of infinite love, that will be indeed a Sanctuary, for manifestation, for oracles, for worship, to the endless ages.

ii. Now let us recall what the paragraph presents to us as some of the steps of truth leading up to this climax of blessing.

First, we reverently remark the uncompromising remembrance, over again, of the *mercy* of salvation. The Apostle cannot let the Ephesians forget the past, lest they mistake the blissful present. He is indeed in the act of reminding them that they have been brought not only into a place of mercy but into all the wealth of covenanted privilege. They are incorporated, out and out, into the true Israel of all the promises; no mere resident aliens, lodged in the suburbs of the holy Zion, but full citizens of the place, aye; members of the royal family of its King. They are one body with patriarchs, and prophets, and high-priests, and psalmists, and with the apostles of the Lamb; they cannot be nearer to God, for they are in His Christ. But then, all this is emphatically, and in their case even eminently, a gift of mere original mercy. They were outsiders once. They had not the slightest claim upon salvation. Not only as they were men, fallen and sinful, but also as they were "Gentiles," they stood upon ground where redemption found them outcast and out-lawed. Sovereign mercy (it was such, of course,) had given Israel long ago a standing in a place of light, hope, and promise; but *they* were not there. And who should dare to say that the Eternal would have been unrighteous had He left them where they were, "dead" as they were "in trespasses and sins," at "enmity" with infinite Holiness? It was mercy from first to last; they must remember this, step by step, as they ascend, in their new life, from strength to strength, from grace to glory. It must be reiterated to them, now in this form of thought, now in that, "lest they forget"; lest their Christian life fatally degenerate by an oblivion of what went before.

iii. Then, the great paragraph is full, in its central utterances, of the glory of the Atoning Work. Mercy has come to them, and lifted them up indeed to God. But it has not come anyhow; its channel is the blessed Cross. Here only in the Epistle is the Cross explicitly mentioned. "By means of the Cross" did the Lord "reconcile the two parties, in one body." "In the *blood* of Christ" did "the remote" become "the nigh." "In His flesh," here with a manifest reference to "the body of His flesh, in death," He "annulled the law of commandments," delivering us from its condemning power; "buying us out from its curse, becoming for us a curse" (Gal. iii. 13). Not by the mere and solitary glory of His Incarnation, no, but by "His meritorious Cross and Passion," the wonderful change of our position was effected. That, and nothing less, lies at the root of our peace, and so at the root of all the blessings which issue from our peace; among them, our spiritual cohesion with our fellow-believers, our growth into a deeper union with them, and so into a larger fitness to become "the habitation of God."

Let this not be forgotten. It comes to us with a peculiar impressiveness, this glorification of the Lord's dying work, *in the Epistle to the Ephesians*. No part of the New Testament deals more than this Epistle does with the inmost, the most spiritual, the most transcendent views of our salvation. We might have imagined *a priori* that it would soar away altogether, or nearly so, from the blood of Golgotha, and the grave at its foot, and deal rather with the serene glories of the Person of the enthroned Redeemer. But it is far otherwise. The Epistle will not let us forget that in order to our salvation the primal need was a righteous dealing with the broken law, a reconciliation of us to God,[1] a proclamation of "peace." And the *sine quâ non* to that immoveable requisite was the Lord's Cross, the Lord's Blood, the atonement of His Death. *That* is the rock on which is set the ladder of our ascent to heaven.

iv. Next, let us notice the prominence in this

---

[1] And in the phraseology of Scripture (see above on ver. 16) "to reconcile to God" means, to provide a way by which God can justly pardon man, and so by which man, coming in repentance to plead that way, can receive salvation.

passage of the deep and living truth of our Union
with the Lord Jesus Christ. For us He died,
vicariously, in expiation, standing in our place.
But that truth can never be rightly taken, never
be fully seen in its tender glory, if it is held
alone, if it is taught without a perpetual reference
to the truth of our living incorporation with Him.
" In Christ Jesus, ye became nigh"; "the two
were constituted one new man in Him"; "in
the Lord, the whole building is growing to be
a holy sanctuary." The work done for us, once
for all, was done with a view to our being
spiritually united to the Worker. And it is
only as we are, in that spiritual Union, "very
members incorporate in His mystical body,"
"joined unto the Lord, one Spirit," that the
finished Work actually avails for our present and
eternal safety.

v. Then, let us not forget but prize as a
chief treasure of the paragraph, its doctrine of
the Blessed Spirit. " In the Spirit," surrounded
and penetrated by Him, the Lord, the Giver of
the eternal life, the Maker to us of the reality
and presence of Christ, "we have our introduction to the Father." The Saviour leads us
in ; but He leads us in as those who have in
them the Spirit who glorifies Him to us, and

makes us one with Him. And so "in the Spirit" the saints are "being built together" for the final Sanctuary of God. That structure and cohesion may have for its *scaffolding* the sacred order of the Church in her visible aspect. But the *cement* is not of these things; it is wholly divine; it is the Spirit, possessing each saint for God, and binding them all together by articulating them all to their Head.

In these days, when longings for the outward unification of Christendom are much in the air around us, it will be well to hold this Ephesian passage in thoughtful remembrance. May we never be found in opposition to *the idea* of external unity, to the utmost degree in which it may be lawfully possible, without sacrifice of revealed truth, without compromise with the un-renewed world. The idea is sacred, and should be a continual guide, among other guiding lines, for our purposes and action. But let us not forget that the true growth of " the holy sanctuary ' is only " in the Lord "; the " habitation of God " arrives at its perfection, stone by stone, only "in the Spirit."

A DIGRESSION: THE GOSPEL, AND ITS WORLD-WIDE SCOPE

ALL, all as one we praise Thee,
Great Giver of salvation!
Whose equal grace nor time, nor place.
Nor language knows, nor nation.
We praise, and wait imploring
Thy hour of final favour;
Call in Thine own, reveal Thy throne,
And o'er us reign for ever.

CHAPTER VI

A DIGRESSION: THE GOSPEL, AND ITS WORLD-WIDE SCOPE

EPHESIANS iii. 1–13

IN the paragraph just closed, we have seen the vision of the spiritual Temple of God. The saints of the Asian Churches have appeared in that vision as stones built one by one into the wonderful structure. Rising upon their foundation in Christ, and compacted in Him their Corner Stone, they are destined at length to form, for ever, the complete and faultless Sanctuary to be inhabited by the eternal Presence, the Shrine for the manifestation of God to the universe in the endless ages.

Toward that "far-off divine event" moves all the work of the Gospel. The labours of the evangelist and the pastor are indeed inestimably precious as they affect the salvation and

development of the redeemed individual. Assuredly, did there exist only one human being,
a unique specimen, race and individual at once,
made in the image of God, and fallen from
Him, the Gospel which should bring to bear
on that one soul the saving powers of the world
to come would do a work worthy of God. But
as the case is, the Gospel has innumerable souls
to deal with. And it has to deal with them
not only as the individual multiplied, but as the
saved, vivified, sanctified, glorified Community.
Its result is to be not only a vast collection of
chiselled marbles, but those marbles, each faultless in itself, constructed into a Temple, with
its courts, and towers, and Holy Place. If the
metaphor may be changed for a moment, the
saints are not to be strewn as scattered pearls
or rubies upon the floor of heaven; they are to
be "made up" (Mal. iii. 17) by the great
Artificer into one glorious brilliant, in which
jewel shall shine upon jewel, and each set off
the whole.

Great and splendid then is the aim which
is to animate the Christian evangelist. He is
working amidst dust and turmoil, but it is for
no less a result than the completed Temple of
the heavenly Solomon. When that temple is

inaugurated at last, he shall be permitted to look upon its symmetry and grandeur, and to think, I too was used in the production of the Habitation of God.

Such surely is the thought of the Apostle at this point in the writing of his Letter. If I read correctly the opening of the third chapter, he was just about to follow up here the theme of the Habitation. But then he turns aside on a sudden to the theme of the Gospel, and of his own part in its enterprise for the world. He was about to say something like this: "You are being built together into the eternal Shrine, the Holy Place, for the residence of God for ever. Therefore, because of such a future, my prayers are going up for you that you may have a corresponding blessing in the present. You are being collected and erected into one Temple, for the abode (κατοικητήριον) of God. I pray therefore that your individual hearts may even now, each one of them, be nothing short of an abode (κατοικῆσαι, iii. 17) of Christ, as the way to your full fruition of every spiritual gift and power. I pray that you may be individually sanctified by the Indwelling now, in order to your being collectively glorified by the Indwelling hereafter." This seems to be the

ultimate connexion between the close of the
second chapter, with its κατοικητήριον, (followed
by the τούτου χάριν of iii. 1,) and the close of
the third chapter, with its τούτου χάριν (ver. 14)
and its κατοικῆσαι

But here comes in this great and memorable
digression. He touches now the thought of his
apostolic commission, his call to gather in " the
Nations " to be built up into the spiritual shrine.
And that touch irresistibly impels him to further
utterances about that commission, and the grandeur of his message, and the wonder in his own
eyes that he, unworthy, should be called to carry
it to the world. So we have to wait awhile
for the precious sentences about the residence
of Christ in the heart by faith, and the love
which surpasses knowledge, and the fulness of
God. But while we wait we listen to an inter-
lude full of spiritual music. St Paul has to
tell us of " the unsearchable wealth of Christ "
poured out upon " the Gentiles," free as the
golden sunshine, and of a " fellowship " for them
all in the long-hidden " mystery " of His salvation, and of the angelic princes of the heavenly
world watching the Church to read there their
brightest, deepest lesson in the " variegated
wisdom of God," and how, in view of such a

glory of grace, he sees himself to be " less than least of all the saints."

It is a digression quite abnormal on strict rhetorical principles. But it is of a kind which carries with it its own peculiar eloquence and impression. Such tangents and excursions of thought are characteristic of overflowing minds, from St Paul of old to Thomas Chalmers in a recent generation ; Chalmers *wrote* his sermons, because he could never *reach the end* of any great subject without the curb of manuscript, so strong was the impulse to diverge into the rich fields beside the road.   And where is the parenthesis of St Paul that does not give the Church some conspicuous treasures of revelation ?

Let us listen then, while we wait :

Ver. 1. **On this account,** in view of such a goal of all my work, and of all your hopes, **I Paul,** yes, no other than this conscious Ego,[1] wonderful as that fact is to myself, **I, the prisoner of our** (τοῦ) **Christ Jesus,** (His prisoner, because my captivity is due to the fact that I belong to Him, and in that captivity am wholly His possession

---

[1] He frequently writes ἐγὼ Παῦλος. So 2 Cor. x. 1, "I Paul myself beseech you"; Gal. v. 2, "Behold I Paul say unto you"; Col. i. 23, "whereof I Paul am made a minister." This is no commonplace *egotism* ; it is the voice of an intense and powerful personality, filled with a vivid consciousness of relation and responsibility.

still,) on behalf of, in the interests of the Gospel for, you, the Nations, (for in you I see, by representation, "*the*

Ver. 2. Gentiles" as a whole ;) if, if indeed (εἴγε), you did ever hear of the stewardship of that grace of God which was given me toward you, even the grace, the sovereign gift, of apostolic commission for labour among the Nations [1]—:

Here on purpose I leave a broken sentence as the close of a paragraph. For it is just here that the line of thought quits the circle at the tangent. The Apostle begins here to dilate on the glory of the Gospel for "the Nations," and the wonder of his own commission, postponing the account of the prayer in which he beseeches for his converts that they may all experience the indwelling of Christ in the heart. That account

---

[1] Εἴγε ἠκούσατε. As I understand this "if," it is the expression of a certain gracious *irony*. The commission of St Paul to "the Gentiles" had been well known through the whole circle of his missions for years, and was notorious of course at Ephesus, and generally in Asia (it was at Ephesus that he first definitely withdrew the converts from the synagogue, Acts xix. 8, 9). And just this notoriety of the fact gives occasion for a gentle, an almost *pleasant*, hypothetical allusion to it : "You may possibly have heard of such a thing as my being the Apostle of the Gentiles ! "

Τῆς χάριτος . . . τῆς δοθείσης. Observe that he speaks here not of the "stewardship" but of the "grace" as the "gift." See for comment the words below, ver. 8, "to me . . . was this grace given, to preach, etc." So probably Phil. i. 7, "partakers of my grace," i.e. of my apostolic work and suffering.

is suspended till ver. 14, where at length we see
him on his knees to the Father, asking for the
promised Spirit, that the saints may each receive
the fulness of the blessing of the Son.   Let us
leave the soul-disturbed construction as it stands,
and proceed :

Ver. 3.   I assume then that you did once hear that,
revelation-wise, by no mere cogitations, reasonings, aspi-
rations of my own, but by the personal, supernatural
information of my Lord, there was made known [1] to
me the mystery, the Secret, undiscoverable except as
revealed [2] ; as I have written above in brief, [3] referring

Ver. 4.   to which utterance (πρὸς ὅ) you are able, you
have the materials, as you read the words over, to per-
ceive my intelligence (σύνεσιν), my God-given insight, in
the mystery, the Secret, of our (τοῦ) Christ ; the hidden
wisdom, the long-buried treasures, stored in His work
and glory.   And what is that Secret ?   It is the divine

Ver. 5.   purpose which in [4] other, different (ἑτέραις),
generations was not made known to the sons of men,
Jewish or Gentile, as (on the scale and with the
unreserved distinctness with which) it has now been

---

[1] Read ἐγνωρίσθη, not ἐγνώρισε.

[2] Such is always the meaning of μυστήριον in the N.T.   See
on i. 9.

[3] Προέγραψα ἐν ὀλίγῳ.   The Greek aorist is here best represented
by our perfect, as the "writing" was so recent.   He refers to
previous passages in this Epistle, i. 9, etc., ii. 11, etc.   Hence our
"above" seems better as a rendering than "before."

[4] Probably omit ἐν.   But the English will be the same.

unveiled [1] to His holy apostles and prophets,[2] the recipients
of His developed message of salvation, who receive it
and proclaim it in the Spirit, in the possessing power,
in the revealing light, of the Holy Ghost.

And now, once more, what is this deep SECRET
of the loving will of God? It is no astounding
but unprofitable curiosity of the unseen world;
nothing which appeals to man except as man
is conscious of himself as a sinner, and awake
to his need of peace and amity with eternal
Holiness, and athirst for present purity and
immortal glory to follow. But let man be thus
awake, and then indeed the Secret of the Lord
is wonderful to him, and is welcome. Let him
be some "Gentile," European, or Asiatic, or
from African Cyrene or Abyssinia, who knows
himself at all, and who has heard indeed of a
God of truth and glory, but only through the
message of the Pharisee; he wonders whether
after all there is room for *him* in the house
of salvation, for him, with all his secular and
uncovenanted conditions; for him, on the wrong

---

[1] Νῦν ἀπεκαλύφθη. Again an aorist, but demanding the English
perfect to represent it, as the reference is to a recent past whose
results are present.

[2] Beyond doubt here the reference is to the "prophets" of the
Christian Church, like Silas and Agabus. See above, ii. 20, and
remarks there.

side of that awful "wall of partition" within which Israel walks in supernatural privilege, on the way to an endless heaven. Let such be the hearer of the apostolic news, (and the heathen world then, even as now, was scattered all over with souls in just such a wistful mood, whatever special form it took in its expression,) and indeed he would hail the Secret as life from the dead. For it is this:

Ver. 6. **That the Nations are,** in God's purpose now at last revealed, after the long age of discipline and reserve, **co-heritors** of the spiritual estate of a common Father, for they are made His children in His Son, **and co-members** [1] in the one Body animated by the new life, **and co-partakers of the Promise in Christ,** the Promise of the full blessing of Abraham, laid up for all who are bound up with Abraham's Lord and Seed, Messiah. And this union with Him has become a fact for them **by means of the Gospel;** that life-bringing message of a Saviour and of a Holy Ghost, by which (1 Cor. iv. 15) man, believing, is "begotten again," and so passes into all that is meant by living union with God in Christ. For it is the message which unfolds at last "the end," the final cause, of that "Law" which seemed as if it were only the barrier between "the Nations" and

---

[1] Σύσσωμα. I sacrifice a literal rendering to preserve the balance in form of the terms συγκληρονόμα, σύσσωμα, κ.τ.λ.

eternal life. It shews the wonderful CHRIST, who was, as it were, prepared and developed within that barrier, now rising and overflowing it, and pouring Himself, like the rivers of Paradise, upon all the world, for the blessing of "whosoever will." This Gospel presents Him to "the Gentile" as no mere casual and accidental, however wonderful, Gift of heavenly compassion ; He is the eternally-intended Lord of *a Covenant* "ordered in all things and sure." Israel was for a season the solitary trustee of that Covenant. But the time has come now for its unreserved conveyance to "all the seed, not to that which belongs to the Law only, but to that which belongs to Abraham's faith" (Rom. iv. 16).

Wonderful Gospel, wonderful in this universality of its covenant-scope! How little do we, so long used to its abundant blessings, understand its *wonder*! But those primeval heathen converts did. And we too begin again to do so whenever, under conviction of sin, we get a real conviction of mercy, and own that all might have been utterly otherwise. The Eternal might have dealt with a disloyal race "according to their works." But He has dealt with them "according to His abundant mercy," according to "the Son of His love," whom He "gave for the life of the world."

The thought of that Gospel fires more and more the heart and utterance of the Apostle.

Ver. 7. **Of which** message **I became minister,** διάκονος, working servant and agent, **according to,** in the spirit and with the strength of, **the free gift** (δωρεά), the benignant boon, of commission and inspiration in my apostleship; the gift of, conferred on me by, **the grace which was given me, according to the working of His power;** yes, according to nothing less than that divine inward resource. I was made the Apostle of the Nations, "according to a gift" as regarded my illumination and commission, and "according to His power" as regarded my capacity to carry through the vast work in all its weight and fulness. Woe to me if I sent myself; but He sent me. Woe yet more to me if I seek to sustain myself in self-born energies and enthusiasm; but He is in me, "working His works" (John xiv. 10). With such a power lodged within me, there is no discouragement, while there is unspeakable humiliation, in the fact that the "vessel" is so truly "earthen," in itself so immeasurably un-

Ver. 8. worthy of its contents. **To me, even me** (the emphatic ἐμοί), **the less than least** [1] **of all saints,**—seen by my inmost self, in all I know of myself, to be no more than that, (a "saint," yes, a true limb of Christ, a genuine devotee to Him; but the really unworthiest among them all,)—**has been given this grace,** this sovereign, unearned bounty—**to the Nations** [2] **to tell as Gospel the unsearchable,** the "untrackable," the labyrinthine

---

[1] 'Ελαχιστοτέρῳ, literally "*leaster*"; a "comparative superlative" coined by his glowing thought for this unique use.

[2] Read τοῖς ἔθνεσιν. note ἐν τ. ἐ.

(ἀνεξιχνίαστον), wealth of our (τοῦ) Christ; the boundless source and resource in Him for all that man needs for the bliss of his whole being, in time, in eternity, in
Ver. 9. life, in death, in glory; and to illuminate all men, to pour round them, whoever they may be, a flood of sunlight, as to what is, in its amazing fact and character, the dispensation,[1] the world-wide distribution, as God designs it, through His servants, of the mystery, the Secret of a world's covenant-blessing in Christ, which has been hidden away, since the ages began, in the God, our God, who created all things,[2] and who in His plan of Redemption has not forgotten that fact of His universal Creatorship.

And this "world-wide distribution" of the tidings of such a mercy, what is it to do? It is to gather in a Church of believers out of universal man. And the work of that Church, what is it to be? A work for extension indeed! It is not only even to illuminate the human world; it is to cast a reflected glory upwards, to the eyes of the watchers of the world above; that
Ver. 10. now, now at last, in the Gospel age, to the governments and the authorities, the "princes" (Dan. x. 21, etc.) of the angelic host, representatives of that host itself, in the celestial regions, may be made known, intimated, given as information (γνωρισθῇ), by means of the Church, by that great object-lesson in what omnipotent Love can do with the material of a ruined race, the variegated, the versatile, the manifold, wisdom of

---

[1] Certainly read οἰκονομία, not κοινωνία.
[2] Omit διὰ Ἰησοῦ Χριστοῦ.

God; the "wisdom" which is never at a loss to carry out its purposes of grace, be the problems presented by its subject what they may.

It is a wonderful scene, as the Apostle lifts the veil, and bids us, like Elisha's lad at Dothan, see the invisible around us and above. Behold "the Church," "the company of the faithful." "Whence came they?" From the Fall, from the death of sin, from the city of destruction, from a profound preference of self to God. Each one of that company, if interrogated, will say that he, that she, was antecedently as unworthy as possible of grace, justly under sentence, "in the flesh," in which "no good thing dwelleth." "Whence came they?" From the real circumstances of mortal life; from the scenes of common toil, and prosaic incident, and everyday intercourse; from the hopes and fears, the laughter and weeping, the births and deaths of time, just as we know them. They have come to Christ "in the body," "in this tabernacle," "being burthened." They have been received by Him so, and kept by Him so, and under these conditions joined together in Him in the wonderful organism of the limbs of the living Head. Men, women, children, behold them there, upon the earth; not in the heavenly future only, as they shall be, but "*now*," in the present, as they are. And then above them see, bending to the contemplation, "the governments and the authorities in the celestial regions." The spirits of immortality are intently studying the mortal scene below them. They possess in their own ethereal consciousness the experience of all the past since they "sang together" (Job xxxviii. 7) over creation. They live where the vision of God is given to them as it is not given yet to us; they "always behold His face"; they "stand in His presence." What then have they to learn *from us*? Ah, they have to learn something which makes them watch us with wonder and with awe. They see in us indeed all our weakness, and all our sin. But they see a nature which, wrecked by itself, was yet made in the image of their God and ours. And they see this God at work upon that wreck to produce results not only wonderful in themselves but doubly wonderful because of the conditions.

It is a thought to inspire the weakest and the least advanced disciple, that he, just as "a man in Christ," is a specimen, an instance, a part and member, of this Object of the attention of "our elder brethren of the sky."

The "angel that excels in strength" has things to learn here which he cannot learn from all he sees among his own bright peers of the celestial Order. He has to learn what grace can do with the mortal nature, and under the burthen of the flesh, as it is carried about perhaps by some poor and despised disciple, some young convert in the lanes of the English city, or in the kraal of the African wilderness. His cloudless intelligence finds matter for profound reflection in the phenomenon of firm and reasonable faith exercised by the man who knows God by grace but is utterly unable, from his earthly point of view, to see through some riddle of his Providence, or to comprehend some dark saying of His Word. In his own immortality, never touched by one drop of our cold river, it is instructive to him beyond all our thought to see his God triumphing over pain and death in some sufferer in the fire of martyrdom, or in the torture of cancer, or in the shipwreck, or just in the silent awe of any form of our departure from the body. " In all these things we are more than conquerors, through Him that loved us." And what He who loved us is, in His " multifold wisdom," is seen thus " through the Church," as nowhere
9

else in the universe, by the Principalities and
Powers.

All this, moreover, this education of heaven through
earth, if we may dare to phrase it so, is a matter of
Ver. 11. the plan and will of God; it is **according
to the purpose**, the programme, **of the ages**, the long
"dispensations" of the slow history of Redemption
leading up to the Church Universal of living saints; the
purpose **which He**, the Father, **formed, in the Christ**, even
Jesus our Lord. For all was planned, as all was to be
carried out, "*in Him*"; "both Idea and Working were
altogether bound up with Him. 'In Christ' God was
to 'reconcile the world'; 'in Christ' the saints were to
'have redemption, in His blood'; 'in Him' to be
'rooted and built up'; 'complete in Him'; 'abiding
in Him'; 'walking in Him'; 'dying in the Lord'; 'in
Christ made alive.'"

"So God hath greatly purposed." And the Principalities and Powers see God working that purpose out
in a material that only illustrates to the utmost, by its
difficulty, His glory.

And now what do they see as the innermost wondei
of the phenomenon they study? They see these fallen
and mortal beings, this Community of the lost and
saved, not only bearing and doing for God here on
earth, but spiritually present with Him in the Holy
of Holies above. The "saints" are in Christ, who is
in God. So they are the intimates of their Father's
heart; His subjects, His vassals, His bondmen, on the
one side, but on the other, His own dear children, who

can *say anything* to Him. For they are one with the
Ver. 12.   Well-Beloved, **in whom we have our** (τήν)
freedom of utterance, παῤῥησίαν, our unreserved leave
of intercourse, **and** our **introduction, through our** (τῆς)
faith in Him (αὐτοῦ).   For this whole wonderful life is
"from faith to faith."   To rely, to confide, to act upon
the promise, is the secret and the means, alike when the
penitent comes first to the feet of divine Compassion,
and when the disciple goes deepest into the recesses
of "the secret of the Presence."

Ver. 13.   **Wherefore I ask you,**[1] I appeal to you, **not to
lose heart,** as in your loving sympathy you might do,
as if you had to feel with me *under a failure,* **amidst**
(ἐν) **my troubles** suffered **on your behalf; for this** (ἥτις)
is your glory.   In the propagation of such a Gospel
the messenger may well be willing to suffer for the
sake of the converts, and they in their turn may well
not be discouraged when they see him suffer for them.
And such a Gospel supplies the very motive to the
spirit breathing here, the spirit which cannot pause to
contemplate its own "troubles" as such, but thinks
only of those for whom they are endured, and of *their*
need of hope and cheer.

So closes the long and magnificent digression.
It has roved from the immediate theme in hand,
but not for a moment has it stepped outside of

---

[1] It seems far better to explain αἰτοῦμαι thus than of prayer to
God. *That* is spoken of in the next sentence, and in much
stronger terms.

Christ.   It is a sudden turn taken in a green labyrinth.   But the labyrinth is all alike the ἀνεξιχνίαστος πλοῦτος, "the wealth not to be tracked by footprints," of our Lord Jesus Christ.

Let us return now, with St Paul, to the original matter of the context.   But let us only the more involve ourselves, as to faith and love, in the glorious Maze of Him whose Name, with all that it contains, is a boundless Paradise of the believing soul.

> Our Garden is a Labyrinth too,
>   Whose paths no clue can tell;
> It spreads about us, ever new,
>   A wealth unsearchable.

PRAYER FOR THE INDWELLING AND THE FULNESS

My prayer hath power with God the grace
   Unspeakable I now receive;
Through faith I see Thee face to face,
   I see Thee face to face, and live:
In vain I have not wept and strove;
Thy nature and Thy name is Love.

C. WESLEY

CHAPTER VII

I HAVE already attempted to explain the structure of this part of the Epistle. If I see it aright, we have in the paragraph, iii. 1-13, a digression from a main line of thought, of which line the characteristic note is Divine Indwelling. If the digression had not taken place, we should have seen the Apostle pass at once from the Indwelling as it concerns the whole Church, and the eternal future, to the Indwelling as it concerns the individual heart, and the present hour ; this second theme being connected vitally with the first, because to the the Indwelling in the Church hereafter for ever the great, the glorious, preparatory step is the Indwelling in the heart now. But the digression broke in upon this sequence, though it did so only to give us a view, among other things, of an "unsearchable wealth" in Christ of which we shall presently speak again. But now, it is over. The stream of thought has run its majestic circuit at the side, and once more it flows straight onward, onward to the sea, to the deep. For it will conduct us to "all the fulness of God," to a power which can, and will, do wonders in us and for us "above all that we ask or think." And on its way to that Ocean it will waft us into the blessedness of the Indwelling of Christ in the Heart.

Look then, and listen. The Apostle is at prayer, "bowing his knees." The Pretorian at his side may or may not kneel also; he may be a pagan scoffer, but quite possibly he may be a convert and a brother. Disciples like Epaphras and Luke may be there, to kneel too; or it may be some time when all such friends are absent. But however, PAUL is on his knees, and pouring out his innermost heart for the Asians. And what he asks for them, he asks for us; for it is for them as *Christians* that he prays. Let us thankfully remember here the marked absence of the local and the temporal in the allusions of our Epistle; it will bring home the truth and glory of the message more fully

upon our own souls.   Not for believers of one
generation, or race, or station, or grade of
civilization, or even of experience, is this man
praying here.   He is praying for Christians
simply as such.   And that means, for us.

We will give ear indeed.   And we will
remember that it is not only St Paul at prayer.
The Lord is in him, that he may intercede.
Never was he more inspired than now.   It is
not he that speaks about the heart, about the
Presence, about the blessing ; it is " the Spirit
that maketh intercession."   We are in the very
line, in each petition, of the will of God.

Ver. 14. **For this cause**, for the sake of your present
blessedness, and your coming unimaginable glory as
the Habitation of God, the " cause " present to my
mind when that same phrase ($\tau o\acute{\upsilon}\tau o\upsilon$ $\chi\acute{a}\rho\iota\nu$) was used
before (ver. 1), **I bow my knees towards**, as looking
up towards, **the Father,**[1] the ultimate and eternal
Ver. 15. Fountain of all blessing, Him **from whom**, out
of whom ($\grave{\epsilon}\xi$ $o\mathring{\upsilon}$), as by a sacred *derivation* of thought

---

[1] The words $\tau o\hat{\upsilon}$ K. $\mathring{\eta}\mu\hat{\omega}\nu$ 'I. X. must certainly be omitted.   The
evidence of MSS. and patristic quotations is against them, and
St Jerome expressly says that the " Latin copies " which contain
them are in error.   And context favours the omission ; the $\Pi a\tau\acute{\eta}\rho$
is here regarded, immediately and mainly, in His relation not to
the blessed Son but to the redeemed Family.   That relation
is indeed only " in " the Son.   But it can be contemplated
occasionally by itself ; and so it is here.

and word, all the Family¹ (πατριά) in the heavens and upon earth, all the company, all the body, of believers here and of the blessed ones above, human and angelic spirits alike, gets its name, πατριά.

And now, what is the petition? It is altogether for the disciples' hearts, and for the Saviour's glory, through the Spirit:

Ver. 16. **That He would give to you, (for it is a sove-**

---

¹ Πατήρ, πατριά : it is a real misfortune that in English we cannot keep the verbal point of the Greek, by words which have a verbal kinship. We might perhaps render πατριά, "*father's-house*," or "*father's-family*"; but it would be cumbersome at best.

The R.V. here renders "*every family*," or (margin) "*fatherhood*." And this would no doubt be right in view of classical usage, according to which "the whole family" would almost certainly demand πᾶσα ἡ πατριά. But the usage of N.T. Greek is not so strict, and we may and must accordingly consult context along with wording. What does context say? Does the Apostle seem most likely here to take up the thought of God's spiritual Fatherhood as the archetype of all family unions, spiritual or not, in earth and heaven? *or* the thought of the family oneness of saints and angels under the "Father of spirits"? To me the answer seems clear for the *second* alternative. All through this great passage he is full of the thought of the spiritual and *universal* community. The phrase, "in heaven and earth," itself (compared with i. 10) suggests such thoughts rather than those of "families" in detail. I advocate therefore the Authorized Version.

The Rabbis called the angels "the upper family" and Israel "the lower." The parallel with St Paul's language is not perfect, but it is near enough for illustration; the phrases may be as old as St Paul's time, and may have partially moulded his language here.

reign gift, under His own covenant of free grace,[1]) according to, on the scale and in the style of, **the wealth of His glory**, the resources of His ever-blessed Nature, manifested to us, **to be with power made mighty,**[2] **by means of His Spirit,** the Holy Spirit of Promise, the Lord of Pentecost, "Spirit of counsel and of might," **deep in the inner man,**[3] the region where the new life moves and grows, the regenerate consciousness itself.

So the prayer is for power, divine in kind, and, as to its operation, penetrating to the depths of manhood. To what issue and effect? Is the result to be convulsive and formidable? Is the operation to come out in words and works of miracle, alarming the world into submission? No; it is a power full of life, life infinite and eternal, but so deep that it is still, with the peace of God Himself, and with a joy which is but heavenly love in movement. This "making mighty with power" is to have for its first and main effect just the opening of the heart's inmost

---

[1] See, on the mighty *gift to the heart* under the New Covenant, Jer. xxxi. 31, and the related passages in N.T.; 2 Cor. iii., Heb. viii., x. See also the close of the present chapter of this book.

[2] Κραταιωθῆναι: observe the aorist, with its suggestion of decision and crisis.

[3] Εἰς τὸν ἔσω ἄνθρωπον: lit. "*into* the inner man." My translation may fairly represent this; the thought is of the inward direction of the Gift; no surface-work.

door to the personal presence of the Saviour, and then, and so, the full apprehension of His salvation :

Ver. 17. So that our (τόν) Christ may take up His lasting habitation,[1] by means of faith, in your hearts ; coming to them in a sense, in a respect, so deep and great, as to constitute a practically new arrival, and remaining where He so arrives not as a Guest, precariously detained, but as a Master resident in His proper home ; and this, " by faith," " by your (τῆς) faith," through your taking Him at His word, taking Him for granted, and opening the door without misgiving to His entrance. Then, at once the ideas of resultant blessing develope themselves from this glorious germ ; **that, in love rooted and founded,[2]** having stricken your root deep into the soil of the Love of God, having built your house of salvation firm upon its rock, **you may**

Ver. 18. achieve strength (ἐξισχύσητε) to grasp,[3] in the insight and appropriation of the soul, **with all the saints,** with an experience all the deeper because

---

[1] Κατοικῆσαι: observe the compound, and the tense. It is to be a *settled* residence, κατοικεῖν. And it is to be a decisive, critical, *beginning*—indicated by the aorist.

[2] Ἐν ἀγάπῃ ἐῤῥιζωμένοι καὶ τεθεμελιωμένοι: placed here at the beginning of a new sentence, the words seem to amount almost to a sentence by themselves, as if he had said, "that you may be in love rooted, etc., and so may be able, etc."—Ἐν ἀγάπῃ : the reference seems almost certainly to be to the Eternal Love. Nothing less in the way of ἀγάπη could be the *soil* of the Christian's root, the *rock* of his foundation.

[3] Observe again the significant aorists, ἐξισχύσητε, καταλαβέσθαι.

consciously one with that of " the whole Family," **what is the breadth, and length, and depth, and height of** that mighty Love just mentioned, and just to be mentioned again, that Universe of blessing, with its vast horizons and its boundless sphere, its Purpose, Work, and Ver. 19. Covenant of glorious grace[1]; **and to know,** with an intelligence now wonderfully developed,[2] **the knowledge - transcending love of our** (τοῦ) **Christ;** yes, transcending for ever, while it invites and allures for ever, all that we call *knowing*, for it is infinite ; so that, as the crown and issue of the whole blissful process of Indwelling, of Intuition, **you may be filled**[3] **unto,** up to, **all the fulness of our** (τοῦ) **God;** your whole happy

---

[1] "Some curiosities of interpretation attach to this verse. Severianus (cent. 4, 5) . . . finds here an allusion to the shape of the Cross, and in that shape to the Lord's Godhead ('*height*') and Manhood ('*depth*'), and to the extent of the apostolic missions ('*length and breadth*'). St Jerome in his Commentary here interprets the words at some length, and finds in the '*height*' the holy angels, in the '*depth*' the evil spirits, in the '*length*' those of mankind who are on the upward path, and in the '*breadth*' those who are 'sinking towards vices. For *broad and ample is the way which leadeth to death.*' The Calvinist Zanchius adopts from Photius (cent. 9) the explanation that the reference is to 'the mystery of the free salvation through Christ of the Gentiles and the whole human race'; called *long*, because decreed from eternity; *broad*, because extended to all ; *deep*, because of the descent of Christ to Hades, and because of the resurrection of the dead ; *high*, because Christ ascended above all heavens." (Note in the *Cambridge Bible*.)

Γνῶναι : again remark the aorist. The whole passage is full of the thought of " *new departures* " in the life of grace.

[2] Once more an aorist, πληρωθῆτε.

nature flooded, as it were, with all which, being Grace
in Him the Giver, can become Grace in us the receivers
of the Gift.

Is this too much to hope, to ask, to take? No,
Ver. 20. because HE is in the question. **But to Him
who is able to do beyond all things,** to carry His work
of blessing to lengths indefinite indeed, **vastly beyond
all** [1] we ask or understand of His wealth and His ways,
yet, all the while, **according to the power** of the Spirit
Ver. 21. which is already at work in us; **to Him be the
glory, in the Church,** (not *by* the Church only, but *in* it,
for it is the occasion and matter of the ascription,)
and in Christ Jesus, [2] who is supremely the Father's Gift,
and therefore supremely the Occasion of His Glory;
unto all the generations of the age of the ages. Amen.
Even so be it, even so shall it be, through that in-
terminable Future which lies waiting for us in His
Eternity; that "age," that "sum and circumference of
ages," ages which again will themselves contain periods
faintly imaged by the "generations" which make up
the centuries of Time.

So ends the Prayer, the "bowing of the
knees," and then the Doxology, which seems to
come less to close it than to waft it aloft into
eternity. This is one of *the great* Scriptures,
the Holy Spirit's words of the first order. Let

---

[1] Construct together ὑπερεκπερισσοῦ ὧν. Observe this grandly
characteristic passage, with its repeated ὑπέρ.

[2] Almost certainly read καὶ ἐν Χριστῷ Ἰησοῦ.

us recall it, let us ponder it, to be ourselves uplifted, and then abased, but only to be the better uplifted again in the power of God.

Adolphe Monod, in his unpretending but precious "Explanation" of the Epistle, writes thus of the profound paragraph before us:

"After the grandest promises which human language can express, the Holy Ghost here closes by declaring that all which can be expressed is infinitely below the reality which is in God. In vain we mount, even in the track of an Apostle; we can only contemplate, after all, 'parts of the ways of God' (Job xxvi. 14), and we must always conclude with 'groanings that cannot be uttered' (Rom. viii. 26). Yes, and nothing other can suffice us than this avowal of insufficiency; nothing less could respond to the vague and vast need of our heart. All that the mind comes to seize distinctly (*nettement*), and the mouth to enunciate with precision, is incapable of satisfying us. This conclusion accordingly, astonishing and unexpected, is just what we required.

"Nothing can restrain or bound the power of God towards us; nothing in Him, nothing even in us; no limits set to His power, for it knows no limits; not even the weakness of our prayers, and the imperfection of our knowledge, for He is able to transcend all our demands and all our conceptions.)

"But alas for us, if this language, infinitely below the reality which is in God, should be infinitely above the reality which is in us! Imagine a practical Christianity conceived according to the text of the Scriptures only, and irrespective of the personal experience of believers; and then imagine a practical Christianity conceived only according to the experience of believers, and irrespective of the written Word. Should we not say that here were two different religions? To pass from Scripture to our experience seems like a fall from heaven to earth—not to say, sometimes, to hell! Let us class (*assortissons*) our Christianity aright. And may the Lord teach us how to bring our experience into harmony with His promises. Truly, we have need of a new baptism of the Holy Spirit."[1]

Reflections like these, the reflections of a saint such as Monod, at once abased and profoundly animated by the words we have studied, may well seem the best commentary upon them. The whole passage calls the believer away from a

---

[1] *Explication de l'Épître aux Éphésiens*, pp. 206, 207.

mere discussion of phrases to the inner chamber
of faith and prayer. "You have your Bible,
and you have your knees; use them"; so said
a venerable Christian, my godfather, Carr John
Glyn, who died in 1896, within twenty months of
his hundred years. Let *us* "use them" indeed,
that the treasures of this Ephesian paragraph
may become in some measure the current coin
of our lives.

But this very end may be advanced by just
such attention to the phrases in detail as may
send us to our knees with more articulate aims
and hopes. So let me take up some few out of
the great words of the paragraph, and point to
them, in all earnest, for faith and for *expectant*
prayer.

i. "I bow my knees to the Father . . . *that
He would grant you.*" So then this is a matter
of divine, personal, benignant *gift*. Free as the
gift of pardon, of justifying righteousness, of
adoption, of incorporation, is the gift of the Indwelling and its attendant bliss. For the moment,
put away other aspects, other sides, other truths;
they will be sure to be remembered in their place,
if we are using "our Bible and our knees."
Think just now of just this; "that He would
grant you," "that He would *give*," ἵνα δῷ.

10

"Cease from thine own works"; "cease from thine own wisdom." This is a gift, free and sovereign; address thyself in simplicity — to receive.

ii. "*To be with power made mighty* . . . that Christ may take up His habitation in your hearts." This is to be the Spirit's operation, "with power to make you mighty," that you may—not shake the earth, but receive the Indweller. And why do we need a supreme *empowering* just in order to receive our Life, our Light? Does the hungry wanderer need power in order to eat the food without which he will soon sink? Does the bewildered mariner need power to welcome on to his deck the pilot who alone can steer him to the haven of his desire? No; but there is another aspect of the matter here. For the heart, though it immeasurably needs the blessed Indweller, has that in it which *dreads* His absolute Indwelling. *Can it trust Him with* complete internal authority? Will He not use it to purposes terrible to the human heart, asserting His position by some infliction, some exaction, awful and unpitying? So the hand, stretched out to "open the door" (Rev. iii. 20), the inner door—for the King is supposed to be already received into the porch,

and hall, and more public chambers of the being—
falls again, and shrinks from that turning of the
key which is to set the last recess quite open
to the MASTER.   Here is the need for the Spirit's
empowering work.   Come, Holy Ghost, and
shew to the hesitating heart " the glory of God
in the face of Jesus Christ," that lovely glory,
shewn in that fair Countenance; then it shall
hesitate no more.   Beholding His love in His
look it shall not dread His power in His grasp.
It shall be strong to welcome Him wholly in,
for it shall see, in the light of the Spirit, that
" *in His presence* is the fulness of joy," that " to
serve Him is to reign."

iii. " That Christ may *take up His habitation
in your hearts.*"   What, has He not been in
residence before?   Can the Ephesian be a
Christian indeed, with Christ still absent out of
him ?   Is it not at Ephesus as at Corinth,
where " Jesus Christ *is in* you, except ye be
counterfeits, castaways" (ἀδόκιμοι : 2 Cor. xiii. 5)?
Well, all that side is vitally true, but there is
another side.   The Lord must, for our salvation
at all, be so in living union with us that we
are in Him, and *He in us.*   But His presence
in us has its degrees and advances, its less
and more, its outer and inner.   To drop

metaphor, a life may be truly Christian and yet far from fully Christian ; the man may have come really to Christ, and have really cast anchor on Him, and have really confessed Him, and be really seeking to serve Him, yet be keeping back, perhaps quite unconsciously, whole regions of the life from Him. He may be living rather as His ally than as His vassal. He may be rather treating Him as an august Visitor in His servant's house than behaving as the loving bondservant in a house where Christ is always the Master at home. And St Paul cannot rest about the Ephesians till they have, all of them, accepted the Lord simply on His own terms in this matter. They will never satisfy their Apostle, for they cannot possibly satisfy the Lord, if they do not welcome the blessed, the beloved, the adorable Indweller *to the heart*, not only to the convictions, or even to the conduct, but to the heart. He must be inducted into the central chamber, for it is His proper place. And He must be always there.

" Christ " must be " hallowed as Lord in the heart " (1 Pet. iii. 15 ; the true reading). " Though all of us is a temple for Him," says the old Puritan pastor, Bayne, of Cambridge, on this passage, "yet the heart is the choir, where He properly sitteth."

There let Him sit, supreme and at the centre. In many a Christian's experience it is as if the Christian life began anew, and in an almost heaven, when the will is "with power made mighty" deliberately and without reserve to seat Him *there*.

iv. "*By faith*"; "by means of *your* (τῆς) *faith*." Take fullest notice of that phrase, so strong in its simplicity. The Indwelling is, from one side, the sovereign gift of God. From the other, it is a matter for the simplest and most personal reception by man. And then, the form of that reception is just this—faith; reliance, submissive trust; not animated action, not exalted aspiration, but acceptance. Wonderful "faith," pregnant of all imaginable blessings, but itself single and simple; pathway to all virtues, but itself no virtue, for it is just the taking of the infinitely Trustworthy at His word; is not this the mere act of reasonable self-preservation?

True, faith is the gift of God—but in order that it may be the act of man. Let it be our act to-day.

v. "*In love* rooted and grounded, . . . that you may know the knowledge-transcending *love*

of Christ." " From faith to faith" (Rom. i. 17)
is the order of the Gospel from one side ; from
love to love is its order from another. The
Apostle prays that in the Eternal Love (I think
we have adequately seen already that it is of
that Love he is speaking) they may so feel
their " root and foundation" that they may look
around from it and contemplate in peace the
universe of salvation, and that now, in particular,
they may " grasp the love of Christ." As if
the apprehension of HIS love were something
very different from only the vestibule and
introduction to the Eternal Love in its highest
aspects ; rather, the soul is seen advancing from
an enjoyment of the divine love in general to
that of the special love of Christ, as to a
sanctuary within the temple.

Wonderful is the testimony of the words, so
placed, to the divine glory of the Redeemer.
Such is His love in kind that to "know" it
is the very hope of the soul. Such is it in
measure that it for ever transcends all our
knowing. If St Paul had written down in so
many words, " Christ is God of God, Light of
Light, very God of very God," he could not
have preached His Deity more fully.

But let us not take the words only as a

contribution to a true Christology. Let us so
receive the Indweller by faith that we may be
for ever knowing this love of His—yes, His
love even to us, just as we are—which yet we
can never wholly know.

> O Son of God, who lovest me,
> I will be Thine alone ;
> And all I have and all I am
> Shall henceforth be Thine own.

vi. "Filled, *unto all the fulness of God.*"
No fanatical rhetoric is here, nor the least
dream of a mingling and confusion of the finite
and the Infinite. "Neither the Church, nor
the soul, can contain the Infinite. But they
can receive the whole, the plenitude ($\pi\lambda\eta\rho\omega\mu\alpha$),
of those blessings which the Infinite One is
willing and able at each moment to bestow
upon the finite recipient." "The idea is of
a vessel connected with an abundant source
external to itself, and which will be filled, up
to its capacity, if the connexion is complete." [1]

> Lord, we ask it, hardly knowing
> What this wondrous gift may be ;
> Yet fulfil to overflowing ;
> *Thy* great meaning let us see.

---

[1] Notes in the *Cambridge Bible.*

> Make us, in Thy royal palace,
>   Vessels worthy of the King;
> From Thy fulness fill our chalice,
>   From Thy never-failing spring.
>
> Father, by this blessed filling,
>   Dwell Thyself in us, we pray;
> We are waiting, Thou art willing;
>   Fill us with Thyself to-day. [1]

So we shut the Apostle's letter once more. Let us do so with that great word of his doxology upon our lips, τῷ δυναμένῳ, "To Him who is able."

To read such a passage, and to look to ourselves, is despair. To read it, and to look "to Him who is able," is "everlasting comfort and good hope through grace."

May it be with us somewhat as it was, a hundred years ago and more, with Dr William Conyers, Vicar of Helmsley, in Yorkshire. Earnest, conscientious, but as yet spiritually unilluminated, he toiled among his parishioners with vast diligence, but always inwardly disappointed. One day, reading his Bible, he lit upon those words which we studied a little in our last chapter, "*The unsearchable riches of Christ.*" They struck him with a profound

---

[1] Miss F. R. Havergal.

surprise, and a strange misgiving ; could the Christ, who had seemed to him hitherto a Figure in his theology so august yet so intelligible, so familiar, be the Christ of those words? And he did not rest till he had found Him indeed in the glory of His salvation, and had felt life transfigured in His light.

You may think, perhaps rightly, that you stand further on in the knowledge of the Lord than Conyers did when he read of the wealth unsearchable. But you can never be so far advanced in it that new worlds cannot yet open before you. For Christ, as to His riches, is a Labyrinth no clue can traverse ; and as to His love, it passeth knowledge.

Thou art able; we adore Thee;
  We ascribe to Thee the power,
And glad anthems to Thy glory
  We would sing each day and hour;
While the joy of now possessing
In Thyself each promised blessing
  Is our glad unending dower.

Miss J. S. Pigott

A RETROSPECT AND REVIEW

THROUGH the meadows, past the cities, still the brimming streams
    are roll'd,
Now in torrent, now expanding into silver lakes and gold,
Wafting life and increase with them, wealth and beauty manifold.

Whence descends the ceaseless fulness, ever giving, never dry?
Yonder, o'er the climbing forest, see the shining Cause on high—
Mountain-snows their watery treasures pouring everlastingly.

CHAPTER VIII

A RETROSPECT AND REVIEW

WE have touched the middle point of the Epistle. The close of the third chapter and the beginning of the fourth mark that point, not precisely in respect of space, for the last three chapters make a considerably longer section than the first three, but in respect of subject-matter. With some obvious qualifications, the first three chapters treat of doctrine, and the last three of practice; the first lead us to the secrets and resources of the Christian life, and the last to its exercise in the Church and in the world.

The connexion of the two sections is vital and profound; this hardly needs to be explained. But it cannot be too earnestly pressed on the attention of the believing reader. For it is a grand illustration of the truth that, in the Gospel, all the doctrine bears upon practice, and all the practice is rooted in doctrine. Or, to put it in terms more living, more personal, more fully true; all the revelation of God in Christ is for the sake of His people's life and service before Him; all the Christian's life and service depends, for its peace, purity, and power, upon his revealed Lord and God, known, trusted, invoked, and used.

But of this we shall see much more when we travel forward into the latter section of the Epistle. Meanwhile, and that we may follow up this theme the better in its place, let us pause a little while here, and look back upon the ground already traversed. We have as it were reached the top of a mountain road; the place invites to rest, and also to retrospect. We shall soon move on towards the plains and cities. Let us sit still for a time under the quiet sky, and contemplate the everlasting hills among which we have ascended, as they lift their heads heaven-wards and pour their waters down the pass at our feet, towards the scenes of human life.

What on the whole then is the view of Christian life, in its source and secret, given us in the first three chapters of our Epistle?

i. We notice first, as we have done before, that the view, whatever it is, has to do not with some disciples, but with all. This is particularly noteworthy, when we remember that in the second part of the Epistle we have a full recognition of the *varieties* of human duty. There we shall find the totally different functions of spouse, parent, child, servant, master, each treated explicitly and apart.   But in the first section nothing of the kind occurs.   The streams are many, the fountain is one.   Whoever and whatever the disciple is, the greatest truths are true for him, for her.   The highest, the deepest, the holiest privileges are his or her possession, in the plan of God.   And he and she are called, each one, to "possess these possessions" to the full, and to enter in experience into the very sanctuary of blessing.

This is a perfectly simple assertion, and manifestly true.   Only, it is so sorrowfully in contrast with the current facts of actual Christian life, (or to speak more exactly, of the actual life of Christians,) that it needs continual re-statement, to keep it really alive as a practical force upon us.

I do not now refer to our nominal, visible "Christendom" in its larger sense, to the multitudes of the "christened" in our own and other regions where the Faith is accepted as the current creed.   Rather, I have in view circles which by comparison are near the centre; the people who in Evangelical parlance would be recognized as "converted," as "decided," as really "in earnest." Is it not true that among Christians thus described, and in whose lives there is much to respect, there appears too often a strange contrast when they compare their inner creed and their deepest experience with St Paul's account here of the "grace and peace" of—not remarkable Christians, but— Christians? Not in formula, no doubt, but practically, have we not allowed ourselves to be content with a life of the soul lived rather in the suburbs than in the sanctuary? A life lived on "religion" rather than on Jesus Christ? At best, a life lived near Him rather than in Him, and in which it would be difficult to find a congenial place for such words as "in the heavenly places in Christ Jesus," "Christ dwelling in the heart by faith"?

Yet the Apostle writes those surpassing phrases with the whole Asian mission in his view. Of every one, without exception, who truly calls upon the Lord, he affirms that the Father has raised that man with His dear Son, and has seated him in Christ in the heavenly places. For all the disciples, without reserve, he bows his knees in importunate and expectant prayer that they may be so dealt with by the Spirit that they may, every one of them, have Christ " resident in the heart by faith "—with all the wonderful sequel of that experience.

Let us not be content with observing, or with owning, this difference, this contrast. *Assortissons notre Christianisme*, as Monod says in the extract quoted in our last chapter. " Let us class our Christianity aright." Is it apostolic, or is it something quite different? And if not apostolic, in its convictions, and (in some genuine measure) in its experience, let us make haste in our turn to "bow our knees unto the Father." " I will not let Thee go except Thou bless me. For I am a Christian, O my Lord, and Thou meanest the fulness of Thy blessing for every one of Thy disciples."

ii. We observe next, coming into detail, that the apostolic doctrine of the Christian life is that it is a life wholly and sublimely heavenly in its source   Truly, as in the warm language of some of our beautiful old hymns, the eternal world is its home of birth :

> Rise, my soul, and stretch thy wings,
>   Thy better portion trace;
> Rise, from transitory things,
>   Toward heaven, thy native place.

11

I do not think that either John Cennick, in that heart-moving song of faith, or St Paul here, means to tell us that we had a personal pre-existence, and lived in heaven before we were born of our mothers here below. But they do mean, the Apostle does tell us, that we believers did exist to the eternal Mind "before the foundation of the world"; that then and there we were "chosen in Christ"; "predestinated to the adoption of children by means of Jesus Christ"; "blessed with all spiritual blessings in the heavenly places in Christ Jesus."

Let us look from our hill-top upon that great Alp of truth, shining all over with the sunshine of everlasting love. It has its precipices, it has indeed. *Cave præcipitium,* " Beware of the edge," was well said by Augustine, great teacher of the sovereignty of grace, and of the mystery of the eternal purpose. But the mountain is as beautiful as it is steep and massive, viewed from the foot of the Cross, and seen *as part* of the great landscape and system of Redemption. It has no frown then for any human soul which in the least degree is seeking God. And for the soul which has found Him in Christ, it only smiles and radiates blessing from all its peaks and glaciers, with the assurance of a salvation nothing less than eternal in its origin, its purpose, and its end. It is the light of Christ which shines upon those steeps and summits. HE looks out upon the believing soul from the mysteries of the choice, and the fore-ordination, and the blessing, and the acceptance. It is no law of fate, no iron destiny, with which we deal; it is the will of the FATHER, manifested and effected in the SON; nothing *there* can be alien, really and ultimately, from eternal Love. So let us dwell in due time and measure, on the revelations of the first great paragraph of the Epistle, with glad and thankful hearts. In the words of the Seventeenth Article of the English Church, " the godly consideration of predestination and our election in Christ is full of sweet, pleasant, and unspeakable comfort to " (note the deep conditioning words) " godly persons, and such as feel in themselves the working of the Spirit of Christ, mortifying the works of the flesh, and their earthly members, and drawing up their minds to high and heavenly things." [1]

---

[1] I quote a few sentences written on this subject in some notes on the Epistle to the Romans prepared for a Bible-reading Union: " The sovereignty of grace is a side of revelation full of awe. . . . Only, we are well assured that it is not *the whole*

iii. Another grand aspect of the inner Christian life, as seen in this section of the Epistle, is that it is a life of supernatural illumination. For his Ephesian converts, for *all* of them, (let us note that point with renewed recollection,) the Apostle prays that the Holy Ghost may so work as the Lord of Light that they may supernaturally see the present and the coming grandeur and wonder of salvation; "the hope of the calling," "the riches of the glory of God's inheritance, consisting of His saints," and also the mysterious force working in them now, even His resurrection-power, the same power which called their Lord from His grave, and set Him on the throne, and made Him Head of the Body.

Let this be observed, as a divine suggestion for the life of all true Christians. The Ephesians

---

of the truth, but one side of it. Whatever it means, it leaves untouched and unhindered the message of John iii. 16. The two no more clash with each other, *in fact*, than the northern side of the Himalaya mountains clashes with the southern. We cannot see both sides at once, either in the mountain-range, or in the system of truth. But God can; and another day he will give us a view-point, in glory, from which we shall see it all in harmony. Meanwhile, faith is nobly exercised, and the believer, having come as simply as a child to Jesus, gets *this* precious treasure out of the rock of sovereignty—that it is *of the Lord* that he (or she) believes and loves; 'not of yourselves, it is the gift of God' (Eph. ii. 8). So, 'where is boasting?' And also, 'where are doubts and fears?' The Giver of the gift is also the Keeper of the gifted one—'through faith, unto salvation.'"

are viewed by St Paul, evidently, as already
abundantly alive in the spiritual sense. "When
ye believed, ye were sealed with that Holy
Spirit of promise"; "You did He make alive,
dead as you were in your trespasses and your
sins"; aye, "He made you sit together in the
heavenly places in Christ Jesus." What more
did they want? In one respect, nothing more
at all, for they had "received Christ Jesus the
Lord," as their eternal Life, by the Life-Giver's
power; and "*all* spiritual blessings" are "in
Christ Jesus," and therefore are in them in
whom He is. But this may be true in covenant,
in provision, and very far as yet from true in
experience, in conscious possession. So, for
these Spirit-sealed disciples, the Apostle prays
for the Spirit—not as for a fresh personal advent
of the Holy Ghost to them, but as for a fresh
putting forth of His power upon them. And the
special result of this is to be that they *know what
they possess.* Their "heart's eyes" (i. 18) are to
be lighted up, to see the landscape of glory before
them, and also the golden treasures, wrought out
of the mines of heaven, actually in their hands
for present use upon the way. He wants them
to be nothing short of "enlightened Christians"
in the highest sense of the term; to be *illuminati*

indeed. They are to be simple as infants in
the sense of need, in the tenderness of penitence, in directness of reliance, and in gladness
of obedience, yet to be " wiser than the aged "
all the while in God-given insight into the
mighty " reason of their hope,' and into the
secrets of God, "revealed to babes," for His
people's present power and joy.

This was the Apostle's standard for common
Christian life in Asia ; and the Apostle was no
visionary. He meant anything in the world but
fanaticism, and fitful ecstasies, and the reveries of
an abstract pietism. But he knew well that for
the fulness of human life in a sinful world nothing
can be more practically useful than the fulness
of the Spirit of God, as He fully manifests to
the believer the depth of man's need and the
magnificence of the Lord's supply.

As then, so now. An illuminated Christian
life is "revealed unto babes" in the nineteenth
century, as in the first. To the young, to the
uneducated, to the naturally slow, the Spirit in
our day, as in that day, "takes of the things of
Christ and shews them," in a way indescribably
different from that of the mere literary and
verbal exegesis of the student. Only a few
weeks ago a Christian friend, widely experienced

in the realities of life, was talking to me of a
man singularly illuminated, filled to a remarkable
degree with divine light, light shed upon the
fulness of Christ, " the hope of His calling,"
and the " greatness of His power " in the hearts
of His disciples. This person's life was outwardly so consistent with its manifest inward
brightness that he was a proverb in his neighbourhood for all that was happy and helpful.
And who was he, who is he? A workman, a
labourer, employed under the County Council of
London to cleanse the sewers in a district of the
East. I have myself sat, time after time, by the
bed of an old man, once the bailiff of a small
farmer in Dorset, and supposed for many a year
to be the type of all that was dull and ignorant.
But Christ, through a saint of His, found the
old man in his latter days, as he lay decayed and
blind in a little room, in a back yard, in a dark
lane. And on the Spirit's work of conviction and
regeneration came down the Spirit's work of " en-
lightening the eyes of the heart," with a wonderful
insight into the hope of the calling, and the
greatness of the power. I have listened to that
feeble old peasant as he got upon his favourite
and wonderful theme of salvation ; self-conscious-
ness was utterly absent from the tone, the manner,

the phrase; humbly, very quietly, never glibly, the words would come. But the Lord spoke through them; His light was in them. Truly, He had " given understanding to the simple," supernatural understanding of the secrets of the kingdom of heaven, the inner verities of our salvation.

Shall we too covet the working within us of "the Spirit of wisdom and revelation in the knowledge of Him"? Shall we go upon the Saviour's explicit promise (Luke xi. 13) and "ask the Father"? "Ask Him!" Such is the brief inscription of a card which, day by day, meets my eye as I sit at my study-table; it was given me not long ago by a Christian friend. Out of the Lord's promise it takes the implied precept. " He shall give the Holy Spirit to them that—ask Him"; therefore, " ASK HIM."

For every department of the revealed work of the Comforter—" ask Him." Ask the Father, in the Name of the Son, at the instance of the Son, on the warrant of His word. Then we too shall live the life which was to be the normal life of all the Asian disciples, the life of those who supernaturally see their hope of glory, and supernaturally experience "the greatness of His power to usward who believe."

iv. But the Apostle, as we have seen, has even more to pray for in the interest of the Ephesians. And again, it is in the interest of *all of them* that he prays. His thought about any of them cannot be satisfied without this supreme result of the Holy Spirit's work within them—" Christ dwelling in their hearts, by faith."

In the proper place I translated that passage (iii. 14, etc.), and gave some comments on its expressions in detail, and on its general message. Here I attempt no fresh particulars of exposition; I only point my reader's attention to two manifest facts in the passage. The first is that the "coming of Christ to reside in the heart, by faith," is presented as a definite thing in itself; a blessing, a gift, an experience, not to be confused with the Christian life in general, but which the truly living Christian may yet greatly need to seek. The other fact is that, unmistakably, St Paul here views this blessing, this experience, as by no means reserved for a select few among the disciples. He is thinking of the whole Church. He is "bowing his knees," with the whole mission-community upon his heart. The people whom he addresses in the last paragraphs of the Epistle are all equally before him here ;

the husbands and wives of Asia, the fathers and
mothers, the sons and daughters, the masters
and the slaves. His prayer is that every one
of them, in all the days of their common-place
human life, in all the strong temptations of
that life to live apart from God, may so live
close to God that this shall be the description,
the formula, of that life—" Christ dwelling in the
heart by faith."

So it was a definite blessing, and it was a
blessing urgently to be sought for by them all.
Observe further that it stood related on the
one side to purely miraculous divine action, and
on the other side to quite simple human reception. It required on the one side that the
Christian convert should be "strengthened with
might by the Spirit in the inward man"; no
power short of that could enable the being to
enter upon this " secret of the Lord." On the
other side, the reception of Christ as Indweller
was to be simply " by faith"; that is, by the
personal reliant welcome of the human affections
and will, opening the door without reserve,
bidding " my Lord the King to come to His
own house in peace."

Is there need that we should remind one
another that these are truths for our century as

much as for the first? There should be no need
to do so, but indeed there is. With simplicity and
humility I do remind my reader, and God knows
I would be daily reminded myself, that *every one
of us* is divinely intended to live a Christian life
of which the inmost secret is this, Christ dwelling
in the heart, by faith; the Spirit strengthening
us thereto in the inner man.

I shrink from an elaborate attempted analysis
of the blessed mystery in itself. I would only
say a little about what must assuredly be some
of its results where it has begun to be. It
must produce a deep and absolutely genuine
humility. It must produce an inner calm which
shall greatly tell upon the air and manner of
outward life, aye, on look, and on tone of
discourse. It must produce an abiding " Christ-
consciousness," at the back, so to speak, of the
manifold experiences of life; with this presence
in the heart, by faith, we shall not find it a
chimerical hope, day by day, and hour by hour,
to "do all to the glory of God." Our life in
its activities and interests may, and very possibly
will, go on as before; we shall walk, and talk,
and work, and rest, and sigh, and smile, as men
really living in a real society. People will find
us doing, not dreaming; attentive, active, full

of the sense of duty and responsibility—only, *kept* amidst it all, by a power not our own, in a tone and temper which mean that "the Lord is there.'

"I sit here and talk to you," said Tersteegen to his friend Evertsen, "but within my heart is the eternal adoration, unceasing and undisturbed. I thank God that He has given me a little chamber into which no creature has entered besides." [1] Tersteegen lived a real and useful life. He did not shun his kind. His mind was fully open to his period; he astonished Frederick the Great by the manly good sense and high ability of a written criticism on one of the King's anti-Christian writings. But behind it all, Christ dwelt in his heart, by faith; and the Indwelling only made his life more real. Have we not known our Tersteegens?

One word more in closing this line of reflection. It is suggested by the words just quoted; "within my heart is the eternal adoration." Yes, this also will assuredly be one precious result and evidence of the Indwelling. Within the heart will be *adoration*. If indeed "the Lord is there," He will be felt there to

---

[1] Mrs Bevan, *Sketches of the Quiet in the Land*, p. 430.

be the LORD.   All His fair characters and
attributes will in their measure be made known
to us; but all will be overshadowed, or rather
overshone, with this—it is the LORD.   "My
Master, O my Master!"   Only, "LORD" seems
to say more than even "Master"; the Lord is
the Master who is the Maker too; who is not
to be served only, even with the most entire
surrender, but to be worshipped all the while.

He knows our frame; He knows that we
cannot be perpetually, with each breath, formu-
lating an articulate *Te Deum* to Him in explicit
words, or even thoughts.   But He can keep
our inmost being, as to its spiritual attitude, for
ever upon its knees.   And He only knows how
greatly He can enable us to *speak* our worship
too, with an instinctive readiness and frequency
which once we could not have imagined.

"Christ dwelling in the heart by faith.'   Let
us clasp and cherish the words, and use them
in the most practical needs of life.   "Not I,
but Christ liveth in me"; "Christ dwelleth in
me."   I listened lately with deep attention to
a Christian man's quiet narrative, given to me
in private, of his experience of discovery in this
matter.   "The fear of man" had been a burthen

to him. It was brought home to him that the secret of deliverance was to recollect that his Lord was in him, and that his Lord was not afraid. Sudden and wonderful was the revolution within. Some circumstances attended it which I cannot for a moment think to be, in God's purpose, normally meant for all believers. But the essence of the thing—is it not meant for all? For it is but an extension and application, in the light of the Holy Spirit, of the truth of the Indwelling in the heart, by faith.

Come in then, Lord, oh come, and dwell, and let Thy presence evermore expand within.

> O Jesus Christ, grow Thou in me,
> And all things else recede;
> My heart be daily nearer Thee,
> From sin be daily freed. [1]

I thus conclude this chapter of retrospect and review. After all, I have only taken a few great specimens from the treasures of our Epistle, to illustrate its view of the inner Christian life. I have said nothing, for example, of the teachings of St Paul here upon the ideal of the Christian Church, in relation to the soul of the Christian

---

[1] From the German of Lavater: *O Jesu Christe, wachs in mir*. The English will be found in *Hymns of Consecration and Faith*.

man. But let this at least be remembered, in that direction. We are living in a period of deep and complicated unrest and perplexity in the visible Church of Christ. There is much to rejoice us in many quarters and many aspects of the life of Christendom. But there are those of us whose hearts often fail them when they contemplate the phenomena, within the Church of England for example, of doubt, of worldly conformity, of grotesque and retrograde superstition.

No thoughtful Christian can look on unmoved; few but must think often over the problem of practical measures for reformation. But let the Ephesian Epistle teach us this, that the deepest of all secrets for strength and cohesion in social Christian life is the extension far and wide in individual Christians of the life hid with Christ in God, the Spirit's light shed in the soul upon the glories of salvation, faith's welcome to the Lord's own Dwelling in the heart.

MAKE my life a bright outshining
Of Thy life, that all may see
Thine own resurrection-power
Mightily shewn forth in me;
Ever let my heart become
Yet more consciously Thy home.

Miss J. S. PIGOTT

HUMILITY, LOVE, HARMONY

THE invisible world with thee hath sympathized;
Be tny affections raised and solemnized.

WORDSWORTH

CHAPTER IX

HUMILITY, LOVE, HARMONY

Ephesians iv. 1-7

THE First Part of the Epistle is now concluded, and the Second opens. We pass from the revelation of doctrine to the development of practice.

Of course this must be said with some qualification. In the First Part we have had practice implied and alluded to; as where (ii. 10) St Paul tells us that we were "created in Christ Jesus *unto good works*," and indeed in the manifest holy bearing of the entire exposition. And in the Second Part we shall find passage upon passage where doctrine is announced and enforced; some of these passages are as important as any of their kind in the New Testament. Altogether we find truth and life, here in Ephesians, as generally in Scripture, so closely, so vitally interwoven that it is impossible to treat either of the two as really isolated. Doctrine runs of itself into practice, in the mind of the Apostles, and practice always feels its footing in doctrine.

Let the suggestion given us by this fact never be forgotten by the Christian teacher. Does he really mean to be a messenger of *the Gospel*? Then let him often remind himself of this double phenomenon of the Good Tidings—that its end is " our sanctification " (1 Thess. iv. 3), in the most practical sense possible, and that it seeks that end through the supernatural means of the message of Christ for us and Christ in us. It is only too possible to forget one or the other of these two sides of the nature of the Gospel. Sometimes we forget that practical holiness, conformity to God's will in real life, and not only security and spiritual enjoyment, is its aim ; and a seriously one-sided type of teaching must result from this. On the other hand it is sometimes forgotten that the grand peculiarity of *the Good Tidings*, properly so called, is to reveal a way towards this aim which is of grace, not nature, of God, not man. It takes man from the hands of the Law, convinced and humbled, silenced into self-despair, conscious to the heart that he can save himself neither from his Judge nor from himself. And then it shews him that wonderful Secret which it was not at all the business of the Law to shew him—the secret of redemption in the blood of the Lamb, and of purity and power in the gift of the Holy Ghost. This, and nothing else nor less, is the Gospel. What leads up to it, by burning into us the sense of the need of it, is not the Gospel, properly ; it is the Law, whether it be the Law as written at Sinai or as spoken in the Sermon on the Mount.[1]

I have heard of great preachers whose perpetual message in the pulpit was the sinfulness of sin, and the profound ramification of sin in the human heart. In all true preaching that stern element should be present ; for the minister of the Gospel is also the vindicator and assertor of the Law. But the teaching which is all conviction is not Gospel teaching. In a strict sense, it is not Christian teaching ; not distinctively

---

[1] The Sermon on the Mount may be described as "the Law glorified." It is an inestimable statement of the essentials of a holy life, " piercing even to the thoughts and intents of the heart." But it is not the Gospel ; "no flesh shall be saved " *by the Sermon on the Mount.* In order to carry out its precepts, in any real sort, we need all the Gospel of the Cross and the Spirit.

Christian. For the peculiarity, the " difference," of the Christian message is not its detection of the disease but its revelation of the remedy. The most soul-searching ministry becomes a ministry of the Gospel only as it goes on to set out the Lord Christ and the power of the eternal Spirit as the hope and liberty of the sinner. Aye, and to be a Gospel ministry indeed it must not only set Christ out but magnify Him, glorify Him, dilating and dwelling upon His " unsearchable riches " in their application to every need of man.

But we have digressed a little, while considering the structure of our Epistle, and the vital inter-texture of its two parts. Let us come back, and observe again (what is obvious) that this inter-texture still leaves the two parts broadly distinguished. On the whole, the first three chapters are doctrinal all along, and the last three are very largely the practical application of the doctrine. If we ask for the picture of the true Christian, for his tangible character, as we shall see it and feel it in life, it is to the second part that we go, not to the first. Come hither then, and watch the Apostle as he draws that portrait.

What will be the first steps of the process?

A painter commonly thinks first of the natural attitude and aspect of his sitter, before coming to the details of feature.   What, in this immortal portrait, will be the chosen and characteristic *position*, the *sic sedebat, sic se gerebat*, of the Ephesian Christian?   The question is the more interesting after our study of the man's position and possessions, particularly after that last stage of our view of them, in which we saw that he was called to live as one "filled unto all the fulness of God." How will he bear himself under such astonishing conditions?   Behold him yonder!   His walk, his look, his manner, whatever else they are, denote one who has indeed learned *the humility of love*.

Ver. 1.   **I appeal to you,**[1] **therefore, I the prisoner in the Lord,** the man whose captivity is due to his union with his Master and yours, and who has thus a sacred claim on your attention, **to set out on life's walk**[2] **in a way worthy of,** in moral correspondence with, **the calling**

---

[1] Παρακαλῶ: perhaps the above rendering is better than "beseech," as παρακαλεῖν usually means "to exhort," "to encourage," and the like.   But I am doubtful.—For a close and beautiful parallel see Rom. xii. 1.

[2] Περιπατῆσαι: the aorist perhaps justifies my rather elaborate rendering.   It is not περιπατεῖν, the continuous course, but *a point* in it; a "new departure" of more assured and conscious consistency.   But I do not press this as if it were the only possible exposition; the aorist sometimes gathers up an idea into a point rather than marks a point of time.

with which you were called, when the heavenly message reached you, and the heavenly grace drew you to close with it.[1] Yes, I appeal to you to take care that your actual tone and bearing answers to the inward transfiguration, to your new standing and your new endowments as the called ones of your redeeming King. Great and wonderful that standing and those endowments are. My exposition of them will aid you to get some yet larger view of them than you had before; yet even so, they are "gifts unspeakable," "wealth unsearchable," a "love passing knowledge," wonders "far above all we ask or think." But then, the grander your place and your resources, the more conspicuous is the sovereign mercy which has conferred them. You look around, and find yourselves "called" to all the peace and all the power of a living union with Christ, planned for you in the deep eternity, realized now in your living persons, so that you are "seated together with Him in the heavenly places." But you remember instantly *how* you are so seated, and so enriched. You were dead, and a boundless mercy has bid you live. You were excommunicated aliens, and God has been pleased in His glorious freedom to give you the citizenship, yea, the nobility of the Israel of God. Ponder your magnificence of condition,

---

[1] See above, on i. 18, for remarks on the proper meaning of καλεῖν, κλῆσις, in the Epistles. Practically, our common use of the word "conversion" nearly conveys the meaning; only with the difference that, while "conversion" rather emphasizes the human side in the great change, "calling" rather draws attention to the divine side, the Voice of prevailing power.

till you begin in some true sense to realize it. But remember how you reached it, and each reflection upon it, while it rejoices your souls with a joy full of glory, and educates you already for the exaltations of the life to come, will only set you lower in your own esteem. "Lord, is it I?" "What have I that I did not receive," even as the destitute wanderer receives the bounty of a prince?

So the very greatness of the Christian's elevation, seen in the light of the Lord, tends directly to his personal humility. It is the profound secret of an abasement (not debasement) which cannot possibly be a matter for merely theoretical estimates ; it must lay the man so low in his own esteem before God that he cannot possibly be other than softened and chastened before his fellow-men. He has been trusted with the riches of his King, and he feels them in his hands. But he remembers that his King has first forgiven him a hopeless debt, many more than ten thousand talents. He is "seated with the princes of His people." But he deserved, in law, to be "delivered unto the tormentors." Are his eyes really open to the greatness of his salvation? Then he sees his own demerit as he could not see it in the light of a salvation smaller and less divinely generous.

The first, the deepest, the all-pervading effect
upon *character*, which must issue from a real
insight into the glory of our "calling," is holy
humbleness. The really illuminated Christian
must be humble, and that in ways which men
around him must find out without mistake. So
the Apostle proceeds:

Ver. 2. **With all lowly-mindedness,** with an *unreservedly*
(πάσης) humble estimate of self,[1] **and meekness,** an
unreserved, simple-hearted, submission under trial, in
whatever form it comes,[2] at once prostrate and at
peace beneath the will of God; **with longsuffering,** the
enduring, unweariable "spirit" (θυμός, μακροθυμία),
which knows how to outlast pain or provocation in a

---

[1] "Ταπεινοφροσύνη . . . is a distinctively Christian grace,
viewed as a thing always to be sought and cherished. Pagan
ethics, at best, just recognized it as right where necessary, but
not as good and happy *per se*. The Gospel puts its obligation
and its blessedness on the same footing for all believers, as
being all absolutely dependent for all true good upon the mercy
of Another. — The corresponding adjective [ταπεινός] is used
(Matt. xi. 29) by our Lord of Himself. Trench [*Synonyms*, s.v.
ταπεινοφροσύνη, πραότης] remarks that we have Him there recog-
nizing His entire dependence as Man on the Father. Not moral
defect, but 'creatureliness,' he says, is the thought there. 'In
His human nature He must be the pattern of all . . . creaturely
dependence.'" (Note in the *Cambridge Bible*.)

[2] See again Matt. xi. 29, where our blessed Master describes
Himself as πρᾶος. His supreme exercise of πραότης was when He
yielded Himself to the prospect of suffering in the Garden, and
to the outrages of His enemies at His trial and crucifixion.

strength learnt only at the Redeemer's feet[1]; the noble opposite to the "short temper" which soon gives way, and whose outbursts are only sinful weakness under the thinnest mask. "With" these fair, tender graces, attended and escorted as it were by their strong gentleness, live up to your "calling," forbearing one another, allowing each for the others' frailties and mistakes, aye, when they turn and wound you, in love, "finding your joy in the felicity of others," and so finding it easy to see with their eyes and, if need be, to take sides with them against yourselves.

And let all this be done not only as right in itself, but in connexion with a far-reaching purpose, affecting your whole community; bear, and forbear, and love, Ver. 3. as those who are giving diligence, aiming in earnest (σπουδάζοντες), to preserve, with a watchful (τηρεῖν) custody, the oneness of the Spirit, the community, the identity, of feeling and of aim, generated by your common experience of the grace and power of the Holy Ghost, in the bond of our peace (τῆς εἰρήνης) That "peace" with God, and in Him with one another, which is in fact Christ Himself (ii. 14), in His sacrifice and His presence, is to form the "bond" which shall maintain you in a holy union of spiritual hope and aim.

To animate the thought, think on the mighty facts connected with this deep oneness; so will they the Ver. 4. better be realized in life.   Remember—One

---

[1] An attempt was made, in the seventeenth century, to naturalize in English the word *longanimity* (like *magnanimity*), to represent μακροθυμία. The Vulgate here has *longanimitas*.

body, and one Spirit; one Organism, and one only, consisting of the regenerated and living members of the one Head, all animated by the One eternal Spirit who first brought each into vital contact with the Lord, and now maintains each and all in Him ; even as you were actually (καί) called, converted, (by this same divine Agent,) in one hope of your calling; so as to find yourselves, whatever your natural diversities as individuals, all included and united " in " the one glorious prospect (ἐλπίς) opened up in Christ. The eternal future, with its oneness, is to bear upon the trials and duties of the present, and to draw the believing Church together in view of it.[1] Yes, in view of your possessions and your privileges, everything contributes to the weight of this

Ver. 5.   holy watchword, Unity ; one Lord Christ Jesus, the same and undivided, Owner and King equally of all His people ; one faith, one identical secret for peace and power, a saving reliance on His one Name,[2] a secret equally necessary and equally open for you all ; one baptism, the same God-given symbol and seal, in every

---

[1] Cp. Col. i. 4 for a parallel. There "the hope laid up for you in heaven " is presented as a *reason why* (διὰ τὴν ἐλπίδα) for "the love ye have towards all the saints." Great indeed is meant to be the binding power of a common eternal hope.

[2] Πίστις is here explained not of the Christian's *creed* but of the Christian's *trust*. I believe this to be required, or at least strongly suggested, by the general use of the word πίστις in the writings of St Paul. Hardly ever, if ever, does he use it distinctly in the sense of creed. Of course some "creed," however brief, is required in order to "trust," if it is to be trust in the trustworthy Object. But this is not in question where we are examining the use of the word πίστις.

case, upon the one saving faith—the same in the sacred simplicity of its Rite, in the holiness of the Triune Name (Matt. xxviii. 19) named therein, and in the riches of the Covenant of which it is the initiation and lastly, crowning all, as the ultimate and infinite glory **Ver. 6.** of all true unity, **one God and Father of all**, of all His individual children equally, of all to whom, in His Son, He has "given authority to become children of God, even to them that believe on the name" of Christ (John i. 12); the Father who is over all His people, presiding, ruling, owning, and, through them all, working out His will by them as His means, and in them all,[1] dwelling in their hearts, and in their community, as in His shrine, His home.

Thus far we have the argument for humbleness and love derived from the watchword *Unity*. Now the Apostle turns to the opposite while vitally related truth, *Diversity*, and draws the same inference from that side also. The Asian believer (and the English) is to "give diligence," the diligence of thoughtful recollection and patient watchfulness, to cultivate the true "solidarity" of Christian life, because its root is one. He is to do this also, and to do it the better, because meantime its branches, leaves, and fruits are many. He is to be prepared for

---

[1] Read ἐν πᾶσιν, not ἐν π. ὑμῖν, and probably not ἐν π. ἡμῖν. But the reference is unmistakable.

a wide diversity in the manifestations of it, and in the functions of those who equally share in it. He is to be more than *prepared* for this; it is to be his happiness to observe and welcome it, for it is the result of his Lord's use of the individualities of His people for the more complete manifestation of Himself.

Let us take the first sentence of this new paragraph, the better to put the complementary truths in their harmony before us; the paragraph as a whole must be deferred for another chapter of exposition.

Ver. 7. But to each one of us was given, when the Master called His servant, when the Head brought the limb into touch and union, grace, the free gift alike of work to do[1] and of power to do it, not in any fortuitous or merely general fashion, but with perfect distributive skill, according to the measure, in a calculated adjustment, of the gift of our (τοῦ) Christ. The " grace " was the " gift," free, full, and sovereign ; it was " the gift of Christ," absolutely His to provide and to dispense. Its allotment, the dealing out of the " talents " from the one great fund, was governed by His own deep design, manifold in detail, one in end.

---

[1] Χάρις is often used by St Paul in reference to the *grant of duty*, though always in connexion with the grant of faculty for it. See e.g. Phil. i. 7, and above, ch. iii 8.

Let each happy recipient take his "gift," and use it, and be glad. And as for the Householder's assignment to a fellow-servant, "What is that to thee? Follow thou Me."

We pause once more in our translation and exposition. In the passage just traversed, what messages emerge as the most conspicuous and weighty? We would fain "hear what God the Lord will speak" in this word of His.

i. All through, as with "the pleasant voice of the Mighty One," He speaks to His people the blissful law of love. That is to say, He bids each disciple forget himself and remember others, in the magic power of "so great salvation." There are many things in Christian life. "But one thing is needful." There are gifts eminent and shining. But there is always one "more excellent way"; it is the way of holy love. Not love anyhow, but love learnt of the love of God in Jesus Christ our Lord; love "worthy of the calling wherewith we were called." Such a love must, if true to itself, be true to its cause. It must be lowly, it must be meek, it must be long-suffering and forbearing. No doubt on occasion it will abundantly prove itself to be brave, to be active, resourceful, practical; "not in word and in tongue, but in deed and in truth."

But all its courage and all its workfulness will have at the very heart of them that grace which the world cannot give, humbleness, meekness, the spirit which has learnt self-abasement in " the secret of the presence" of a perfect Saviour.

Be this remembered by us all in these days of hurry, of unchastened liberty, and abundant self-advertisement. Alas, such "days are evil" for close intercourse with God in Christ, and deep insights into His covenant-treasures, as by souls which "have an unction from the Holy One." Therefore all the more those who seek to be disciples indeed must watch, and pray, and ponder the often neglected Word, that they may "know the hope of their calling," and then may " walk worthy of their calling"—with the walk of humbleness and love.

ii. The paragraph speaks to us all along of the deep sacredness of Christian Unity. " Behold, how good and pleasant a thing!" From every point of view the happy duty is enforced, of " giving diligence," of being in earnest, for unity. Its deadly enemy, the spirit of self, is here commanded to depart in the name of our " heavenly calling," which, "calling" us to Christ calls us immeasurably above the miserable self-seeking and self-assertion which dislocate and disintegrate the union of souls. The celestial friends of unity are here called to the front— the recollected oneness of our new life in Christ, of our faith within, of our baptism without, of our Master, of our Father.

Beyond question, the Apostle means a unity which is tangible, practical, working. His mention of our Baptism may remind us of this, if we need it; the oneness of the sacred outward Rite suggests at once a community of life which in some measure must express itself externally and publicly. "One baptism!" said a venerable Hindoo convert a few years ago to a Christian visitor, who, sitting by the old man's sick-bed in the mud-hut in Bengal, had just recited to him the words of this Ephesian passage. The Englishman reached the phrase, "one faith"; the ex-Brahmin, who had been literally worshipped *till he was baptized*, and then at once treated "as the offscouring of all things," quietly, but with indescribable impressiveness, took up the next words, "one baptism!"

Indeed the Apostle has in view a unity which does not satisfy itself with sentiment. It prizes all possible actual coherence of order, and organization; all such methods of worship as may best aid the believing company to enjoy

13

a public fellowship together before God as true
and general as possible. Easy and ill-considered
separations, even in things most external, are
assuredly wounds to such unity, and in that
respect are sins. The Christian Church should
reflect as much as may be outwardly the holy
inward principle and power of unity in Christ.

Yet let us on the other hand earnestly
remember that the context and the terms of
this passage alike lead us, for the heart of the
matter, to a region of things far other than that
of authority, administration, succession. For his
basis of unity the Apostle goes to the height ot
heaven and to the depth of the sanctified soul.
He has in his deepest thought not a Society
founded by Christ on earth to convey His grace,
but the Church written in heaven, and the
Lord of it present in His every member's
heart, welcomed in by personal faith, under the
power of the eternal Spirit, in response to
imploring prayer.

Such was our Master's own thought ot Unity,
in the great High Priestly Prayer :—" that they
may be one *in Us* ; that they may be one *even
as We are One.*" Poor and unsatisfying are
the results where " Unity," " Corporate Life,"
and the like, are the perpetual watchwords, but

where they bear *a primary* reference to order, function, and succession in the ministry of the Church. One cannot but ask the question sometimes, when contemplating phenomena of an ardent ecclesiasticism, is *this* the worthy goal of ten thousand efforts, of innumerable assertions of " catholicity "—this spirit and tone, these enterprises and actions, so little akin either to the love or to the simplicity, the openness, of the heavenly Gospel? Suppose such "unity" to be attained to the uttermost, beyond even the dreams of Rome. Would it contribute at all to making " the world believe that the Father hath sent the Son, and hath loved us even as He loved Him " (John xvii. 23)? No, it would not.

But the manifestation of the presence of the Lord in all who bear His Name, so that they forget themselves in Him, would do so to a degree now inconceivable. It would tend more than all ecclesiastical schemes to an external and operative cohesion. But it would do so not by policy, but by grace; not by the universal acceptance of a hierarchical programme, but by " the life of Jesus manifested in mortal flesh."

PARTAKERS of the Saviour's grace,
The same in mind, in heart,
Nor joy nor grief, nor time nor place,
Nor life nor death can part.

C. WESLEY

DIVERSITY AND HARMONY OF GIFTS AND SERVICE

SAINT PAUL in his Epistles has written more fully and wisely of virtues and good works than all the philosophers.

LUTHER

CHAPTER X

DIVERSITY AND HARMONY OF GIFTS AND SERVICE

EPHESIANS iv. 7-16

Ver. 7. **But to each one of us was given grace, according to the measure of the gift of our Christ;** in perfect correspondence to His plan for each and for all, and as Ver. 8. His own sovereign endowment. **Wherefore,** (because the spiritual fact and the Scripture promise of it *must* tally,) **it saith,** the prophetic Oracle saith, as with a living voice,[1] **Ascending on high, He led captive a captivity,** a host of captives, **and gave gifts to men,** to mankind, τοῖς ἀνθρώποις. Words whose phraseology lends itself, in the light of Christ, to an interpretation exactly appropriate to Him who, for our salvation, came so immeasurably far *down*, that He might then and Ver. 9. therefore mount so immeasurably high: **Now**

---

[1] It seems better to explain λέγει thus than by "*He* saith," as in A.V.—For an example of the many passages in which, in Scripture, Scripture is almost personified, cp. Gal. iii. 8: "The Scripture, *foreseeing* . . ., *preached* before the Gospel unto Abraham."

189

the phrase, "He ascended," what is it, what does it mean, if not that He also descended,[1] aye, to the lower regions of the earth, to the subterranean Sepulchre, and to that hidden Separate State of which the Sepulchre is the Ver. 10.   portal and the type?[2]   The Descender, He, He and none other (αὐτός), and He because He descended, is also the Ascender, the Conqueror who went up, far above all the heavens, all the spheres and regions of blessed creature-life, to the Uncreated Glory itself, to the Throne, to the Majesty on high; that He might[3] fill all things, the Universe and its contents, τὰ πάντα—fill them with the presence and the power of One who, being God over all, is now also the Son of Man, and Ver. 11.   the Lamb that was slain.[4]   And He, none other than He (αὐτός), this wonderful Descending and now Ascended Christ, in the virtue and the prerogative of His Sufferings and His Glory, forthwith "gave," as

---

[1] Probably the word "first," πρῶτον, of the Received Text is to be omitted.   It is most likely an early explanatory note.

[2] Some have interpreted τὰ κατώτερα μέρη τῆς γῆς to mean merely *the earth*, considered as a region lower than the heavens; "the lower parts, consisting of the earth."   So Bp Pearson.   But the reference to the Grave seems both more suitable to the context and more congenial to the phrase.   Cp. Ps. lxiii. 9: "They shall go into the lower parts of the earth."   And see the grand spiritually-parallel passage, Phil. ii., where the Saviour's Exaltation follows upon His "obedience even to the length of *death*."

[3] Lit. "may," πληρώσῃ: but usage favours our rendering.

[4] "There is no reference here to a diffused and ubiquitous corporeity, but to a pervading and energizing omnipresence. . . . Christ is perfect God, and perfect and glorified Man; as the former He is present everywhere; as the latter He can be present *anywhere*" (Bp Ellicott).

we have seen (ver. 8), "gifts unto men." What were those gifts? In brief, they were a Spirit-filled Ministry, with a view to the development of a Spirit-filled Church, united in the Spirit to the Lord Himself. **And He gave some men as apostles, some as prophets,** prophets of the Christian order, **some as evangelists,** devoted expressly to the *extension* of the Church rather than to its internal edification,[1] **some as shepherds and teachers**—two sides of one work; men who were set over the local "flocks" of believers to be their leaders and instructors in the Lord. And these "gifts" were given not to terminate in the ministers themselves, but altogether for the sake of the Church at large. And they were given for the Church at large on purpose that "the Ministry" might not absorb or monopolize ministration, but might promote its exercise through the whole Body. For what do we read as the aim and object of the giving? **With**

Ver. 12. **a view to the equipment,** the adjustment, the adaptation and furnishing (καταρτισμόν), **of the saints,** of all the true members of the Head, **for work of service,** for active and fruitful enterprise and labour in their Lord's Name and for His glory; all summed up in the parallel phrase, **for the upbuilding of the Body of our** (τοῦ) Christ; for the winning of new "members" to the

---

[1] "This passage would lead us to think of the Evangelists as standing between the [apostles and prophets, pastors and teachers;] sent forth, as missionary preachers of the Gospel, by the first, and as such preparing the way for the labours of the second" (Smith's *Dict. Bibl.*, s.v. *Evangelist*). This would fairly describe, from one point of view, what appears to have been the function of the "evangelist" *Timothy* (2 Tim. iv. 5).

living Organism, and for the deepening and developing
of the cohesion of the whole, by all holy influences of
word and work.

A noble process, with a glorious goal! All was to
be aimed at nothing short of the production of an
ideal community of ideal members, each and all alike
animated and sanctified by saving reliance on the Head
Ver. 13. and sanctifying acquaintance with Him; till
we attain (καταντήσωμεν), the whole number of us (οἱ
πάντες), to (εἰς) the unity of, the unity generated and
conditioned by, our (τῆς) faith in and our (τῆς) true
knowledge (ἐπιγνώσεως) of the Son of God, (in whom we
too are the sons of the Eternal Father;) yes, (to put
the same prospect in more concrete terms,) to a full-
grown (τέλειον) man, a "man" in the sense not of
humanity only (ἄνθρωπον) but of matured and strong
humanity (ἄνδρα); even to the measure, the standard,
of the stature of the fulness of Christ. For nothing short
of this is to satisfy our hopes; the Christian is to grow,
and the Church is to grow, in spiritual maturity, till
the result is no less than "the fulness of Christ," the
attained ideal of all that is meant by "CHRIST." And
what is that? It is that which shall be when the
glorious Head shall have for the vehicle of His action
a mystical Body complete and perfected, faultless and
immortally mature.[1]

---

[1] "Cp. the phrases, 'fulness of the Gentiles' (Rom. xi. 25), and
'fulness of the time' (Gal. iv. 4). The phrase here appears to
be analogous: *the total, at length attained, of what is meant
by Christ.* And 'Christ' in this passage (so full of the idea of

Such is the grand maturity, the developed and full-grown "manhood," of the ideal Body, as it shall be. And it is to be always more and more approached and realized even now. Even now the purpose and the process are to issue in a noble relative strength and

Ver. 14. fulness of holy character; that we may be no longer infants, "childish" in respect of ignorance and the weakness of ignorance, borne on billows and drifted about by every wind of the teaching which would beguile us, in, in the sphere and influence of, the dice-play, the unscrupulous religious cozenage, of men, (these *mere men*, who have no Christ, no God, behind them;) in their cunning, with a view to, to reach the ends of, the scheming of their (τῆς) deceit. For alas, there are those around you who not only do lead you astray, but mean to do it, laying deliberate traps, and arranging well-drawn methods, on purpose to guide you away from the Christ whom they do not love. The purpose of the great Giver's plan is the opposite to this; it is, as we have seen, that you should not be exposed helpless

---

the oneness, in and with the Lord, of His mystical Body) is, in effect, Christ and His Church . . . as in 1 Cor. xii. 12, 'as the body is one, and hath many limbs, so also *is Christ*.' The Lord the Son becomes in accomplished fact all that He wills, and is willed, to be, only when He is the Head of a perfected mystical Body which lives by His sacred Life and is His incorporate 'limbs.' . . . So He and they are guardedly and reverently spoken of as One Christ; with full reservation, from other Scriptures, of the truth of the undying personality of each individual 'limb' of the glorious Head, and of His divine Personality." (Note in the *Cambridge Bible*.)

Ver. 15. to these wiles, but, being followers of truth,[1] in love, not in bitterness and prejudice, but purely seeking the glory of God and the good of man, should grow, with an ever deepening and more vivifying contact, into Him, in all respects, as to your whole being and your whole life—into Him who is the Head, our (ὁ) Christ. The more you thus "grow into Him," with an ever closer cohesion of faith, and hope, and love, the nearer will your union with one another be, and the better the
Ver. 16. whole condition of your organism ; for out of Him,[2] with resources ever drawn from His fulness, all the Body, getting[3] adjusted together, and getting braced together, through every joint of, every *nexus* which is a channel for, the supply of life and power from the Head, according to His working, in the measure of each part, effects (ποιεῖται, a fuller word than ποιεῖ) the increase of the Body, its development alike in stature and in strength, to the upbuilding of itself, in love. For love is the inmost condition of the whole work—"the love of God, which is in Christ Jesus our Lord," the sunshine in which the true life basks and grows.

Here is indeed a paragraph pregnant of truth and life. The comment shall take the form of

---

[1] Ἀληθεύοντες : Alford renders the word as above. It certainly means more than " truth-*speaking*," though of course it includes it. It surely points, *in this context*, to " the *Truth* " of the Gospel and the Christian's devotion to it.

[2] I change the relative (ἐξ οὗ) here into the demonstrative, to relieve the length of the sentence as paraphrased.

[3] Observe the present participles here.

detached remarks upon some of its greater contents.

i. What strikes us first is the citation from the Psalm, made to illuminate and enforce the thought that grace, in its oneness and its variety, is "*the gift* of Christ." The Apostle takes us back, for a prophetic verification, to Psalm lxviii., and shews us the Conqueror ascending, after battle, to the throne. He leads a host of captives with Him, helpless beneath His mighty hand, to vex His people no more. And He "gives gifts to men." Here, says St Paul, in effect, is Christ—Christ who went down first from His throne on the eternal hills to the plain, nay, to the dark valley of the conflict, and who thence returned, Incarnate and Glorified, to His heavenly seat again, and from that seat dispensed the gifts of Pentecost, and particularly now the gift of the Pentecostal Ministry in the Pentecostal Church.

Two problems present themselves. The first is one of translation; for the Hebrew, as familiar to St Paul as the Authorized Version, or the Prayer Book Version, is to us, runs here: "*Thou didst take gifts in man*"; that is, "*amongst men.*" The path to St Paul's rendering (which is not that of the Septuagint) is smoothed by that of the Chaldee Targum, or Paraphrase, perhaps of the Apostle's date : " Thou hast given to them gifts, even to the sons of men." And the key to these renderings may well lie in the thought that the Conqueror *took* that He might *give*; He *gave* what He first had *won*. " In man," that is, among His human subjects, He distributed *the spoils* of victory. His bounty was not only bounty ; it was conquest first.

The other difficulty is a more general one. Does the sixty-eighth Psalm, as we read it, claim (so to speak) a Messianic reference? Are we to think that the Psalmist, David or whoever he was, foresaw the Lord, and sang of Him ? I should for myself be very slow to answer that question. To say that he did *not* do so would be to say what we cannot possibly be sure of. Some sorts of modern criticism glide much too easily into theories of the composition of Scripture which practically eliminate all supernormal conditions from the consciousness of its writers. But literature, far outside the Bible, offers abundant evidence for the possibility of totally supernormal conditions in human minds, foreseeing and foretelling ; the records of the " Second Sight " are full of such things. I cannot say but that the author of this wonderful Psalm really was lifted above the horizon of time, and saw Messiah, however far off, in His glory, in His victory, and then sung about Him in mysterious verse.

But I am not careful to assert this. After all, his "first reference" may have been to some great event of his own time, some triumph of the old Israel, in relation to which he seemed to see, above the rejoicings on earth, above all the festal chorus of the Temple, with its minstrels and singers, and shouting people, the everlasting KING Himself, Israel's true Lord, leading HIS triumph in the skies. But all the while the Poet's true Possessor and Inspirer would have had *His* view beyond the temporal horizon, and under the veil of the national story would have indicated in His own way the coming Triumph of Redemption.

The "consciousness" of Psalmists and Prophets is a deeply interesting study, so far as it is possible. But it is secondary. The primary thing is the "consciousness" of their Inspirer. And our Lord Jesus, *in His risen life*, as much at least as before He suffered, bore abundant witness to the fact that the Inspirer filled the Old Scriptures, the Psalms included, with "things concerning Himself" (Luke xxiv.). "We feel free to recognize any 'first reference' fairly provable; but also bound to believe that the Divine Author worked through the human author, so as to convey eternal and permanent truth through his imagery and words, and so as to make the whole terminate on Christ, whether the human author was aware of it or not." [1]

ii. We take note of some remarkable *data* presented to us here, for true views of the Christian Ministry.

We have, first, its Divine Institution. From the Apostle to the Pastor-Teacher, it is "the gift of Christ." Perfectly true then is that view of the Ministry (only it must be rightly applied) which sees in it, as to its essence, not an emergence from below, a mere product of the needs of the Church, developed in merely "natural" ways, but a gift from above. Let that thought both awe and animate the true Minister, and give the private Christian a due sense of honouring love towards the Pastorate.

On the other hand we observe that the emphasis of the passage lies upon the truth that the ideal Ministry is a Ministry of spiritual power. We have here, of course, indications of grade and order; and the thought of the distribution and difference of functions is the main thought of the context. But the "gifts" are all alike

---

[1] Note in the *Cambridge Bible.*

in this, that they are given by the just-ascended
Lord; they are Pentecostal gifts. This calls
attention supremely to the witnessing work of
the Christian Ministry. That Ministry has many
sides to its duties and commission; the "shep-
herd" must needs be in some sense the guardian,
and the "teacher" the guide. But the Pentecostal "gift" was above all things a gift *for
witness*; "Ye shall receive power, by the coming
of the Holy Ghost upon you, and ye shall be
witnesses of Me" (Acts i. 8). Again and again
in the Acts the Apostles themselves appear as,
above all things, witnesses. Such, to the end,
is the Christian minister, in his true idea. His
characteristic function is profoundly different from
that of the Aaronic priest. Distinctively, (let me
deliberately say it, with the New Testament
open,) it is not "sacerdotal" at all. It is prophetic; it is the function of the Christ-given,
Spirit-filled, witness to the Lord and His Word,
before the Church and before the world.

We observe again, as another and most
momentous side of the matter, that a Ministry
so conditioned cannot possibly absorb into itself
the spiritual functions of the Church. Rather,
it will quicken and develope in the Church the
sense and exercise of spiritual functions. The

14

one purpose of the Ministry mentioned here by
the Apostle, its one great *raison d'être* in his
view here, is this.   Note the translation of
ver. 12 : "With a view to (πρός) the equipment
of the saints for (εἰς) work of service."   Who
are "the saints"?   Briefly, all believers.   A
saint, in the Epistles, is just the Christian as
he should be ; the disciple assumed to be true
to Christ and (Rom. viii. 9) possessed of His
Holy Spirit.   He may or may not bear public
office in the Church.   But is he a member,
a limb, of it?   Then he exists for "work of
service" ; he is to "yield himself unto God,
and his members as instruments of righteousness
unto Him."   Whatever the details of practice,
this is the principle.   And the function of the
true pastor and teacher is to help him, to equip
him, for such a life ; to do all he can to quicken
the "saint's" conscience in the work of the
Lord, and to animate his zeal, and to welcome
his activity, and in all wise and kindly ways
to seek to make the most of it by guiding and
combining it.

In the modern Church countless illustrations of
this truth happily exist.   More and more, in many
quarters, it is being recollected that "the laity,"
ὁ λαός, the holy People, *are* the Church, for which

the Ministry exists, and that the Christian layman, and woman, has an all-important place in "work of service"; not only in the "serving of tables," but in witnessing and teaching. But there is still grave need for a larger recognition of that fact, alike by the pastorate and the laity.

There certainly was once a time when pious men of strict Church opinions dreaded the least approach to such work of service. A veteran Christian, a layman of high position and culture, told me lately that fifty years ago he asked an Oxford friend what he thought of his (the narrator's) work among his poor neighbours as a voluntary Scripture-reader. Might he read the Bible to an old cottager? Yes, certainly. Might he, if she said she did not understand, explain it to her? No, certainly not; that would be usurping the work of the priesthood.

Did Priscilla then (Acts xviii. 26) usurp it? Assuredly not, in St Luke's opinion; she was doing "work of service" as a member of the Church of God.

Meanwhile, let this passage remind us that the ideal of the matter is that "the saints" should indeed do "work of service," and contribute their labour and witness to "the upbuilding of the body of Christ"; but that they should not

therefore slight order, cohesion, and the loving
guidance of the spiritual Ministry. I am very
far from saying that there is no place in the
Lord's work for the "free lance" worker; lives
upon which His blessing manifestly abides are
evidence enough to the contrary. But I do say
that this is the anomaly, not the rule; Scripture
and reason alike assure us of this. "Prophet,
evangelist, pastor-teacher," are, *in the rule* of
the Master's will, necessary to "the saints" for
their "work of service"; as on the other hand
"the saints" are utterly indispensable to the full
work of the Christian minister.

How easy, in view of these remarks, to
suggest problems of difficulty, and cases of
impossibility, on either side! Yes, but the
principles abide, and their silent influence, under
the Lord and the Spirit, will be of infinite value
in the Church Visible, with all its confusions
and distresses. *Solvetur ambulando cum Deo.*

iii. The passage gives us some invaluable
messages upon Christian maturity. The Apostle
glides from the topic of work—the work of the
spiritual Ministry and the work of the believing
Church—to that of character, the character of
the Community. To be sure, the character of
the individual is not forgotten; it is impossible

to read verses 13-15 and not to feel that what is true of the Body must be true also of the member ; for no community can be really mature and stable in spirit and tone unless it consists, prevalently at least, of mature and stable individuals. But the main thought is of the Body. And St Paul, we see, views the Christian Body as one which is to be always growing towards an ideal whose great features are an adult and well-grounded fidelity to the revealed Gospel, such as to resist and throw off the assaults of subtle error, while yet maintaining a spirit of love, full of the love of God.

There is a point of view from which the Christian character cannot be too *child-like*—at the Master's feet. But there are points from which alike the man and the Church must avoid to the utmost the *childish* in thought and faith. For the Lord's work and witness, there is an urgent need of the mature, the intelligent, the man-like, if the cause of Christ is to be adequately maintained and advanced in " this naughty world." St Paul evidently strove to cultivate this spirit (the opposite of conceit and self-importance) in his converts. " I speak as to thoughtful persons ; judge *you* what I say" (1 Cor. x. 15); such are his words to the

Corinthian community, over a matter of profound doctrinal and practical moment. Alike towards the " pastor-teacher " within, and towards the advocate of "another Gospel" from without, he would have their attitude to be that ot *men* ; men conscious of their maturity, aware of their reasons and their convictions, while at the same time sobered and humbled by an adult sense of their responsibility and their imperfections.

I do not forget that the bright ideal of ver. 13 cannot be fully realized till the pilgrim Church steps into the world of glory. There only, most assuredly, will be actually attained " the measure of the stature of the fulness of Christ"; bright, magnificent, blessed hope! Yet the context here bears mainly not upon eternity but upon time. It deals mainly with a period when errors and dangers are still around, and when the Body is still in process of "upbuilding." Its reference, then, is to an " adultness " rather relative than absolute. It animates us with the thought of a manhood in Christ attainable now, while yet from another aspect it is only a step to the full and immortal manhood of heaven.

iv. Lastly, here as everywhere, we find all that is said of Ministry, and of Saints, and of Body, and of corporate Life, ruled and glorified

by what is said of Jesus Christ. Verses 15, 16,
take us altogether to HIM. The remarkable
imagery of ver. 16 does this in a way peculiar
to itself. For it puts before us the Body, in
its multiplicity of articulation ; yet it suggests
the thought that each limb lives by a contact
with THE HEAD, immediate and personal. The
material figure bursts, as it were, and gives
way, and leaves to us the view of an organism
such that the limb does not live, ultimately,
by its contact with other limbs, however full
of life, but by having its own "joint of supply,"
its own individual point of contact with the
Head. So it grows, and thrives, and works.
And HE is also the secret of growth and energy
for all its fellow-limbs. Therefore, because of
Him, as the inmost Secret, there is cohesion,
continuity, harmony, in the whole organism.

After all, the supreme requisite for life and
labour is personal and immediate union with
the Lord.

Wonderful picture—a Church, a Body, indeed!
It is alive all over. Everywhere there is "work
of service," promoted in *every* limb by those
limbs whose function is in any special sense
that of leadership. Everywhere there is a

steady growth of adult intelligence and purpose. Everywhere there is the pulse of love, as the whole Organism feels the vital warmth of the eternal Love. And the secret of the whole is the blessed HEAD, "into" whom the limbs "grow" with ever-deepening contact, and from whom they draw all His fulness for all their need.

> To know, to do, the Head's commands,
>   For this the Body lives and grows ;
> All speed of feet and skill of hands
>   Is for Him spent, and from Him flows.

THE OLD MAN AND THE NEW

A CHRISTIAN praises God for His justice, and yet fears Him for His mercy. He is so ashamed as that he dares not open his mouth before God, and yet he comes with boldness to God, and asks Him anything he needs. He is so humble as to acknowledge himself to deserve nothing but evil, and yet believes that God means him all good. He is the most lowly-minded, yet the greatest aspirer; most contented, yet ever craving.

BACON: *Characters of a Christian in Paradoxes.*

CHAPTER XI

EPHESIANS iv. 17-24

ST PAUL pursues the theme of practical Holiness. He draws nearer and nearer, as he pursues it, to the duties of the common day, to the application of eternal principle, eternal blessing, in the intercourse of the city, the street, the home. He has led us, as we saw in the last chapter but one, from the mysteries and bliss of our heavenly life with Christ and His living presence in us, to the resultant precepts of humility, of mutual forbearance, of watchful avoidance of the separatism which comes of selfishness. In view of the oneness of believers in their glorious Head, he has gone on, as we saw in our last chapter, to speak of a living unity whose growth and exercise are aided by the diversity of the members in their gifts and

functions in the Body. Alike their spiritual
fulness in Christ, and their limits and imperfections of experience, and their differences of
practical gift and mission, are to draw them
nearer to Him, and nearer to one another.
"Growing into Him," they will indeed each
individually grow, with a rich maturity of the
soul, and they will mutually contribute each to
the whole Body's growth, in its cohesion and
its capacity.

He now draws closer to the thought of
"holiness in common things." He cannot speak
only of the larger aspects of life and relation;
he must deal in minute but firm touches with
the individual's call to purity, and truthfulness,
and fidelity, and the spirit of forgiveness. It will
not do only to soar into true conceptions of the
mystical Body, and to remain aloft; we must
come down to be "sweet at home."

The close practicality of the appeal, meanwhile,
will have all along the support of the recollection
of eternal truths; it will root itself in the doctrine
of the Old Man and the New.

Ver. 17. This then I say and protest (μαρτύρομαι), calling
you in as it were as *witnesses*, by the response of conscience, to the eternal facts of grace and duty, in the
Lord, (for I am in Him, and you are in Him, living

limbs of the One Head, and therefore related Christ-
wise to each other in everything,) that no longer should
you walk, live, act, converse, as once you did (μηκέτι),
in the way in which actually (καί) the Nations[1] are
walking all around you. And what is the character
of that "walk"? It is in the vanity of their mind,
under an *illusion* (ματαιότης)[2] beclouding their reason;
for the principles of it can only seem good to man's
mind when the eternal facts are hidden from it, and
sin, the great failure of all failures, seems to bring
freedom and gain. They "walk" as those who have
Ver. 18. been and are darkened in their (τῇ) understanding,[3] aye, as alienated from the life of God, dis-
located from man's ideal union and communion with
the blessed Creator who is his true "Life Eternal";
on account of the ignorance which exists in them, ignorance of their great need and of His fair surpassing
glory of love and holiness; in other words, on account of
the hardening[4] of their heart, the loss of the sensibility

---

[1] Probably omit the word λοιπά before ἔθνη.

[2] No idea of "self-*conceit*" resides in such "vanity." It is
the emptiness, the delusion, the "vain shew" of substance without reality. They mistake lie for truth, sin for happiness.

[3] "[Διάνοια] may fairly be said to be the reason [νοῦς] in action.
Here accordingly the phrase defines, so to speak, the phrase just
previous; the general illusion of the reason comes out in obfus-
cated acts of thought" (*Cambridge Bible*).—"*Have been and
are*" is an attempt to render ἐσκοτωμένοι ὄντες. (It seems better,
in view of rhythm, to connect ὄντες with ἐσκοτωμένοι than with
ἀπηλλοτριωμένοι.)

[4] Πώρωσις: the word means failure of sensation in general;
"blindness" is one phase of such failure, but only one.

of their inner being (καρδία) towards the Highest Good, under the dreadful *anæsthetic*, sin.

Do we ask for visible evidence of the existence of such a condition? Look at the characteristics of the developed grace-less life; they who live it are such as,[1]

Ver. 19. having got beyond the pain (ἀπηλγηκότες) of doing iniquity, gave over[2] themselves, yes, themselves by their own act,[3] to wantonness, the scorn of all moral restraint; ("Who is Lord over us?"); resulting in an active dealing in all impurity, in a spirit of greed; yes, the pursuit of evil becomes in time a business, a trade (ἐργασία), followed up with all the keen and unscrupulous pertinacity of the selfish hunter after gold.

It is a tremendous picture. Do we hesitate to accept it as it stands? It is inevitable that we should feel some difficulty in so accepting it, unless we read altogether without thought. For who is not aware that, even among the most abandoned, there are differences in actual sinfulness? And who is not aware that in heathendom,

---

[1] Οἵτινες: "ὅστις is more than *qui* and less than *quippe qui.*" It does just more than merely *denote*; it borders upon *description.*—The translation here is a little paraphrastic, to bring out the meaning better.

[2] Observe the aorist. An ideal crisis is in view; a definite choice; "evil, be thou my good." In too many an experience such crises are actual, not only ideal.

[3] Ἑαυτούς is emphatic by position.

ancient and modern alike, there have been and
are manifestations of the power of conscience,
and exercises of the human will on the side of
virtue, which we cannot possibly put down as
so much falsehood and illusion? Are we indeed
to think, in view of all this, that "the Nations,"
in their countless numbers, have all "got beyond
the pain" of sin, and have "given themselves
over to wantonness"?

In reply, we may first remark that assuredly
the Apostle is here speaking broadly and generally, as regards a developed and manifested
wickedness in the world. His own words and
actions on occasion assure us that he did not
as a fact look upon every pagan person as an
advanced and abandoned transgressor. "I am
not mad, most noble Festus"; these are words
which indicate, as they come from an absolutely
truthful man, a certain moral regard for the
person addressed. So with Sergius Paulus in
Cyprus, so with the Athenians on Areopagus,
so with the Lystrians in their turn; the tone
is that of one who speaks with candour and
sympathy, as well as with fidelity and decision,
in his appeal to man for God. It seems reasonable to say that here, to the Ephesians, he is
speaking of a broad phenomenon of open sin,

yet with a full recollection, behind his words, of reserves and exceptions.

But then, other things are to be remembered. First, as regards the actual condition of heathenism, of heathen society in its mass and its rule. Is it easy to overrate its horrible corruption? Those of my readers who are familiar with classical literature will surely bear me out when I answer, No. I appeal for justification not only to deliberate pictures of wickedness, drawn by Greek or Roman pens, but to passing allusions to current morals in all kinds of places in the old authors. Is it not rare to find an amatory poem of theirs which, however beautiful in form, is also pure? Are not the biographies of even comparatively worthy personages, for instance, the Galba of Suetonius, defaced with unblushing allusions to sins now unnamable? Is the taint of even that deep pollution absent from the Platonic page itself? But if such things can be said of circles where things were at the best, what must have been the corruption of the mass?

One thing is certain, that the early literary " Defenders of the Faith," the " Apologists," do not hesitate to appeal to their heathen readers to confess the conspicuous moral difference

between the Christians and "the Nations."
Notably is this the case with Aristides, in the
second century; and his witness is the more
impressive because he appears to stand on a
sort of border-line, and not yet to have cast in
his lot personally with the Lord and His people.
He recites the sins of "the Greeks" in terms
which compel a translator for general readers
to leave frequent gaps in the translation;
summing up with the sentence (ch. xxvi.): "I
have no doubt that the world stands by reason
of the intercession of the Christians.   But the
rest of the peoples are deceived and deceivers;
and they grope as if in the dark, and are
unwilling to know the truth, and like drunken
men they stagger, and thrust one another, and
fall down.   The Greeks practise foul things, and
then turn the ridicule of their foulness upon the
Christians."[1]

And is the non-Christian world of our own
time better than that old world?   I fear it is only
an optimistic dream which finds in it anything
greatly to modify the estimate of an Aristides.
Everywhere, still, as St James tells us (iii. 9),
men are "made after the similitude of God,"

---

[1] I quote, somewhat freely, from the excellent translation of
Aristides by Mrs Rendel Harris.

15

made in the mystery of a moral personality;
conscience and will are present everywhere. But
everywhere man is fallen. And the developments
of the fallen state, left really to themselves, are
awful still. As I write, I hear of a recent
laborious and accurate examination, by an
American student, of the actual moral condition
of non-Christian peoples, which tends to bring
this out in the light of provable facts; certainly
with sufficient fulness to silence in candid hearts
the thought that pagan humanity can do without
the Gospel.

But before we leave this passage let us remember that it points, with its deepest meaning,
not only at the actual sinfulness of the dark world
but at its potential evil. It speaks, in universal
terms, of gross iniquities. Those iniquities are,
in the divine mercy, largely restrained from their
natural developments, even in the non-Christian
regions, by the presence of conscience. But they
are all latent, all implicit, in the awful *principle
of sin* in (not some selected human hearts, ex-
ceptionally bad, but) *the human heart*, fallen
from dependence upon God. Does my reader,
in some real measure, *know his own heart*?
Has he, in serious earnest, I do not mean in
a morbid restlessness of conscience, but with a

conscience soberly and fully awake, learnt to weigh his motives, and to watch the play of his thoughts? Has God drawn near to him in conviction "of sin, and righteousness, and judgment"? Then I need not write at any further length to give moral proof of the point.

Before we leave this stern paragraph, let us however remember that even through its darkness shine the rays of salvation. For what does it imply concerning this terribly fallen and sinning world? That it is a world, a race, a mankind, which by the very fact of its *fall* bears witness to its having been made by a Blessed Creator for infinitely better things. True, it is lost, it is condemned, it is dead in trespasses and sins. It is "alienated from the life of God"; "ignorance is in it"; "blindness of heart." But those very terms imply that in its origin as a race, in the idea of its being, it was altogether otherwise. "Man," in his *idea*, was once in communion with "the life of God," or he could not be said to be "alienated" from it; who can be alienated from a position he has never occupied?[1] If so, we

---

[1] I would be careful not to be misunderstood, as if I could mean that the individual, I for instance or my reader, began his personal life in harmony with God, and therefore holy and good,

have here not only an account of ourselves as
men which should drive us in awe and penitence
to the feet of God, crying, " Unclean, unclean " ;
we have a hope put already into our hands.
Were we but " stones," He could " raise up of us
children to Abraham." But we are not stones.
We are ruined *men* ; and Man was made to be in
contact with " the life of God." Will it not be
the Maker's *joy* to restore us ? Shall it not be to
Him no " strange work," but divinely congenial,
to act for us in our awful need, in His Son, and
according to His promise ?

From the very depth of our discovered iniquity,
then, *de profundis*, let us look up to Him. We
deserve only His death-sentence. But He created
our nature on purpose for life and holiness in
contact with Himself. And in the Second Man
He has provided for what is indeed, from one
side, a " New Creation," altogether new, but from

and *then* personally fell from holiness to sin. Scripture and
consciousness alike witness against the Pelagian theory. But
the Race, the Nature, was " created upright," and fell by its own
act. And that most mysterious fact is as it were reflected in
each individual by the equally mysterious (but not less certain)
fact that we freely speak of ourselves as *"fallen"* beings.
We are *where our nature was not made to be*—in personal
sin. And this is at once an alarm and shame, *and* the condition to a blessed hope, for every individual who looks up to the
Restorer.

another, the Restoration of ruins which still bear, in their polluted fragments, the impress of His hand.

But let us take up the Apostle's words again. He has given us a view of the awful darkness; he passes now to the light, and to the children of the light.

Ver. 20. **But you did not so,** in such sympathy with the deadly tendencies of sin, **learn our** (τόν) **Christ,** when, in your conversion, you found in Him the true Subject-matter of His own Gospel, the "hidden wisdom" of

Ver. 21. pardon, holiness, and heaven; **if indeed,** taking it for granted that,[1] **it was He whom you heard,**[2] as the Message spoken to your souls, **and if it was in Him that you were taught,** so that your teachers' words were all summed up "in" Him, and you, as hearers, found yourselves learning "in" union with Him as Saviour and Head; **even as in our** (τῷ) **Jesus,** and in Him only, **truth is.** For indeed there, and only there, is truth to be found; the lines of solid *fact* and spiritual *reality* meet nowhere but in Him, in this divine CHRIST who is also "the Man Christ JESUS,"

---

[1] This is the practical meaning of εἴγε (as in iii. 2). It does not imply any doubt, necessarily, but calls the reader to verify the statement.

[2] Αὐτόν is emphatic by position. And the accusative after ἀκούειν suggests "hearing Him" rather as Message than as Teacher.

as historical as He is eternal. And what line in particular did the "hearing," and the "teaching," and the "truth," take, for the purpose before us now, this purpose of practical holiness? It was all with reference

Ver. 22. to your putting off, your laying aside, (as regards your former course of life, in "regard" of the need of a revolution and conclusion for that dark "course,") the Old Man, the old, the former, the now past, state of things for your humanity, in which, as unrenewed sons of Adam, you were under the death-sentence of the broken law and under the bondage of sin within; that "Man," that personified state of you men, which is decaying, corrupting, like a moral corpse, on its way to final ruin, according to, in the fashion inevitably due to, the desires of its (τῆς) deceit— the lusts which respond to the wiles of temptation with which it plays and parleys. And the "teaching" and the "truth" were not negative only, speaking only of a "putting-off"; they were positive, with the glorious watchwords of renewal and investiture: with

Ver. 23. reference, on the other side (δέ), to your being renewed, in a holy process[1] of new development, the bright antithesis to the process of "decay" now arrested and reversed a "renewal" in respect of the spirit of your mind—your spiritual life and faculty coming out in *mental* action; your human spirit awakened and enabled to grasp saving truth, and so to find the secret of an abiding blessing. And along

---

[1] 'Ἀνανεοῦσθαι : a *present* infinitive.

Ver. 24. with this, the "teaching" had reference to the fact that you did put on[1] the New Man, the new, the grace-given, state of things for your humanity, in which, as re-generated members of Christ, you have exchanged doom for peace and moral bondage for spiritual freedom ; that " Man," that personified state of you " men in Christ," which, true to God (κατὰ Θεόν), "answering His great idea," was created, constituted, when it was provided in Christ Jesus, the Second Man, in righteousness, in loyal correspondence to the Will of God, and sanctity, piety,[2] of the truth, the truth of the Gospel; for to that truth " sanctity " belongs, as a fruit which the truth ever tends to produce, and as the fair adornment of its holy stem.

The passage thus before us is important in more than one respect.   It is instructive in the first place as an example of what the Epistle has already so often illustrated to us, the con-nexion of doctrine with life.   St Paul is intent here upon the practical holiness of the Ephesians. He is unalterably desirous that in every detail of daily life they shall " walk uprightly, and

---

[1] I paraphrase freely here, to bring out the force of the *aorist* infinitive, ἐνδύσασθαι, and the reference (which I believe to be intended) to not a *duty* but a *fact*. The "putting-on," like the "putting-off," is viewed, I believe, as *fait accompli.*

[2] Ὁσιότης : see Trench, *N. T. Synonyms*, series ii., § xxxviii. It is the virtue which " reverences everlasting sanctities and owns their obligation."

work righteousness, and speak the truth from the heart" (Ps. xv. 2). How does he approach this matter, with all its infinite importance for the realities of human intercourse? By taking his disciples inward and upward to the secret things of the grace of God. He conducts their thought, that he may conduct their faith, straight to the personal Christ, to the wonderful Lord Jesus, as the meeting-point of all the lines of truth. And then he reminds them (it is a reminder, not a new announcement; he must be referring to lessons given long before in "the school of Tyrannus") of facts and principles which sound at first as visionary and far away as possible, but which are potent for immediate use. He speaks to them about an Old Man and a New Man, and about "putting off" the one and "putting on" the other, as of facts in a mysterious biography of the human spirit.

How dreamy, how exquisitely unpractical, says the wisdom of the world! But the Apostle is wiser than that wisdom. He is speaking practically, for he is speaking of facts which are as solid and operative for the spirit as gravitation and magnetism are for the body. He knows that behind the term "the Old Man" lie *facts* deep as man himself, of sin, righteousness,

judgment, guilt, bondage—a chain which no force
of the human will can break, if only because it
can have no adequate fulcrum apart from Christ.
And he knows that behind the term " New
Man " lie all the solid treasures of redemption ;
Christ for us, Christ in us ; a contact with
eternal love, and with divine power for victory
and freedom in the soul, which can work with
glorious practicality in the hour of present-day
temptation.   So he takes the Asian believer in
to the hidden place, and bids him take out of
it, clasped firmly in his hands, the facts of his
supernatural salvation, in order to a supernatural
result—a life of heavenly purity and love lived
amidst perfectly earthly circumstances.

Do we not know in experience, in our measure,
what this means?   True it is that nothing is
more lifeless than a theory of life without practice.
But nothing is more living than a life really
lived with a strong, sure, theory behind it.   The
man knows the law of action, as well as the
line of it, and loses no time in fumbling for
his resource.   He has learned the nature of his
weapon, and the use of it ; so far from his being
encumbered by his knowledge, in the hour of
conflict, it is just his knowledge which makes
him move and strike with decision.   Did we

never experience, in our own inner history, a time when, after long uncertainties and confusions, we came (perhaps on a sudden) to find that our way to inward conquest was a way quite definite and quite supernatural, that is to say, Christ used by faith? And was not that discovery instantly applicable to "the next thing" in the path of common duty? Was it not our delight to spend it upon the most concrete difficulties— to find it act upon the next solicitation to impatience, to envy, to unfaithfulness, to cowardice, to indolence, to impure thought?

Mystery may stand in the closest possible relation to all that is practical. Who can tell us all about the physical mystery of electricity? But for all that, there is no unreality about the electric telegraph, and the electric lamp, and the electric carriage. These are things practical enough to be matters of common use, commercial investment, and state legislation.

In conclusion, we note a point or two in the phraseology of the passage.

i. "The Old Man"; "the New Man." It seems important to observe that these terms are not synonyms for "the flesh" and "the Spirit" respectively. They are such that the Apostle here contemplates our definitely and altogether

quitting the Old Man to enter the New. On the
other hand he contemplates (e.g. Gal. v. 16, 17)
the abiding presence and counteraction in our
being of "the flesh" and "the Spirit," though
he expressly reminds us that the divine purpose
is that the Spirit shall be the continuous
Conqueror of the flesh.

"The Old Man," "the New Man," are not
elements or presences in us; they are, highly
personified, relations and connexions attaching
to us. As such the one may be definitely left,
the other definitely entered.

ii. "Put off," "put on." If I have understood
and expounded aright, the immediate thought of
the Apostle, in the ἀποθέσθαι and ἐνδύσασθαι, deals
with the "accomplished facts" of divine Redemption; the provision for us in the Lord Jesus Christ
of a complete transference and emancipation, so
that the believer, once "in the Lord," *has* stepped
out of the old position and *has* entered upon the
new, however imperfect his consciousness of it
may be, and however much he may have to
learn of the further possibilities of his present
position. This is an aspect of truth which
needs often and earnestly to be remembered and
used. A grasp of the facts of the Covenant of
God, a handling of our present possessions in

Christ, is one of the mightiest secrets of the disciple's life of faith.

Only, that aspect will continually translate itself into another; the recollection of covenant possession will pass on into the action of conscious acquisition. The man who knows that he possesses Christ will evermore resolve, in experience, to find Him. The man who knows that, by the grace of God, he has put the New Man on, will therefore rise up, in working experience, in view of each hour's need, to " put on the Lord Jesus Christ."

TOTAL ABSTINENCE FROM SINNING IN THE FORGIVEN LIFE

Je n'ai plus de force que pour m'occuper de l'amour ae Dieu. Dieu nous a aimé : c'est toute la doctrine de l'Évangile. Aimons Dieu : c'en est toute la morale.

MONOD, *Adieux*

ORDER my footsteps in Thy Word,
  And make my heart sincere;
Let sin have no dominion, Lord,
  But keep my conscience clear.

WATTS

CHAPTER XII

TOTAL ABSTINENCE FROM SINNING IN THE FORGIVEN LIFE

EPHESIANS iv. 25—v. 2

IN the last chapter we watched the Apostle's
actual approach to the treatment of the
practical holiness of the disciples, and his first
words about some great details. In particular,
he has put his readers face to face with the
awful facts of the corruption of man's heart apart
from God, and so of the unspeakable corruption
of current human life. And he has reminded
them that they " have not so learned our Christ."

Yet still we have had to wait for the full
stream of explicit precepts. The Epistle to the
Ephesians has been powerfully characterized, I
think by the late Dr C. J. Vaughan, as a writing
so full of eternity that, even when it stoops to
the earth, its heavenly wings, by their slightest

waft, bear it aloft again to the regions of transcendent truth. So here the Apostle, laying down for his converts the rule of purity, rises for a moment to the mystery of the Old Man and the New, and so to the wonder of our vital union with "the Second Man" as the ultimate account of our power to be really holy at all. Here, as everywhere, such digressions upward are pregnant with the suggestion of the living bond between the really spiritual and the really practical. Nothing indeed is meant to be more matter-of-fact, or, if I may use the phrase, more workmanlike, than the Christian's attention to right-doing in his common life this hour. Nothing is more remote from his Master's mind, or from the mind of his Master's Apostle, than that he should think it really a "stoop to the earth" to be careful to be pure and true in the next little thing, as if it was something greater and higher to muse upon eternal principles. Yet it is as certain as both revelation and experience can make it that a sure grasp upon eternal principles is of infinite importance for the really right doing of the duties of time. Of this we have been just reminded, then, and we shall have it set before us again and again in the remaining pages of the Epistle. But now comes

in at length the fuller and more particular treatment of duty.   The long wings of the angel of
truth are folded, though ever ready to expand
again, and his white feet walk upon the familiar
surface of our common life.

Ver. 25. **Wherefore, because you have** "learned Christ,"
and have "put on the New Man," coming out of the
polluted darkness into the clear, clean light, **laying aside**
decisively (ἀποθέμενοι, aorist) **the falsehood,** τὸ ψεῦδος, the
whole class of thought and speech which falls under
the head of untruth, **speak truth each with his neighbour,** particularly now his Christian neighbour, his
fellow-believer ; **because we are one another's limbs,** one
spiritual organism in our Head, and thus vitally related
to each other, with an absolute obligation to serve each
other's good.   To all men, indeed, you will act as under
the law of truth, for you belong to Him who is the
Truth itself ; your lie, to the veriest pagan, would *belie
Him.*   But this wider circle of duty will be all the
better fulfilled for a special fidelity to the inner circle,
the family of faith.   So glorify God by a truthful
tongue.   Glorify Him also by a kindly temper. **Be angry**
Ver. 26. **and do not sin**[1]; if wrath must sometimes

---

[1] "The words are verbatim the LXX. version of Ps. iv. 4.
The literal Hebrew there is, '*tremble, and sin not.*' And the
verb rendered 'tremble' may denote the tremor of grief, awe, or
anger indifferently. The question of interpretation thus becomes
one of context, and it has been suggested (by Dr Kay) that
the reference is to the temptation to David's followers, during
Absalom's rebellion, to give way to unholy wrath against the

16

be, (and it sometimes must be, while wrong is in the world,) see to it that it is unsinful wrath, wrath in the line of God's will, pure displeasure at evil, not partisanship for self. And where there *has* been failure of patience, be prompt to return to love; let not the sun set upon your exasperation [1]; lay feeling of all grievance at the Lord's feet absolutely, before you part for the night; dare not to refuse your " neighbour " a farewell

Ver. 27. in the peace of Christ ; nor give place to the devil, who, " wherever he finds a heart shut, finds a door open," and who knows too well how to use it, till he fills the inner chamber with his dreadful presence, and the man " who hateth his brother knoweth not whither he goeth " (1 John ii. 11)—from sin to sin.

As with truth of word and gentleness of temper, so Ver. 28. with honesty and honour. The stealer, the man once used to pilfer or to plunder as if it were but a foible—" everybody does it ! "—let him no longer

---

rebels. Bishop Perowne, though saying that the LXX. Greek is ' certainly a possible rendering,' refers the words to the tremor of awe before God. And he remarks that St Paul gives here the Greek version ' not in the way of direct citation,' [but as using its words as the vehicle of his thought]. This last remark is important. The N.T. does not necessarily endorse a certain version of the O.T. by adopting its wording for a special purpose *without* the decisive formula, ' it is written,' or the like. Still the suggestion of Dr Kay is noteworthy in itself, and it would give a peculiar point and force to the words here." (Note in the *Cambridge Bible*.)

[1] " Wetstein quotes a parallel from Plutarch . . . who says of the Pythagoreans that it was their rule, if betrayed into angry reviling, to shake hands before the sun set." (Note in the *Cambridge Bible*.)

steal; let him put a quiet, decisive, close to the whole
habit in every form. Nor only so; let him aim at a
positive and not merely a negative repentance; let
him resolve upon a life-long course of reparation, in the
way of active distribution of his own to others [1]; rather
than the slightest further trifling with the old sin, let
him be a toiler, labouring hard (κοπιάτω) as for a main
object, working with his own hands (ταῖς ἰδίαις χερσίν)
what is good, making honest gains by honest pains, that
he may not merely "recover his character" but have
what he may share with the man who is in want,[2] and
so reverse the past into a delightful contrary. Then
again, let the disciple remember to sanctify his tongue.
He has been warned already to use it only for what is
true; let him equally take heed to use it only for what is
Ver. 29.   pure. All speech corrupt,[3] all talk tainted with

---

[1] Assuredly St Paul would desire, as in the case of Onesimus
(Philem. 18), that, wherever possible, restitution should be made
to the *injured party*. See Zaccheus' words (Luke xix. 8); "*I
restore him* fourfold." But he is here concerned with the widest
and most permanent aspects of the case. The man who has
ever been a defrauder of others must all his life now feel bound
specially to be the benefactor of others.

[2] Μεταδιδόναι is not only to "distribute," which might be done
by a mere agent or official; it involves the thought of share-
and-share between giver and receiver.—Ἵνα ἔχῃ . . . τῷ χρείαν
ἔχοντι. It is just possible that there is an intended antithesis in
ἔχῃ and ἔχοντι—one *has* the need, the other *has* the supply. But
the phrase χρείαν ἔχειν is too common to make this very probable.

[3] Σαπρός : lit. "corrupt, putrid." The Latin Versions render
simply *sermo malus*. And the Greek word is certainly used
with considerable latitude. But here, surely, is the very place
for its more proper and narrow meaning. The thought is of

moral decay, the miserable innuendo, the vile *double entendre* of sin, as well as more avowed impurity, let it not issue out of your mouth; see that " the Lord's watch" (Ps. cxli. 3) is set before that mouth ; *that* will absolutely bar such outgoings. But no artificial silence, meanwhile, will be the alternative ; the mouth, perhaps once greatly defiled, will now " give goodly words." While the " speech corrupt" is for ever hushed, let there issue from you whatever speech is good, tending to upbuilding in faith and purity, as the need may be,[1] that it may give grace to those who hear it; " giving," as an instrument in the Lord's hands to benefit the souls and wills to which you speak. Thus living, thus speaking, see to it that you " walk and please God ";

Ver. 30. and put not to pain the Spirit, the Holy Spirit, of our (τοῦ) God, wherein (as you were *embraced in* His [2] gracious power) you were sealed—as the purchased property of your King[3]—in view of the day of redemption, that bright day, the goal of hope, the stimulus of holiness, when He shall claim the property He has purchased and has sealed, to take it home with Him for ever for His own heavenly use.

---

the sort of speech which reeks of moral pollution, coming from "the throat which is an open sepulchre" (Ps. v. 9), "full of all uncleanness."

[1] Lit. "towards upbuilding of the need"; i.e. towards such spiritual and moral benefit as the particular occasion calls for.

[2] I do not hesitate to indicate in the paraphrase the Personality of the Holy Spirit ("*His* gracious power"). Only a Person can be "put to pain" by moral wrong.

[3] See above, i. 13.

As the Apostle pauses, his thought gathers up
the whole matter again into one comprehensive
appeal.   He calls for a *total abstinence* from sins
of temper, and of tongue ; for the deep secret of
the peace of the Church, and of the home, and
of the heart, in a life of love learnt at the Lord's
own feet.

Ver. 31.   All bitterness of spirit and tone, and wrath
(θυμός), the habitual readiness to be inflamed, and anger
(ὀργή), the eruption of the habit, and all outcry of intem-
perate, uncontrolled, assertion of grievance, and railing,
abusive words against others, aye, even down to the most
easily allowed expressions of harsh and loveless criticism,
let it all be taken away from you, lifted clean out of your
lives, as a thing utterly incongruous with a Christian's
first rules of conduct, with all malice, all the wretched
native soil of these miserable growths, all the underlying
unkindness from which spring the careless anger and the
cruel word.[1] Yes, let it be dealt with in a holy in-
tolerance ; in the Lord's name *take it away* ; bid it be
gone ; give it over to Him who knows how to " lift it
out of " your spirit and your practice, and to place Himself
Ver. 32.   where it was.   And so become, grow ever more

---

[1] Kακία : sometimes the word signifies " evil " in a very general
sense, as when we have " the evil of the day," " the trouble the
day brings " (Matt. vi. 34). But in a passage like this, where
vices are spoken of in some detail, the narrower meaning is more
appropriate ; it is " malice," the deep *unkindness* of the self-
centred, Christless heart.

and more, in a developed manifestation of His power within you, **towards one another, kindly, gentle-hearted,**[1] **mutually forgiving**[2]—that duty so easily confessed but often so impossible to flesh and blood, impossible without a divine motive and a divine power. And here that need is supplied ; **just as actually (καὶ) our (ὁ) God, in Christ, did forgive you**[3]—in that sublime "accomplished fact" of pardon. It was done in eternity from one view-point ; it was done at Calvary from another ; from yet another, it was done on your personal coming into union with Christ by faith; but from all points of view it was an act towards you of immeasurable and wholly unmerited mercy, which must for ever give tone to all your thoughts when you have to consider the duty of forgiving. Yes, it calls you to an "imitation," which shall penetrate to the very springs of life, and shall always find its possibility in the fact of your own salva-

Ch. v. ver. 1. tion. **Become ye therefore, with the perpetual "becoming" of a still developing practice,**

---

[1] Εὔσπλαγχνοι : the σπλάγχνα are the "nobler" interior organs of the body, including the heart. Hence the word and its cognates, in figure, signify much what we signify by "the heart" and its actions.

[2] Lit. "forgiving *yourselves*," ἑαυτοῖς. But the idiom is well known, and unmistakable here. It differs from the same construction with ἀλλήλοις only by somewhat accentuating the "solidarity" of the parties concerned; the forgiveness would as it were circulate within the complex "self" of the deeply united community. This however, in view of the familiarity of the construction, must not be pressed far.

[3] Note the aorist, ἐχαρίσατο, as it points to an act past and done.—"You": another reading, with considerable support, is ἡμῖν, "us." Internal evidence is in favour of ὑμῖν.

imitators of our (τοῦ) God, in a life in which (in a sense of entire reverence and humility) HE is reproduced, in His essential Character; as children beloved, children of such a Father, shewing the family likeness of the Home
Ver. 2. of Grace; and, in this condition, in the joy and power of this divinely given relationship, **walk** along the path of actual human intercourse, with all it brings to you to do or to bear, **in love**, the spirit which "seeks its happiness in another's good," **just as actually** (καί) **our** (ὁ) **Christ did love us,**[1] in all our lost and polluted estate, unlovely and unloving, **and gave Himself over on our behalf, an Offering and Sacrifice to our** (τῷ) **God, for an odour of fragrancy**; "a savour of repose," in the language of the ancient Law,[2] the vehicle

---

[1] Another reading, with considerable but not decisive evidence, gives ὑμῖν, "you." But there is no doubt that ἡμῶν, five words below, is the right reading there; and it is most unlikely that in that short space the Apostle would vary the reference. Ἡμῖν, "us," should be retained here accordingly.

[2] רֵיחַ נִיחֹחַ, *réach nîchôach* (see e.g. Lev. i. 9). The altar-victim was regarded as emitting, so to speak, its "savour" to the Deity, as a token of submission and surrender; so the thought of the Deity's pleasure and pacification was conveyed under the imagery of a welcome odour, "redolent" of the "repose" of restored relation between the Deity and the worshipper. "Pagan sacrificial language has many parallels; see e.g. Homer, *Il.*, viii. 549. Cowper renders this passage—

'Next the gods
With sacrifice they sought, and from the plain,
Upwafted by the wind, the smoke aspires,
Savoury, but unacceptable to those
Above, such hatred in their hearts they bore,' etc."
(Note in the *Cambridge Bible*.)

and the token of the wonderful reconciliation of offended
Holiness to us miserable sinners, who now for ever must
live as those who owe all to the mercy and the love
which provided, which made, and which accepted, the
Atonement of the Cross.

Here let our paraphrase pause awhile. It is
difficult, in this context, to say of any given
sentence that it is the climax of a paragraph,
so intimate and pregnant are the connexions.
We go forward at once from this verse, for
example, into precepts about purity which have
the closest possible relation to the fact of our
salvation by the mysterious mercy of a holy God
who accepted the sacrifice of " the Son of His
Love " on our behalf when we lay condemned.
But we may lawfully pause here, if we remember
meantime that the delay is only provisional.
For here, with this second verse of the new
chapter of the Epistle, closes the special reference
to the Lord's Sacrifice, which began to be made
at the end of the chapter previous. And it
does so in immediate connexion still with the
theme of forgiving love which was the matter of
appeal there.

What shall we say then of the messages of the
portion now before us ? They group themselves
into messages of eternal truth and of minutest

present duty.   In the order of statement, the
words upon duty come first, and the eternal
truths are given at the close.   But let us work
backwards in our meditation, and think a little
first of the Apostle's language upon "the Sacrifice
of the Death of Christ, and the benefits which
we receive thereby."

.i. We observe first how the whole subject
comes in here incidentally, and for a special and
practical purpose.   He is wholly intent upon
bringing home to their wills and affections the
blessed duty of a loving life, which forgets self
and remembers others, and meets if need be the
wrongs done by others with love in the form
of forgiveness, full and free.   To give that duty
all its sacred weight upon their hearts he brings
in two sublime facts of salvation, infinitely
mysterious, perfectly genuine.   The first is the
love of the Father, who has forgiven us, and
with so great a forgiveness, nothing less than
a forgiveness lodged "in" His dear Son, and
therefore given "in" the gift of HIM.   The
second is the love of that Son, "our Christ,"
who, in order to make that forgiveness actually
ours, in fruition, offered Himself up on our
behalf, as an altar-sacrifice.

ii. We notice that we are not to expect here

a complete and reasoned exposition of the Atonement ; if we seek that, we must go rather to such Scriptures as Isaiah liii., (holding the lamp of the New Testament to our feet as we traverse it,) or Romans iii., or large portions of the Epistle to the Hebrews; remembering that even there we never get, in any one place, the subject treated from *all* its sides. Here, manifestly, one side only is prominent in view— the side of Example, the Example of the Father, and the Example of the Son, as illustrating the glory of the law of love, and the infinite obligation upon us to be forgiving. Very little is said here (almost nothing required to be said, in this view) upon the truth of the Atonement with regard to its eternal principles, its line of efficacious action, its precise regard towards God, or towards our race, as a sacrificial act. All that was needed was the solemn reminder that it was a process, a work, of immeasurable mercy, springing out of the depths of divine forgiving love. And may that aspect of it be ever present, ever living, in our hearts, as a thing far too deep within them to need to be quickened into operation by a perpetual restatement of the dogmatic certainties of the sublime " plan " of mercy. May we " walk in love " along our

common path, as those who habitually breathe
the air and power of just that fact—I am wonderfully forgiven ; freely, fully, certainly, but withal
wonderfully ; in the words of the Moravian
hymn,

> "It is mere mercy;
> Remains a wonder
> Of Christ's longsuffering, when thereon I ponder,
> Now and always."

iii. But then all the more observable it is that
into such an incidental, passing, reference to
atoning mercy the Apostle cannot help (so
to speak) putting much which illuminates our
doctrinal vision of the mystery. Here, for
example, we have emphasized that fact, ever
prominent in Scripture, that it is distinctively the
Lord's Death which is our pardon and our peace.
Not Incarnation *per se* but the Death of the
Incarnate is our redemption. He "gave Himself
over for us"; words which obviously point to
that supreme surrender when He "took the cup
of trembling," and willed to die, with all that
death meant for Him, "a ransom for many";
assuredly because, for eternal Holiness, no other
and smoother way was possible to liberate eternal
Love upon a rebel race. Further in the same
connexion manifestly, we see Him self-given to

be an "offering and sacrifice *to God*"; not merely an exhibition of divine love to melt the hard heart of man, but a sacrifice, an altar-sacrifice, θυσίαν, *to God*. *God-wards* first looks the work of Calvary, that then, and not before, it may look *man-wards*. "The savour of rest" must ascend to the throne of violated Holiness, before the rainbow-shower of infinitely willing forgiveness can come down from that throne upon our guilty heads.

iv. Then, for the actual possession and fruition of the blessing, that we may indeed drink in that "great rain of His" love, we have here the revealed law that we get it only *in union with* our atoning Lord. "God *in Christ* did forgive you." "For Christ's sake," says our Authorized Version there; and the words are absolutely true. Their truth depends not so much upon one passage, or upon several, as upon the whole view given us in Scripture, first of the Father's infinite and eternal complacency in the Son, then of the Son's undertaking our cause as Propitiation and as Advocate, "the Just for the unjust." "For His sake" is a phrase inadequate indeed fully to express that truth; but it is true to the idea. But here we have, in the literal and just rendering, this *and more*. "*In Christ*, He did forgive." The forgiveness is what it is—for His sake. It is imparted, in all it is, not only for His sake, but—to those who so come to Him as to be embodied, involved, " in " Him, taken up into membership with Him their blessed Head. Such is the Son to the Father, that the Father en-spheres His actual mercies all in the Son. Such are we to the Father that He welcomes us, poor sinners, for pardon, holiness, and heaven, into the depths of union with the Son ; that He may " love us " with no mere benignant amnesty, but " even as He loveth Him " (see John xvii. 23).

v. So we come, stepping backwards, to the opening verses of our paragraph, its precepts of holiness, the holiness of truth, of purity, of kind speech, of self-forgetting love. As the paraphrase proceeded we have seen something of their in-cidence in detail. So our only comments now shall be summary, general, and of the briefest.

1. Observe afresh, and carry it into every hour of waking life, yes, every hour, that we are called here to total abstinence from sin ; " *let all* be put away " ; " *let all* be lifted off."

2. Observe, similarly, that we are called, with equal directness, to a positive practice of good, always, as well as to a perpetual abstinence from evil.

3. Observe, lastly, that the idea of such a life will be the mockery of all our hopes, and our very Christianity will be embittered by a long inward disappointment, unless it is lived in the full sunlight of personal forgiveness, enjoyed in personal union with the Christ of God. Lived there, it will be life indeed, loving, lasting, overcoming, serving, even to the end.

THE WORKS OF DARKNESS AND THE FRUIT OF
LIGHT

HE who examines is startled to find that the phrase, 'fear of the Lord,' is woven into the whole web of Revelation, from Genesis to the Apocalypse. Well and blessed would it be for this irreverent and unfearing age, in which the advance in mechanical arts and vice is greater than that in letters and virtue, if the popular mind could be made reflective and solemn by this great emotion.

SHEDD, *Sermons to the Natural Man,* § xvi.

CHAPTER XIII

THE WORKS OF DARKNESS AND THE FRUIT OF LIGHT

Ephesians v. 3-14

Ver. 3. But fornication, a sin so lightly thought of among the heathen as hardly to be held by them a wrong or shame at all,[1] and all impurity; all, absolutely all, which falls under the same class, sin of the soul against the body, all that is unworthy of the "children beloved" of the All-Pure; or greed of whatever is another's, but now specially *sensual* greed, directed towards the ruin of another's purity,[2] be it not even named amongst you, as beseems holy ones, men and women dedicated to the Holy One, His purchased and surrendered possession. No, let not such things even play upon your lips. True, those lips may sometimes need to refer to them, quite explicitly, (even as in these very sentences they are referred to,) to expose, to condemn, to warn. But even so, let the mentions be as

---

[1] And too lightly thought of in our modern nominal Christendom, to judge by much of its public opinion and of its legislation.

[2] See on iv. 19 above for the wider and narrower meanings of πλεονεξία.

brief and as reserved as may be, or they may hurt both speaker and hearer ; and as for any lighter "naming" of them, any treatment of them in talk as mere inevitable incidents in human life, or any lingering round them in conversation, as round what has the slightest attraction to the mind, any talk such as dresses them in colours of sentiment or romance, beware ; put the thing utterly away. In such "naming" there is always a sinful motive behind, however little realized ; and the "naming" reacts upon the motive, to develope and to quicken it. All round the circle of such evil let the same absolute rule prevail ; "name" not ever filthiness,

Ver. 4. *αἰσχρότητα*, vice in its aspect of deformity, hideousness, that aspect which by a dreadful law of evil sympathy can become positively attractive to a once tainted imagination ; nor fool-talk, the horrible trifling and soulless "frankness" over what is bad which marks the fool of fools, who makes a toy of "the abominable thing which God hateth" (Jer. xliv. 4) ; nor jesting, the wretched pleasantry, as different as possible from the play of pure and wholesome mirth ; the pleasantry of unclean badinage, of epigrammatic allusion to vice, of half-meanings wholly foul, which defile not only common talk but many a brilliant page of literature ; things, all of them, which are not befitting, unutterably unseemly to the sinner who has become in Christ a saint. And let not your abstinence, here again, be merely negative. Let your Lord so fill your hearts that

---

[1] The construction is continuous in the Greek : καὶ αἰσχρότης, κ.τ.λ. ; but I have broken it for the purposes of the paraphrase.

from them to your lips shall rise not only no pollution but the clear sweet stream of glad thankfulness, pervading all your talk with its light and life. "Name" not evil, but rather "name," utter, as out of an inner abundance, thanksgiving.

We rest a few moments upon that word, in its deep significance and fitness here. Why does St Paul, just in this passage of awful insistence upon purity of speech, call for a habit of thanksgiving in the Christian's lips? He does not mean, of course, that we are never to articulate any words but those which speak gratitude to God; we have, in the path of duty, to talk upon countless matters, and often upon matters that sadden the speaker to the heart; the Apostle is at this moment doing so himself, with that sort of speech which flows through the pen. But he does plainly mean that our talk is to have a habitual tendency to the utterance, somehow, of thankful love to God. Is not the reason this, that "thanksgiving," as a fact, so it be pure and genuine, and not fatally spoiled by artificial motives, is both a symptom of inner wholesomeness and a means to its development? It is the positive exercise of spiritual health, the instinctive movement of holy happiness. It is the outcoming of the "joy of the Lord"; and that joy is not only our "strength" (Neh. viii. 10) for toil and suffering, but our strength too, in a wonderful measure, against the very subtlest and the very fiercest forms of temptation. Who that knows at all the power of even one minute's joyful consciousness of what the Lord Christ is to him, and he to Christ, does not understand this without explanation? Is it too much to say that the Christian is (in a practical sense) invulnerable to the poisoned dart while he is "giving thanks," with a true heart, for a great and a present redemption, or rather for a great Redeemer, present in all His fulness to him? The classic legend is in point here. Orpheus, the minstrel of the Argonauts, when the ship passed near the island of the Sirens, and their sweet but fatal song was audible to the mariners, and began to tell upon their wills, struck his harp and raised his voice aloft *in praise* of the heavenly Powers. The better song overpowered the worse, with its pure positive. Let us practise not Orphean but Christian music in our hearts, and we shall find its power upon the enemy, so that it be music really learnt from the sight of our Redeemer.

Nor let us fail to notice that the Apostle here

is enjoying not only the feeling within but the expression without.   Thanksgiving is to take the place of the " naming" of evil with our lips. Of course, in this matter, as in every matter, there are rules of wisdom as well as of love. Circumstances are very easy to conceive in which an audible utterance of spiritual gratitude would not only do no good but would do much harm; above all, if that expression were in any degree forced and mechanical.   But far oftener, probably, than we think, the modest but free expression of a really happy soul would do the deepest good. And it may and it does react in a wonderful way, rightly exercised, upon the heart from which it comes.

The application of the thought is obvious, meantime, to the united and public expression of Christian thanksgiving.   More will be said of this below by the Apostle (v. 19, 20).   Here it is enough to remember that holy hymns, whether sung in the congregation, or in the home, are powerful means of grace in the hand of the Spirit, and above all when they are hymns of praising gratitude.

> "Sing, till you feel your hearts
> Ascending with your songs;
> Sing, till the love of sin departs,
> And grace inspires your tongues."

But let us return to the Apostle's text, as he passes from precept to urgent and anxious warning :

Ver. 5. For this you know with clear recognition,[1] as a tremendous fact, resting upon eternal and inexorable truth, that every fornicator, without exception or extenuation, and [2] unclean man, whatever his *form* of moral foulness, and greedy man, with the "greed" denoted above (ver. 3), which means (ὅ ἐστιν) idolater, (for his "greed" is a dreadful and debasing worship of the creature, or rather of his own vile pleasure in the creature,) possesses no inheritance in the kingdom of our (τοῦ) Christ and of God. No ; let him flatter himself as he will ; his willing sin precludes absolutely his *title* to entrance and to place in that kingdom, and as absolutely negatives his *capacity* for its life. He cannot possibly be a genuine subject of the holy Saviour and the holy Father now, happy in that blessed Rule loyally welcomed, and that sovereign Protection thankfully enjoyed. And when that kingdom passes into its eternal development, when the throne of God and of the Lamb is the centre of the Holy City (Rev. xxii. 3), and the blessed ones for ever and ever serve around it, with the Name on their foreheads, "where shall the ungodly and the sinner appear ?" (1 Pet. iv. 18). " I

---

[1] Τοῦτο γὰρ ἴστε (not ἐστε) γινώσκοντες : "you know (as fact), knowing (with insight into the reason)."

[2] Lit. "or" (ἤ) ; and so in the next words. But our idiom seems to require "and."

never knew you ; depart from Me, ye that work
iniquity" (Matt. vii. 23).[1]

The Apostle urges his warning home, for
he knows that there is need. Now from the
heart within, now from outward influences, as
conversation, literature, or what not, comes the
suggestion that things are not so bad as the
prophets of judgment paint them. Sin is not
all that they would have it ; is it not after all an
incident of our finite nature? Is it not perhaps
even a step upwards, (though it stumbles on
the slope, and finds the ground miry,) in the
development of that nature into a larger experience? Anywise, the large, the boundless,
insight and sympathies of an all-benignant Power
will preclude the "taking of strong measures in
the Universe." *Tout savoir c'est tout pardonner.*

---

[1] "What is the ' Kingdom ' here? On the whole, the glorified
state, the goal of the process of grace. True, the word often,
with obvious fitness, includes the period of grace in this life,
in which most truly the Christian is a subject of the King (see
e.g. Matt. xi. 11 . . .). But usage often gives the word a special
connexion with the final state, glory ; cp. esp. Matt. xxv. 34. . . .
See also the passages, closely akin to the present, 1 Cor. vi. 9, 10 ;
Gal. v. 21 ; where the '*shall* not inherit' . . . points to the
idea of *a coming* ' Kingdom.' . . . The practical meaning here
then is, ' no such moral rebel can be, while such, a citizen of
and pilgrim to the heavenly city." (Note in the *Cambridge
Bible*.)

We are poor unfortunates at the worst, who have gone astray under very dark skies, on very rough ground. There will be a large indulgence on the part of "the good God." He will arrange that this world shall somehow be set happily to rights in the next. So let us walk, though at a moderate pace, along the broad road still; certainly let us not be too unhappy, too despondent, too full ot forebodings, about those who are upon it, whether or no we go along with them there.

" Ye shall be as God, knowing good and evil. Ye shall not surely die."

It is remarkable how soon, however, in the depth ot some hearts at least, these " vain words " get hushed into an awful silence, when other words come to meet them. Perhaps it is a record, simple and authentic, of a case of conviction of sin; possibly of some hour, unutterably dark, within the outskirts of an infinite night, when a dying man tells those around him that he finds he has put God off just too long, and no argument of love, no pressure of divine promises upon that heart, appears to have the least effect, save to evoke answers, terribly pointed, repelling the inference of mercy. Perhaps it is the very simplest statement,

unattended by the least circumstance of terror,
of eternal moral principles; the absolute and
formidable difference of right and wrong; the
distinction between divine Love in its essential
harmony with divine Holiness and a loose benevo-
lence, weak and vague. Perhaps it is a simple
re-perusal of some of our Lord Jesus Christ's
own urgent words about sin and the judgment
upon sin beyond death; above all, His "depart
from Me," His "I never knew you." We may
have come to take "liberal" views of the Bible,
till we hardly know what it is to approach the
Bible except as its critics. Yet on a sudden
this Book turns upon us, rises as it were in
new and awful life from the dissecting-table
and speaks to us with even more than its old
authority about temperance, righteousness, and
judgment to come, till we tremble all through.
We begin to know again that sin is something
other than development, or than misfortune, and
that the wrath of God has an awful element
in it that is very far from remedial, and that
somehow time has terribly much to do with
eternity, and that all this is true for us. "Vain
words" of fallacious reassurance, poor parodies
of the true message of a love and a mercy
unspeakable, but holy, can, as I said, sink into

dead silence in face of such replies. But they
will be always ready to revive, and talk again.
So we need often to recall the counter-words,
the tender, awful warnings of the holy Book,
" lest we forget." Here then is one of these.

Ver. 6. **Let no one deceive you with empty words,** true
successors of the fatal words of the primeval Temptation ; " empty " of the eternal facts of the unknown
horror of sin, of the sure, tremendous law of retribution,
of the dread reality of divine wrath, of the certainty,
deep as all truth, that divine love will never bend divine
holiness aside, no, not for a hair's-breadth, nor for a
moment. All such words are empty, all such teaching
is deceiving. **For on account of these things,** because of
these lightly tolerated sins, these " frailties," these
" irregularities," these " falls upward," **there is coming**—it
is already on its stern, straight way—**the wrath of our God,**
the personal, infinite, energetic displeasure and hostility
of the revealed Holy One against sin and against the
wills that choose it ; **upon**—as a resistless force marches
" upon " a doomed town—**the sons of this** ($\tau\hat{\eta}s$) **dis-**
obedience, the beings who have linked themselves, by
their choice of evil as their good, to the cause of rebellion
against Him. " As it was in the days of Noah ; as it
was in the days of Lot." All things looked " peace and
safety " ; there was apparently a " silence of God " deep
and permanent, a tolerance, an indifference, an absence.
But " the wrath was coming," and at length, without
mistake, it came.

Ver. 7. **So do not become sharers along with them;** "*becoming*" such, by allowing temptation to "become" transgression, and the acts to grow into the habit; do not become "sharers" of their fatal "disobedience," and so of their hopeless ruin—"consumed in the iniquity of the city." Let not "empty words" allure you into that complicity. No, nor let holy words do so, misused to the purposes of the enemy. Let not the blessed revelations of this very Letter do so, its messages about an eternal and electing love, and a completed salvation, and a session with the Lord in heavenly places. Whether or no you apprehend the sublime harmony, (which there is,) between the song of salvation and the thunder-voices of warning, *listen to each in its turn* with the whole heart. And, however, use the certainty of your Lord's love and mercy wholly and only in the interests of your Lord's will. You *have* His blessings, and are invited to the fullest assurance of them; you know what you were, and what you are; therefore live

Ver. 8. wholly in His will. **For you were once darkness**, not merely in the dark, but impregnated and as it were identified with the "darkness" of ignorance and sin, **but now**, in the blessed present of the converted life, **you are light;** not merely in the light, but filled and as it were identified with the sunshine of knowledge and of holiness; **in the Lord,** in your grace-given union with Him who is the Light; in whom is now your home, your sphere, so that if His radiance does not consciously fill you it is only that you do not open your eyes to take it in. So, as Light's children, walk, live out your real life, in the real world of duty and temptation, as those who are in living and intense connexion with the truth and the purity that is for you in Christ. In that "childhood," break utterly with "the sons of disobedience," and take that narrow path which "is as the shining light, that shineth more and more unto the

Ver. 9. perfect day" (Prov. iv. 18). For the fruit of the Light,[1] the blessed outgrowth of our knowledge of Him in whom we see God, is, consists of, and is developed in, all goodness, every form of all that is the pure opposite of evil,[2] and righteousness, holy regard of the rights of others, in respect of both honesty and purity, and truth, the deep reality and sincerity of purpose which is the one possible basis for a right life.

Thus "walk," at once in holy liberty and in the exactest correspondence to its "perfect law" (Jas i. 25), the will of God, which alone secures our emancipated happiness. And as you do so, watch; for on the King's highway you still have both clouds and enemies to

Ver. 10. reckon with. So go on, testing by the touchstone of His "sweet, beloved will," what is well-pleasing to the Lord; that question which will ever be rising in

---

[1] A.V., "the fruit of the *Spirit*." So Gal. v. 22; (where note the phrase, "the *fruit* of the Spirit," not "*fruits*": the graces make one beautiful and perfect whole). But here the evidence decidedly supports the reading φωτός, not πνεύματος, "light," not "Spirit." Happily the ultimate message of the two is the same; it is only by the Spirit that we have Him who is the Light.

[2] 'Αγαθωσύνη: the word tends to the special meaning of kindliness, beneficence. But its wider original meaning seems more in place here.

the heart which loves Him ; not with the weary feeling,
"What will be the next restriction, the next imposed
chain, the new addition to the load upon my shoulders?"
but with the responsive look of love, the "asking eye"
which would gladly anticipate His perfect purpose and
infinitely beautiful desire, so dear to His loving bondservant's heart. "How can I please Thee in this thing,
and in that? How can my thought meet Thine, and
my will have the joy of being laid along the line of Thy
good pleasure?" Happy they who thus "walk," thus
"testing"! Their souls acquire more and more a holy,
prescient instinct ; a sympathy in the very depths with
God.

Yet again the Apostle returns upon his warnings ; so great is the risk, so infinitely important
the escape.

Ver. 11. And have no part and lot in the barren works [1]
of the darkness, the actions and habits congenial to the
life of sin, things awfully "barren," for their "harvest is
a heap in the day of desperate sorrow" (Isa. xvii. 11) ;
their "end is death" (Rom. vi. 21). Rather even, going
beyond a mere *abstinence*, however total, bring them to
conviction, ἐλέγχετε, bring them to book, *evince* their
dreadful fallacy and mortal futility by appeals to conscience in the name of God. There is need for such

---

[1] Ἔργοις: just before we have had καρπὸς τοῦ φωτός. Possibly
the collocation is intentional, as in Gal. v. 19, 22, where the
weary "*works*" of the flesh are contrasted with the genial,
living, "*fruit*" of the Spirit.

aggression on "the darkness," and you will find souls
there conscious of their degradation, and so far ac-
Ver. 12. cessible; for of the things secretly done by them,
by the miserable rebels there, it is a shame even to
speak; the details could only defile the teller; "let them
not be named."[1]

Is such a field hopeless then for the influence of the
Christian? Is it *practical* to seek to "bring to conviction" such works of the darkness? Yes, if it is done
in the right way, done *by the light*, by those who are not
merely censors and denouncers, but "light in the Lord,"
speaking first and most with the convicting eloquence
of transfigured lives in Christ. It is "a shame to
Ver. 13. speak of the things done in secret." But all
things which are brought to conviction are by the light
made manifest; nothing but the light will do the work;
and you are now light, in Him who is pure Light.
Therefore, while you watch and pray against infection
from the darkness, *shine into it*; let the Lord's light in
upon it, in any way possible, the light of holy truth with
holy love, and then shall the inhabitants of the darkness
(such as you once were) become "light" too; for everything which is being manifested,[2] exposed to the pure
day, is light; that holy Day cannot but transform

---

[1] Only too well is this charge borne out by many a black line
in classical literature and art. But is not the same charge
awfully true in a Christendom which is all too much "the world,"
decorated with certain Christian elements in thought and
practice, but at heart in "the darkness" still? See above, ch. xi.

[2] So certainly we must render; not. "whatsoever doth make
manifest."

where it really gets entrance. Happy they whose word
and whose life, acting together, pierce those shadows and
carry there the Lord's life-giving light!

Ver. 14. Wherefore, in view of this work of life by light,
it, the Scripture, says, Awake, sleeping one, and rise from
out of the dead, and our (ὁ) Christ shall dawn upon thee.[1]

So we find a paragraph again, and make
pause a little while. May He who is the everlasting Light, and ' in whom is no darkness at
all,' so shine in us that the awful darkness may
be kept, by His presence, outside our wills,
outside our lives. And may He so shine from
us that we may be the blessed vehicles for
carrying His transforming radiance even to the
inhabitants of the night.

---

[1] The passage chiefly in view, we can hardly doubt, is
Isa. lx. 1, "Arise, shine, for thy light is come, etc." But other
Scriptures appear to blend with this in the Apostle's inspired
thought; as Isa. lii. 1, 2, "Awake, awake, put on thy strength,
O Zion," and li. 17, "Awake, awake, stand up, etc." See Kay
on Isa. lx. 1. And cp. Edersheim, *The Temple and its Services*,
for a possible reference to Jewish liturgical language at the
Feast of Tabernacles. Some have suggested that we have here
the words of a primeval Christian psalm. But the phrase "*it
says*," λέγει, seems to prove at least an ultimate reference to
Scripture itself. St Paul writes, " *Christ* shall dawn upon thee."
But to him this would be no unfaithful citation of the words,
"the glory of the LORD is risen upon thee." See St John's
reference to Isa. vi. 1 (John xii. 41), and St Peter's to Isa. viii. 12, 13
(1 Pet. iii. 15, where read, "the Lord *Christ*").

BRIGHTLY beams our Father's mercy
From His lighthouse evermore;
But to us He gives the keeping
Of the lights along the shore.

BLISS.

THE CHRISTIAN'S WATCHFULNESS, TEMPERANCE, AND SONG

THE first said to him, Thy sins be forgiven thee; the second stripped him of his rags, and clothed him with change of raiment; the third also set a mark upon his forehead, and gave him a roll, with a seal upon it, which he bade him look on as he ran, and that he should give it in at the celestial gate. Then Christian gave three leaps for joy, and went on singing.

Pilgrim's Progress

CHAPTER XIV

THE CHRISTIAN'S WATCHFULNESS, TEMPERANCE, AND SONG

EPHESIANS V. 15-21

THE Ephesians have learnt much now of the details of the holy life, and the last words which they (and we) have heard about it have pointed the thought full upon an element in it which is vital to its health—holy action, holy service. The believer, " light in the Lord," is to shed the light which he receives. There is to be a warm hearth-fire in his own soul's chamber, and a lamp fed with heaven's own sunshine is to hang from its ceiling. But it is also to be a radiant point in the dark world, finding way for its searching beneficent brightness through the windows of the soul, from the beacon-tower of the life. The range of

265

penetration may be vast, or it may be very small. It may command a great region of the earth, or many regions ; it may fill an age of time, it may affect all the ages ; such was the range of St Paul's radiation, for example. Or it may light up one small neighbourhood, one poor home, the visitors to one sick-room ; it may be limited in time by only a fragment of the disciple's one short life ; such was no doubt the range of radiation for many an Asian saint then, as it is for many an English saint now. But the point is that there *is intended to be* radiation outward where there is light within. The Master's service is to be the dear object of the redeemed life. The sacred light is given indeed for the being's own bliss, rich and large ; but it is never given to terminate there. And they best meet the Master's will who most willingly and most continually so keep the windows clear that the light within may radiate around, for conviction, and for gladness, just as freely and as far as may be.

Happy they who, by His grace, so serve Him. Do we not know such lives ? They " cannot be hid "—not because they advertize themselves ; that is the very last thing they do. But it is unmistakable that they are enjoying a great light

within, and it "will out."   Such (to keep close
to our own time, and to no very extended
circle) were William Pennefather, Arthur
Blackwood, Frances Havergal.   Such was that
great light-bearer so recently called from us
D. L. Moody.   Such are cherished names still
among us, known to thousands who owe them
more than they can ever tell, for the light
brought by them into the thick darkness of
worldliness, sin, doubt, and fear.   But there
have been, and there are, countless others whom
no Christian history will ever name, but who
live in transfigured hearts on which they have
shone.   Their "record is on high."

The Apostle comes now to a few more lines
of general caution and precept, before he
approaches his final topic, the Christian Home.
He has to appeal again for a grave remembrance
that the "walk in the light" is no mere prome-
nade, smooth and easy, but a march, resolved
and full of purpose, cautious against the enemy,
watchful for opportunity for the King, self-
controlled in every habit, and possible only (if
it is to be a reality) in the power of the
eternal Spirit.   It is to be a walk, onward and
onward, of holy and habitual praise, of fellowship in spiritual help, and of a mutual submission

which means forgetfulness of self in the recollection of others, in the Lord.

Ver. 15. See therefore, with eyes spiritually open to the path and its environment, **that you walk** (it is the seventh time that this pregnant word has been written) **accurately;** recollecting the importance of detail, fully aware that life is made up of steps and incidents, and that nothing in it lies outside the claims of God. Spend watchful thought upon duty and opportunity ; think nothing trivial in such matters as use of time, manner of act and speech, consistency in common things ; **not as unwise men,** blind to the import and occasions of the passing day, and the relation of time to eternity, **but as wise men,** with that holy wisdom which comes of heart-concord with the will of God, and with a watchful use of thought and of every faculty for its ends. As you walk, make all you can of the events of life, to use them for Him ;

Ver. 16. buying up the opportunity, as it evermore occurs, " buying it *out* " (ἐξαγοραζόμενοι) from alien ownership, from the mere use of self, securing it for your Master *at the expense of* self-denying watchfulness.[1] Do this, remembering that you *will need* to do it if you are to be

---

[1] " The same phrase occurs (Aramaic and Greek) Dan. ii. 8 : ' I knew of a certainty that ye would *buy the time* ' ; where the meaning plainly is, ' that ye would get your desired opportunity *at the expense of* a subterfuge.' . . . In Col. iv. 5 the special thought is of opportunities in intercourse with ' them that are without.' " (Note in the *Cambridge Bible.*)—Here surely it is the same. The thought of seizing occasions to let in " the light " upon " the darkness," that it may become " light," is still in view.

really serviceable to Him ; it will not do to let things
drift, as if circumstances would take care of themselves,
and automatically serve the Lord's servant ; because the
days are evil ; the " days " of your human life in a sinful
world do not *lend themselves* to holy uses where the
man who lives them does not watch for opportunities.

This precept is for all time. No doubt there
were special conditions in Asia at that date which
may have led St Paul to write it down with a
heart centred upon peculiar and acute difficulties.
In many respects the " days " at Ephesus were
" evil " as they are not now, at least for those
of us whose lot is cast in lands which bear the
Christian name, and are full on their surface of
the Christian tradition.   But then, to the age, as
to the day, " sufficient is the evil thereof."   We
have *our* characteristic obstacles, here and now, to
the active doing of the Master's work, and to the
silent diffusion of His light ; among them is the
Christian tradition itself, where it exists along
with spiritual death in men's wills and affections.
So now, as distinctively as then, " the days are
evil " for the full Christian enterprise.   And the
" evil " must be reckoned with, now as ever, by
the merchants of the King, " seeking goodly
pearls " ; they must be on the watch, and " buy
up the opportunity " at a real cost.

We may be sure on the other hand that St Paul does not mean, for in the wisdom of the Spirit he could not mean, that we are enjoined *to force* occasions for our witness or appeal. The imagery of purchase looks just the other way ; it points to a lawful acquisition, though at a real cost. We have need to ask as earnestly for wisdom as for courage and persistency in life and work for Christ. But then, that thought is not to be the miserable excuse for a contented silence. Rather, it is to be our deep motive for such a close personal walk with God, such a readiness, through the prayer of faith, to spend and be spent for Him, such a maintained consciousness that His holy service is our true *raison d'être* as Christians, that when the opportunity is ready for us we shall be ready for it. More than half the price of the " purchase " will thus be paid by our own secret watching and prayer over our own unhindered communion with God.

To usefulness and power
There is no royal road ;
The strength for holy service
Is intercourse with God.

Ver. 17. **On this account**, because you have such a work to do in such a field, **do not become** (γίνεσθε) **foolish**, mindless, witless, as regards duty and its conditions ;

do not "*become*" such, by a permitted *habit* of forgetfulness, deepening till it fixes; but understand (συνίετε)
what is the will of the Lord; with that understanding,
that intuitive perception, which can be got only in the
way of spiritual wakefulness and watching, while the
disciple does indeed use "sanctified common sense," yet
takes care that it *is* "sanctified," by nearness to God
and real accord with His will. Then, and only then,
will you be humbly sure that this or that circumstance
is the signal of His purpose and His call.

Ver. 18.   And do not intoxicate yourselves with wine, in
which, as if lying hidden in that dangerous vehicle, is riot,
"dissoluteness" (ἀσωτία), the miserable licence which
bursts the bonds of conscience with dreadful ease, and
breaks up the whole moral order.

It is not apparent at first what brings in this
grave precept here.   Bengel strikingly remarks
that St Paul "fitly follows up a warning against
impurity with a warning against intemperance";
words which every worker for God among the
"lapsed" will verify from experience.   And has
not many a worker known something, in personal
experiences of temptation, of the awful relation
between the one evil and the other?   But St
Paul has not been dealing so explicitly with impurity in just the last few sentences as to give an
obvious place to Bengel's note.   I would venture
to suggest rather that at this moment in the

Epistle there already rose on his mind the subject of the Fulness of the Spirit, as the profound
requisite to a life of light and of light-giving
power; "the Spirit's calm excess"[1] was present to
him; and this suggested, while he was still occupied with the warning side of truth, this brief,
imperative word upon that "excess" which comes
not from heaven but hell. So brought in, and
indeed whatever was the precise suggesting
reason, it stands here related to *every* foregoing
appeal; for the "riot" which lurks in the cup
of the drunkard annihilates equally, so far as it
prevails, *every* bond of duty. All experience tells
us that it tends to obliterate the very faculty to
speak the truth; it can harden the heart, however
affectionate by nature, against the nearest, the
dearest, the most pathetically dependent; it can
let loose the tongue to speak all sorts of evil;
it can fan the spark of lust into a furnace.
" It biteth like a serpent, and stingeth like an
adder" (Prov. xxiii. 32), at the very heart of
virtue.

I have no purpose here to discuss the grave
problem of " total abstinence." For many long

---

[1] " Læti bibamus *sobriam*
    Ebrietatem Spiritûs."
ST AMBROSE (*Splendor paternæ Gloriæ*).

years, in view of the terrific ravages of intemperance in English life, and wishing to contribute the atom of a personal experience and example on the other side, I have "totally abstained," till the very reminiscence of any "self-denial" in the matter has faded away. But I have never dared to lay down my rule for others, or to think those who take another course to be therefore unfaithful to their Lord. I cannot forget, nor elaborately explain away, the frequent allusions in Scripture to a certain use of wine; remembering however that God has suffered local and temporal conditions to affect the surface of His holy Scripture, so that it is lawful to qualify such allusions, in their bearing upon *English* life, by the thought that "drink" was not the curse in the East then which it is with us now. But I cannot forget also that this same tolerant Scripture, with its ample recognition of the genial side of human life, contains some of the most urgent warnings that can be written against the horror of intoxication, conveyed sometimes in language which the most intolerant of total abstainers could not surpass. One such I have quoted just above in part; let me recite the whole (Prov. xxiii. 31-35, R.V.): "Look not thou upon the wine when it is red, when it giveth its colour in the cup, when it goeth down smoothly : at the last it biteth like a serpent, and stingeth like an adder. Thine eyes shall behold strange things, and thine heart shall utter froward things. Yea, thou shall be as he that lieth down in the midst of the sea, or as he that lieth upon the top of a mast. They have stricken me, shalt thou say, and I was not hurt ; they have beaten me, and I felt it not : when shall I awake ? I will seek it yet again."

This was written in the East, where the plague of intemperance is not as it is with us of the North. Awful is the caution which it conveys to us, for whom indeed, in this matter, "the days are evil."

Ver. 18. **But be filled,** with a fulness habitual, normal,[1] always supplied and always received, **in the Spirit.**[2] Let the Holy One, your Sealer and Sanctifier, so surround and possess you that you shall be as it were vessels immersed *in* His pure flood ; and then, yielding your hearts without

---

[1] The verb (πληροῦσθε) is in the present tense, and thus gives the thought of continuance.

[2] I do not hesitate to supply the definite article, "*the* Spirit" (so R.V. text). So above, i. 17, ii. 22. The context assuredly demands it, for we need a word which shall be an antithesis to the "wine" of the previous clause. It would be no antithesis if we rendered here (as R.V. margin), "be filled in spirit," i.e in the sphere or receptacle of your human spirits ; without specification of *the thing which was to fill them.*

reserve to Him, you shall be vessels not only immersed but open ; " *in* Him," and "*filled*" in Him," as He, continually welcomed, continually occupies and hallows all parts of your nature, all departments of your life.

Let us remember well that this great clause is not a teaching merely but a precept. As distinctly as it is enjoined upon us not to be intoxicated with wine, so is it enjoined upon us to seek, in earnest, "fulness in the Spirit." May nothing blind us to the fact and the significance of that precept ; no, not the unwise and perhaps even fanatical things which have been sometimes heard in the Church in connexion with the sacred Fulness. We may be very sure that the command means nothing which shall "unhinge" the Christian's life, and cast it loose from the noblest sanity and the most steadfast order. As a fact, we find it here imbedded amongst precepts laying down the great laws of self-control, and it comes just before the special directions which the Apostle gives for the quiet sanctities of the Christian home. It must be a thing, whatever it is, full of all that is just, true, lovely, and of good report ; full of virtue and of praise (Phil. iv. 8). But then, all the while, it is a thing supernatural. It is a state of man wholly unattainable by training, by reasoning, by human wish and will. It is nothing less than—God in command and control of man's whole life, flowing everywhere into it, that He may flow fully and freely out of it in effects around.

"O Thou from whom *all holy desires* do proceed," give us the great gift of the desire, ever deeper, for "fulness in the Spirit"; that we may with joy lay claim to the mighty, benignant gift. For Thou hast promised "Thy Holy Spirit to them that ask Thee." It is the unspeakably vital requisite to the full blessing of the soul. It is that which the Church needs with a need that cannot be uttered.

We must not forget meanwhile that the thought of this Fulness is here connected, in a special degree, with that of the joy of the Lord and its expression. As the miserable exhilaration of the drunkard comes out in the song of "riot," so the "calm excess" of the man "filled in the Spirit" will come out in song too. It will come out always in the song of the life, the melody and harmony of a character and conduct gladdened by the blessed Presence. But it will tend often too to come out in the song of the lips, and above all when Christians, thus "filled," meet together before their Lord. So in close connexion, he proceeds:

Ver. 19. **Talking one to another** [1] **in psalms, and hymns, and spiritual odes**; in every variety of sacred song, the Psalms of the elder Church, the rhythmic praises or meditations of the Church of the Gospel,[2] anything, everything, that offers itself as a true vehicle for this precious exercise, "the song of the Lord"; **singing and making music,**[3] **with your heart, to the Lord.**

Not that the hymnody was to be *only* internal, "in the heart"; or how would they thus "talk to one another"? Voice and perhaps instrument too were to be fully audible;

> "No voice exempt, no voice but well could join
> Melodious part; such concord is [from] heaven!"

But all was to be internal also. The sounds were but to express the praising souls. And all this was to be done, not as "music-worship," (God forbid,) but as worship full of music, paid to the remembered, adored, loved, present Lord.

Such singing—and no other—is audible upon the Throne;

> "that God's own ear
> Listens delighted."

---

[1] Ἑαυτοῖς: lit. "*to yourselves.*" See the note on the same word and idiom, above, iv. 32.

[2] It seems out of place too elaborately to analyse and classify. The Apostle evidently means here to emphasize variety and comprehension, not to instruct as to classes of composition.— Some details are given in the note here in the *Cambridge Bible.*

[3] Ψάλλοντες: properly, the word should refer to instrumental music. And so it may; strings or pipe would often accompany the Christian hymn.

Such singing—and no other—is a sure means of grace to singers and to listeners; the Holy Ghost is in it.

Ver. 20. Giving thanks always over all things; for everything has His love in it, upon or below the surface; " all things work together for good " for His people ; **in the Name of our Lord Jesus Christ,** resting on Him, using Him, as Mediator and Advocate ; **to our (τῷ) God and Father,** " ours " in Him.

We have seen already (ch. xiii.) the deep connexion between thankfulness and holiness. Here the sweet subject well recurs, in this passage where the fulness of the Spirit is seen to issue in the sacrifice of song. And now, in deep and beautiful connexion, comes one last word, in which the souls so happy in their Lord, so full of His praise, are found happy in their relations with each other, in a self-forgetting mutual loyalty :

Ver. 21. Subjecting yourselves to one another, in God's fear. For nothing so withers pride as pure thanksgiving.

Happy in God, with a joy full of worshipping "fear" to grieve the all-blessing Love, the disciples yield, without an effort, each to the other's claim upon his help and kindness ; loved, and loving ; blessed, and blessing.

THE CHRISTIAN HOME; HUSBAND AND WIFE

MASTER JOACHIM MÖRLEIN has pleased me well to-day with his sermon, for he spoke of the office and vocation of a wife, and of a maid-servant—namely, that a wife should think she lives in a Holy Order, and that a servant also may know that her works are good and holy works.

LUTHER

CHAPTER XV

" SUBJECTING yourselves to one another."
So the last paragraph has closed. Now
opens the theme which St Paul seems to have
reserved lovingly for the last, in this Epistle as
in that to Colossæ: the theme of the Christian
Home. That sentence about mutual subjection
is the fittest possible introduction to it. For we
shall see that the Apostle's philosophy ot the
happiness and holiness of Home is centred
precisely here—in the mutual loyalty of its
members, the recollection by each ot the others'
claims and of self's sacred duties.

Here is a subject as pregnant and far-reaching
as it is in itself beautiful—the Christian Home.
It is not too much to say that the perfecting of
Home is the masterpiece ot the Gospel, in its

work of social blessing. Nothing on earth is so beautiful as a perfect home; and it takes the Name of Christ and the grace of His Spirit to produce the full phenomenon. And then, where the home is really perfect, it is beautiful with a beauty which must diffuse itself in good around. For home is the school of mutual unselfishness and duty, where love is continually learning its true work, namely, the finding its happiness in the felicity of another. And such a school cannot but send its scholars forth, in one way or another, to practise the blessed art outside the doors; carrying on the campaign of love extended from that happy base. The home where the Lord reigns is " a watered garden," fresh, fragrant, and in order. It is also " a spring of water, whose waters fail not," making glad the region around it [1] which needs so sorely the gracious stream.

It is with the deepest reason then that the closing paragraphs of an Epistle like this are devoted in so large a measure to domestic life. At the first glance there is a surprise about it, a sort of anticlimax. The Epistle, as we certainly do not need at this stage to prove, is concerned, in an almost unique degree among the

---

[1] See Jer. xxxi. 12.

Epistles, first with the most transcendent aspects of Redemption, as it is seen to be the eternal purpose of the Infinite Mind, and then with its largest and most comprehensive sphere of realization, in a Church which is "the fulness of Him who filleth all in all." The first three chapters are exclusively devoted to such great aspects of the faith and of the life of Christians. What shall be the climax of such a message? Shall it not be that unfathomable future where "God shall be all in all"? Shall we not be directed towards the light of eternal fulfilments, and in it see everything absorbed, as it were, and blended into the one prospect of the final state, almost losing, in the vision of the glory of the Throne, all distinct sight even of the multitude that loves, worships, and serves around it? Instead of such sublime exaltations of prospect, we have here as a fact just the persons and relations of a little circle within the doors and walls of an Asian dwelling-place. Even the city around it, Ephesus, Smyrna, Hierapolis, is left unmentioned, almost unthought of. The home is for the moment everything; as much as if the whole earth had for its population just one domestic group, and all human duty and all human hope were lodged there, and there alone.

Yet this paradox is the truest issue of the glorious antecedent passages.   For this home circle is the genuine and abiding unit of human society.   And the Gospel, in all its depth and wonder, as well as in its simplicity and tenderness, brings to man a salvation whose blessings can only be fully realized in social human life.   So the glorious rays of the eternal Purpose, and the achieved Redemption, and the Sealing by the Spirit, and the Life of the Head in the Body, are all focussed from above upon this one spot, that we may see them in their fruits just where those fruits shall best be generated and developed, for the delight of God and man.   If we see the process in its lovely efficacy *there*, we have the true pledge that it can yet be efficacious everywhere, in all the true relations of human existence upon earth, in which man is training for his final and endless life in "the Father's House," which is also "the Holy City."

This aspect or the matter will be brought before us in a way as tender as it is sublime, in the paragraph we are about to translate.   The immediate subject is the married state, man and wife in their Christian relation, in a human home as unfigurative as possible ; in Ephesus, in London.   But so is the transcendent truth of

the Heavenly Wedlock woven into the whole
texture of the passage that the expositor turns
to these sentences almost as much for his doctrine
of the relation of the Church to Christ as for
his account of how husband should think of wife
and wife of husband in a mortal home. And
why? Not by any accident or arbitrary juxta-
position of subjects, but by a holy law of truth
and thought. How *are* those conjugal partners
to think of one another in their home-life, day
by day? With all possible practicality of considerateness, with all cordial devotion of human
affection, with a recollected attention to one
another which will regulate their intercourse of
word and conduct far more minutely than the
longest code of rules could do. Most true; but
that is not the whole of the matter. This
attention, affection, watchful consideration, this
mutual loyalty and love, is to be perfectly human;
but also, if it is as it should be for *Christians*,
it is to be inspired by what is perfectly divine.
The two persons are genuine man and woman,
in an entirely human home-life; no pagan pair
can be more so. But their entire humanity is
entirely joined to the Lord their Head, in that
mighty union which His Body, the true Church,
has with Him, and which every member of it

has with Him, and through Him with all the others. They are each, and both, in Christ. They can never therefore think quite truly or fully of one another apart from that wonderful position and condition. So the illustration— backward and forward—of their married state by the Heavenly Wedlock, and of the Heavenly Wedlock by their married state, is not an accidental thing ; it is of the essence of the facts. The life of holy matrimony, and so the life of the home which is its outcome, is raised to its ideal, to its truth, not only by general religious considerations but by the profound and special relation to it of that very mystery of the Eternal Purpose of which the earlier passages of the Epistle were so full, the relation of the glorified Lord to the Company of His Saints.

Pregnant indeed is the passage, thus regarded. And never more than in our time did its sacred lessons touch the very point. Home, that word so dear for long generations to our English race, is still, God be praised, a mighty factor in our modern life. But, like everything else established among men, it is assailed, and from many sides, and not without visible dangers and losses. The stress and also the manifold dissipations of life in our day, when artificial conditions affect more and more what we do, are both alike unfavourable to the full strength and life of the home. Too often parents are too hurried to be parental, and even children are too hurried to be filial. Sometimes it is the labour of actual toil, in handicraft or profession, sometimes the labour of over-wrought school-competition, hardening and hurrying the young existence, to its lasting loss ; sometimes it is the toil and service of what is known as pleasure. By one means or another innumerable homes are not what their predecessors were ; the world's loud and open life has thrust the door ajar, and stands inside it, before the time. What is the best antidote, the true succour, for the true preservation or restoration of this inestimable thing, God's own primeval gift, man's Home? It is the recollection and use of the glorious Christian principle of its life. It is the old, eternal story of the Lord Jesus Christ's relation to home. We Christian parents must solemnly remember again before God that our union is the holy counterpart to the Heavenly Wedlock, which is to govern its action and experience every day. Then we shall be the better able, by word and very far more by life, life lived in the keen sight of our sons and daughters, and of our domestic helpers, to hold home in a true unity together, till it is diffused to reproduce itself in other homes, knit together by the same invisible but mighty bond.

But now, let us come to the Apostle's wonderful message. We have talked over it ; it waits to speak for itself. St Paul's last precious sentence has uttered the far-reaching precept of mutual "subjection"; the natural attitude of will to will where both have been taken in hand by the grace which dethrones self-will to install the Lord. So the words go on to the conjugal case at once.[1] The wife is the first addressed, as the party of the two who, in the order of nature, appears as rather follower than leader. But be it observed that the appeal to her, quite as much as to her husband, is based only on the noblest spiritual truths, presented for the open-eyed and free acceptance of her spiritual nature. The very precept lifts her into the altitude of the highest freedom ; for it comes to her as one who has to be approached with no less an argument than the transcendent truth of the eternal Matrimony.

---

[1] And so directly that it is at least likely that we should omit, in the Greek, the verb ὑποτάσσεσθε in ver. 22. It has to be supplied mentally, *from the* ὑποτασσόμενοι *of ver*. 21. The R.V. accordingly prints "be in subjection" (ver. 22) *in italics*.

She is called to an allegiance to her partner
which is nothing if not free, with the freedom
of regenerate reason. She is asked to recognize spiritual facts and to assent to them as a
spiritual being, fully in Christ.

Ver. 22.   **Ye wives, to your own husbands**[1] **subject yourselves**, with a " subjection " specialized, so to speak, from
that which Christian always owes to Christian (ver. 21) ;
as to the Lord, who is, in some special respects, repre-
Ver. 23.   sented to you by them.[2]   **Because the husband
is head of the wife, as our** (ὁ) **Christ too is Head of the
Church**,[3] with a Headship which is rooted in a living
Union, where the two are one, while the One is Leader,
with a leadership infinitely remote from all that is harsh,
tyrannous, or alien from the noble intercourse of highest
sympathies.   Such, and only such, is to be " subjection "
and " headship " in your conjugal Christian life ; its one
true *norma* is to be seen in that glorious Union,
which you *both* share, with Him who is, for all His own
in their blessed conjunction, " Head " indeed ; **Himself
being Saviour of the Body**,[4] with a *Saviourship* (of rescue
and of safeguard) which has vitally to do with *Leadership* ;

---

[1] The assumption evidently is that the Christian law is, *one*
husband, *one* wife : τοῖς ἰδίοις carries this on its face.

[2] " She sees [in the attitude of wifely submission] a special
reflection, as it were, of her relations to the Lord Himself.   Her
attitude has a special sanction thus from Him." (Note in the
Cambridge Bible.)

[3] See of course i. 22 above.

[4] Read, αὐτὸς σωτήρ, not καὶ αὐτός ἐστι σωτήρ.

to *save*, He must be trusted, with the *obedience* of
Ver. 24.   our faith.[1] But, leaving that thought for the
moment, as the Church subjects herself to her (τῷ) Christ,
with an allegiance which is at once and absolutely the
act of inmost love and highest reason, **so**, with full
reservation of the aspects in which the Lord's Leadership infinitely, of course, transcends that of the mortal
husband, yet truly " so," within that limit, do **you wives
subject yourselves to your husbands in everything.**[2]

Now the appeal turns to husbands; and to
them too it is still, in its essence, this—" subject
yourselves," in the sense of an entire and self-
sacrificing devotion. Note well that not one
syllable is said to them about their rights; no
hint is here of "insisting upon the marital
position"; assuredly no sanction of any "right
divine to govern wrong." The whole thought

---

[1] I incline to think that there is a sidelong intimation here that
the husband is likewise to be the wife's (temporal) "saviour,"
to the best of his power, from life's ills, and so similarly must,
in some sense, in order to this, have her loyal and free allegiance.
My note in the *Cambridge Bible* takes another line. The question
is so far from easy that I speak still with uncertainty.

[2] Here again, as in ver. 22, the verb has to be mentally supplied
in the clause αἱ γυναῖκες, κ.τ.λ. It may be supplied (from the
ὑποτάσσεται just before) either in the second or third person.
I prefer, on the analogy of ver. 22, to assume it to be ὑποτάσσεσθε
rather than ὑποτασσέσθωσαν.—"*In everything—*": "This great
rule will always, of course, be *over*-ruled by supreme allegiance
to Christ; but its spirit will never be violated in the Christian
home." (Note in the *Cambridge Bible*.)

is directed upon the husband's sacred and
cogent duty, in his high relation, to live " not
unto himself."   No denunciation of domestic
tyranny (the curse of many a home where
nominally the Lord is acknowledged) could
possibly speak so absolute a condemnation as
this appeal does over the morose, selfish, self-
indulgent, capricious, arbitrary, "masterful" man,
who has presumed to ask for a woman's love
and life, and then sinks to the depth of being, in
any sense or measure whatsoever, her oppressor.
He is called to be her self-forgetting servant ;
doing her the service of " saving," preserving,
protecting, love, in the noblest of all possible
fellowships of life.

Ver. 25.   **Ye husbands, love your wives,** with a love warm
always with the first summer of its pure human gladness,
but kept high and true meantime by an ideal great as
heaven, **just as our** (ὁ) **Christ too did love the Church, and,**
such was that supreme affection, **did give Himself over on
her behalf,** "over" to His unutterable Passion, that she
Ver. 26.   **might live ; yea, that her,** emphatically her,
going as it were out of His sacred Self to her great
need, **He might** [1] **hallow,** dedicate to union with Himself,
cleansing her by the bath of the water, in, attended and

---

[1] Lit. "that He may." The Greek idiom *presentiates* the
past, in the thought which is recorded,

conditioned by, an utterance, the utterance of that
Covenant Name of her salvation which alone gives
significance to the " bath " which seals her blessing.[1]
And this the celestial Bridegroom did with a love not
only self-sacrificing but such as to reach, in its mighty
scope and permanence, into the eternal state ; that He

---

[1] Some points in this important verse call for remark in detail.
(*a*) ἵνα αὐτὴν ἁγιάσῃ καθαρίσας : verb and participle are both aorist,
and Greek usage favours our attaching them both to one time or
crisis. The " hallowing" and the " cleansing" are in thought
contemporaneous ; we may express it by saying that the " cleansing" of the divine pardon and acceptance is *ipso facto* the
"hallowing," the dedication to God, of the accepted ones, and
here of the accepted Church, their ideal Unity. (*b*) τὸ λουτρὸν
τοῦ ὕδατος : " the bath, (or bathing,) of the water." Baptism is
assuredly referred to. The great question remains, what is the
relation of the rite to the blessing in question, which is, here, the
spiritual "cleansing" of the Church—a cleansing, primarily,
from the guilt of sin, remission (1 John i. 7 ; Heb. ix. 14) ; the
avenue to all covenant blessings. In the broad light of scriptural
teaching in general, we venture to affirm with confidence that the
relation is rather that of seal to promise than that of pipe or
conduit to fluid. It is a natural turn of language to speak, under
such a view, of the rite as if it actually effected the reception of
the blessing, while in fact it (divinely) seals (cp. Rom. iv. 11 on
circumcision) the certainty of its reception by faith direct from
the Heavenly Giver. See further, the note here in the *Cambridge
Bible*. (*c*) ἐν ῥήματι : " in an utterance," a word meaning something more isolated, so to speak, than λόγος : a declaration or
proclamation *ad illam rem*. The bath is "*in*" this, i.e., by a
familiar Hebraism (see e.g. ἐν σάλπιγγι, 1 Thess. iv. 16), it is
attended, conditioned, by it. Are we not right in referring here
to the great baptismal Commission, Matt. xxviii. 19, where the
rite is to be done "into the Name of" the Triune God of
Salvation ? The confession of that " Name," in its glorious
saving significance, the proclamation of its treasures of grace to
the believing, is that which makes the " bath" what it is, not a
mere action but a divine embodied warrant of blessing to faith

Ver. 27. might Himself[1] to Himself present the Church
arrayed in glory, at the Marriage Feast of heaven ; He
both bringing her and welcoming her there, bringing
her as her one blessed Rescuer and Preserver, saved
wholly by Him from guilt and from sin for ever, and
welcoming her as her eternally faithful Spouse, "rejoicing
over her" (Isa. lxii. 5), as[2] not having spot of wrong, or
wrinkle of decay, or aught of things like these, in that
pure eternity, but that she might be holy and unblemished,
completely hallowed to His will, finally like Him in His
spiritual beauty—glorious issue of the supreme Conjugal
Fidelity of the Husband of His redeemed.

Now from the heavens to the earth, but with
no moment's break of continuity, for the whole
thought moves "in Christ."

Ver. 28. So, with a love akin to this, and inspired by
nothing less, the husbands are bound to love their own
wives, just as their own bodies, (which indeed, in a
mysterious sense, they *are* ;) "so," for thus Christ has
loved the Church, as at once His Body and His Bride.
So devoted, with such sacrifice of self for the beloved
Object, with such an intimacy of sacred union, with such
an indissoluble fidelity—this is the type and kind of the
Christian husband's love. He who loves his own wife
loves his own self, in the fair ideal of their union, which

---

[1] Read αὐτός, not αὐτήν.

[2] Μὴ ἔχουσαν : not οὐκ. The negative μή gives not only the fact,
but the fact as a condition.

in Christ can be the real. So are they "sanctified and joined together," spirit, soul, and body, that the affection resulting is to be of the order of sinless, natural, self-love; not the self-love which sins against others by vanity, or pride, or greed, but the self-love which, by a profound law of being, recognizes the personality as the living centre from which it looks on all things, and shrinks with a true and necessary horror from its pollution or Ver. 29. destruction. For no one ever, under normal and natural conditions, hated his own flesh[1]; no (ἀλλά), he nourishes it, developes its good condition, and comforts it, studies its well-being, its healthful comfort; just as our (ὁ) Christ[2] nourishes and comforts the Church.

Ver. 30. For remember that He has joined us to Himself in a union which makes it—may we dare to speak the word?—His sacred instinct to deal thus tenderly and faithfully with "the blessed Company"; limbs are we, nothing less or more distant than limbs, of His Body, as it were developed out of His flesh, and out of His bones[3];

---

[1] It seems almost needless to point out that such a statement allows for (*a*) abnormal states of mind, insanity or frenzy; (*b*) abnormal circumstances in which (as in the case of martyrs) a man may be called to "hate" his life (Luke xiv. 26), in the obvious sense of acting *as if he was* its enemy, giving it up to pain and death. The Apostle states a great law of nature in its broadest aspect.

[2] Read Χριστός, not Κύριος.

[3] "Three important MSS. (A, B, ℵ), supported by other but not considerable authority, omit these words, ['out of His flesh, etc.']. It has been suggested that they were inserted by transcribers from Gen. ii. 23, as the next verse certainly is quoted from Gen. ii. 24. But the phrase here is not verbally close enough to

produced, in our new life, out of the fact of His
Incarnation.   Remember the words of the primeval
Scripture (Gen. ii. 24) in which is shadowed forth, under
the holy principle of human wedlock, that yet greater
thing, the Lord's coming forth from the eternal Home

Ver. 31.   to seek His mystical Bride : **On this account,
in order to realize the high idea of conjugal union, man
shall forsake father and mother, and shall cleave to his** (τῇ)

Ver. 32.   **wife,**[1] **and the two shall come to be one flesh.   This
mystery,** this holy secret, revealed only by God's Word,[2]
is great; its terms lead us soon beyond our full comprehension ; but do not wonder ; for **I,** emphatically I,
as distinguished from any reader who may mistake me,[3]
am speaking with reference to Christ, and to the Church.

---

that in Gen. ii. 23 to make this likely.   *A transcriber* would
probably have given word for word ; while the Apostle would as
probably quote with a difference. . . . And the difference is
significant.   ' We ' are not said here to be ' bone of His bone,'
which might . . . imply that our physical frame is derived from
that of the Incarnate Lord, but, more generally, 'limbs of His
body, *out of His flesh,* etc.'   Our true spiritual life and being is
the derivative of . . . the Second Adam in a sense so strong and
real as to be figured by the spiritual derivation of Eve from
Adam. . . . 'We,' the believing Church, as such, are, as in the
case of Eve and Adam, at once the product of our Incarnate
Lord's existence as Second Adam, and His Bride.''   (Note in
the *Cambridge Bible.*)

[1] Read, καταλ. ἄνθρωπος πατέρα καὶ μητέρα, καὶ προσκ. τῇ γυναικί.

[2] This is, in brief, what μυστήριον always means in N.T.   The
Vulgate here has *sacramentum* (as in i. 9, iii. 9).   See note in
the *Cambridge Bible.*—Cp. further here Grimm's *N.T. Lexicon*
(Thayer) under the word μυστήριον.

[3] Or perhaps, as distinguished from Moses, in the primary
reference of Gen. ii. 24.

The immediate theme is the holy marriage of man with woman ; but this stands related to an Archetype which " hath not entered into man's heart to conceive," the Bridal of the Lord and His People ; at once sublimely transcending and unspeakably hallowing the thing of which it is the Archetype. And now, to return again earthward, while still " in Christ " :

Ver. 33. Only, leaving the sacred premises in order to act upon them in the practical logic of a true married life, do you too, in humble imitation of your Lord, all and several (οἱ καθ᾽ ἕνα), each love his own wife just as his own self; while the wife—let her see that she reverences [1] the husband.

---

[1] Φοβῆται : lit. " fears." But the A.V. " reverence " seems best to express the thought *in this context.*

THE CHRISTIAN HOME: PARENT AND CHILD, MASTER AND SERVANT

"As for me and my house, we will serve the LORD."

Joshua xxiv. 15

A SERVANT with this clause
    Makes drudgery divine;
Who sweeps a room, as for Thy laws,
    Makes that and th' action fine.

HERBERT

CHAPTER XVI

THE CHRISTIAN HOME: PARENT AND CHILD, MASTER AND SERVANT

EPHESIANS vi. 1–9

THE Christian Husband and the Christian Wife stand now before us ; two noble portraits, making one. We contemplate them again, one in their absolute mutual loyalty and love, one, in a sense as deep and sacred as it is warm with affections created by Him who is Love itself, holy and everlasting. We see them "devoted" to each other, each in the respective conjugal position. We see that heart "devotion" at once chastened, deepened, and profoundly secured by the thought all around it of the *duties* in whose line it moves and glows ; a thought to which every true heart that knows the interior life of Christian wedlock will respond with joy. Above all, we see them walking

along their one path, "one soul in two bodies,"
as those who see upon that path, at every step,
in all its relations, its duties, its sorrows and
its joys, a glory shed from the "great mystery"
of the Heavenly Wedlock which has joined
them each to the Eternal Bridegroom. Yes,
upon their common domestic duties, the affairs
of the household in its most prosaic aspect, a
radiance falls, elevating, purifying, gladdening,
hallowing, from very far aloft, even from where
there shines

> "A light upon the shining sea,
>   The Bridegroom with His Bride."

It is good for the soul to gaze upon this
portrait ; it is good for the whole human heart.
For it all illustrates the power of the spiritual
Gospel to act with full benignant force upon
the social life ot man. It has sometimes been
thrown as a reproach upon the advocates or
ambassadors of that Gospel that they have
occupied themselves too much with the message
of personal salvation and too little, or not at
all, with the salvation (so to speak) of society.
Let them not be afraid of that reproach it it
only means that they have firmly refused to
forget that their first and vital message is to

the fallen and sinful soul of man ; " Be recon-
ciled to God." They do well to resolve never
to let this be exchanged for any programmes
and enterprises of social reform and amendment
which at all ignore man's sin and scarcely
contemplate his immortality as a practical prospect in the matter. But let them take good
heed to the criticism if it means that they have
not diligently drawn social inferences out of
personal salvation, perpetually reminding those
who have believed that they are " saved to
serve," and that out of that fact flows a whole
life of social usefulness as the Redeemer's will
for His redeemed. Let them resolve, if need
be, that if they have neglected this vast side
of their work they will do so no more. And,
if they would go the right way to work, let
them, in a sense most particular and definite,
" begin at Home." Make the Christian feel
that the inmost and most heavenly truths of
his wonderful personal salvation bear direct
and full upon his life at home, upon his
married character and conduct, and you will
have taken a long step towards the leavening
of all social relations, so far as that individual
can in the least touch them, with the power
of Christ

As we pass on, let us note in this portrait of a Christian married pair what may escape our notice as a distinctive trait. I mean, the simple injunction to the man *to love* his wife. Few of us, perhaps, realize how remote—at least how separable—from the pagan idea of marriage was the idea of love. There would be love of brother and sister, of parent and child ; there would be the passion of lovers, alas how often quite apart from the restraints of the law of virtue. But marriage was essentially a matter of arrangement, contract, convention. It was a necessity of human society. It was the required antecedent to the succession of generations and the devolution of property. But it was not at all understood to involve love, before its consummation, or after, as a thing essential. In Hebrew life it is far otherwise; who does not remember Jacob and Rachel ? And who has not observed that the teaching of the Old Testament leads directly up to the truth of the Heavenly Wedlock of Christ and His Church, by the long stream of appeal and prophecy about the Marriage of the LORD and His Israel, full of the thought of an eternal conjugal affection ? But it needed the consummated revelation, the full truth,

as it shines out in this Epistle, to bring home
to a universal Christendom not only the
mystical truth of the supreme Bridal, but also
the hallowed and hallowing affections and
tender duties of the married life of man and
woman, here and now.

But the Apostle has much yet to say about
home. Necessarily, he has spoken first of its
heads and leaders, because the whole tone of
the circle, children and household, must so
vitally depend upon what they are, each in
his and her personal life, and both together
in their life mutual and one. Nothing but a
miracle of abnormal grace can make the home
company happy and holy when the Parents are
not *towards one another* living the full Christian
life. So not till that has been depicted does
he say one word about children, or about servants. To them now it is time to come.

Ver. 1. **You children, obey,** with the listening ear[1] of
unhesitating attention, **your Parents,** mother as well as

---

[1] Ὑπακούετε : not ὑποτάσσεσθε, as above (ver. 22). So again,
ver. 5, where the servant also is bidden ὑπακούειν. We gather
that both child and servant are to yield an obedience different
in some respects from that of the wife ; in her case equality and
union give another quality to the "obedience."

father, in the Lord; obeying thus, with a motive far
above that of dread of penalty, or anything which
severity can produce; it must be nothing less than the
remembrance that you and your parents are alike " in
the Lord," in covenant union with Christ, limbs of His
Body, and so bound by *supernatural* relations to the
willing, spiritual, acceptance of all true *natural* relations.
Act thus, as the deep, steadfast, living law of conduct;
for this is righteous. It is not beautiful only, or befitting;
it is in the line of the holy Will and Law of God, alike
in Nature and in Revelation. So speaks that Law, in
its twelve-fold Edict of primary human duty (Exod.

Ver. 2. xx. 12 ; Deut. v. 16): **Honour thy father and thy
mother**, with an " honour " not of emotion only but of
practical allegiance ; **a commandment such that it is** ($\mathring{\eta}\tau\iota\varsigma$
$\mathring{\epsilon}\sigma\tau\iota$) **the first of the Ten attended by** ($\mathring{\epsilon}\nu$) **a promise**, that

Ver. 3. promise which thus runs, **That it may prove
well for thee ; and thou shalt**, thus behaving, **be long-lived
upon the earth**; reaping, in the normal course of God's
benignant providence, human peace and permanence
from loyalty to His first law of human order. For the
promise, made to the national Israel in special reference
to their " promised Land," was but a limited instance of
a universal and perpetual principle, having its bearing
not only upon Hebrew family life, or even upon only
Christians, but upon mankind.[1]

---

[1] It has been remarked that nowhere is family loyalty more
universally honoured, at least in theory, than in China; that
"long-lived" Empire, which seems to tend always to persist and
survive, even under such shocks as the last few years have
brought it.

So St Paul lays his command, or rather his Lord's, upon the younger members of the Christian Home. It seems superfluous to say much upon the weight and point of his words for our own time. " Disobedience to parents " is repeatedly named in the Bible as a symptom of formidable evil in human life, as in Rom. i. 30, and 2 Tim. iii. 2, where it stands as one of a black catalogue of developed evils. Is it too much to say of this, amongst other phenomena around us, that the Apostles,

> " noting down
> The features of the last degenerate times,
> Exhibit every lineament of these " ? [1]

Is it not too true that in this respect, far and wide in our modern England, the mournful words are more fully verified than ever,

> " Fireside, the heroic wealth of hall and bower,
> Have forfeited their ancient English dower
> Of inward happiness " ? [2]

Let no exaggerated word be said about it. There are still among us countless homes where sons and daughters not merely are " fond of " their

---

[1] Cowper, in the lofty closing passages of *The Winter Walk at Noon*.

[2] Wordsworth, Sonnet *To Milton* (written 1802).

parents, but inwardly reverence them, and actively
" obey " their precepts, and also their example ;
homes whose children go out in due time to serve
God in their own generation, and their elder
friends say of them with joy that they are
" treading in their fathers' steps." And further,
it would be unwisdom indeed to demand that
home " obedience " should be a thing which
should forbid and exclude the least development
or modification of word or habit by which a
younger generation can vary upon its prede-
cessor. Never since human life began has such
a mechanical repetition been quite possible, as
it has never been desirable ; certainly not since
Christian human life began, with its inner principles of freedom and growth under divine law.
But when all due recollections and allowances
are made, it remains true that this command of
filial obedience, the honouring loyalty of sons and
daughters towards their parents as such, is at a
very low ebb not only in the world at large but
in what is called the Christian world as a whole.
" Development " and " modification " of word and
habit too often mean now a restive or a reckless
indifference to the first elements of common attention and modest bearing towards God's appointed
leaders of young life. Affection itself too often

takes the form rather of a premature and crude
familiarity, as different as possible from the
loving, cordial, but yet " honouring," freedom
with which the child *is* meant to have " access
with confidence " to the parent's heart. The son
or daughter, forgetting all that is tender and all
that is noble in the filial state, is at once " as
free "—as " free and easy "—in manner with
father or mother as if the parent were a junior
and less experienced acquaintance, and as strange
to the parent's real heart as if they had scarcely
yet been introduced to one another.

I do not think that I am overstating the facts
of many, very many cases, to be observed and
lamented in even Christian family life to-day.
How much we need then the Apostle's firm,
tender, deep-toned precept, which is but the echo
of his blessed Master's,[1] and which lays down
a rule glorified, beatified, by the " subjection "
of the Son of Mary in the home of Nazareth.
When that Example is out of date, and not
till then, shall we have outgrown the Law of
Moses and of the Lamb, " Honour thy father
and thy mother." He who set that Example
through long years of home-duty knew that it

---

[1] See the *Corban* passage, Mark vii. 10-13.

was for the very life of human righteousness and happiness.

One further remark is suggested by the wording of this passage. The children of the Christian home are to "obey" "*in the Lord*." So it is assumed that they are, of course, "in the Lord.' Here I observe that this cannot mean, if the teaching of the New Testament as a whole is remembered, that every child of such a home would be, as a fact, necessarily, in that spiritual and inward union with Christ which only personal holiness can evidence to others. But it does on the other hand remind us that there is *a* covenant connexion with the Lord which is to be taken as a fact in the case of every child of such a home, and to be made without reserve the ground of spiritual appeals, without waiting for evidence of heart-conversion to God. To me, this consideration has a plain bearing on the right of all children of the Church to the Baptism of the Covenant. But on this I do not dwell here.[1] I refer to the matter only to emphasize the rightness of such appeals on Christian principle to our children as children

---

[1] I may refer to a brief treatment of the subject in *English Church Teaching* (p. 109).

of Christians ; so that it be done with Christian common sense.

But the Apostle has an all-important word for us parents in this matter.

Ver. 4. And you fathers, fathers as the responsible leaders in home authority, though let not the mother's inestimable rights and influence be forgotten,[1] do not irritate your children, by an exercise of your authority void, for one hour, of sympathy and of love, forgetful of the fact that you were children once, and should carry the child's heart in you for ever. Never claim a right for yourself where you are not manifestly mindful of the sacred right of your son, your daughter, to your own unselfish affection. Your authority is not for your gratification, but for their good, entrusted for a season to your guardian hands. No, bring them up, "*educate*" them, "lead them out" and on, in the development of good into better, in the Lord's discipline and admonition ; using restraint, and using warning, but not what your own caprice dictates ; it must all be " the Lord's," learnt by you first in His school, and animated with His love.

A brief but priceless word for the parent's heart. It lays a fresh stress upon his responsibility, reminding him that he *must* do his duty in the guidance and the forewarning of his child ;

---

[1] Πατέρες is used of *both parents* (of Moses), Heb. xi. 23.

but that the spirit of self must be banished from the work if it is to be done indeed.[1] The LORD must take its place.

But the home may contain other members, besides father, mother, son, and daughter. There will be the servants; what about them, and the mutual relation raised by their existence? Are they mere accidents of the life, "*employés*," machines for saving trouble, sometimes at the cost of giving a great deal of trouble on the other side, beings whose function is to do as much as they must, and who might preferably be automata if that could be?

This is a conception of the matter absolutely non-Christian. In the principle of the Gospel, "neighbourhood," whatever be its place, involves "love," whatever be its proper exercise. The servant is very much a neighbour, above all when the service, as here, is domestic. The servant therefore is placed by the Gospel within the love-relations of the Christian home.

---

[1] I seize the opportunity to refer to an admirable chapter in Dr A. Whyte's *Bunyan Characters*, in which the fine passage in *Pilgrim's Progress* where Charity questions Christian about his dealings with his family is developed with great depth and force. For parents who would fain do their whole duty to their sons and daughters the suggestions are invaluable.

I need scarcely remind my reader that the
"servant" here in immediate view is the δοῦλος,
the bondservant, the slave. The Gospel found
slavery in the world; and in many regions,
particularly the Roman and the Greek, it was
a very bad form of slavery. The Gospel began
at once to undermine it, with its mighty principles of the equality of all souls in the mystery
and dignity of manhood, and of the equal work
of redeeming love wrought for all souls by the
supreme Master. But its plan was—not to batter,
but to undermine. It absolutely declined to
patronize, still less to stimulate, political or social
revolution[1]; its majestic method is that of social
reform, generated from within man, by bringing
him near to God in all his conditions and
relations. So while the Gospel in one respect

---

[1] See Lightfoot's *Introduction* to the Epistle to Philemon (and
I may refer to my own, in the *Cambridge Bible*, and in *Colossian
Studies*). See also a masterly tractate by Mr Goldwin Smith
(1863), *Does the Bible sanction American Slavery ?*

"The great Gospel doctrine of the believer's "slavery" to his
Master, Christ, . . . would inevitably tend to a peculiar mutual
rapprochement between Christian masters and slaves, . . . and
would do infinitely more for the abolition of slavery than any
'servile war.' . . . With impartial hands it . . . sanctifies subordination to constitutional authority . . . and meanwhile ennobles
the individual, in respect of all that is highest in the word liberty,
by putting him into direct . . . relations with God." (Note in
the *Cambridge Bible.*)

21

left slavery alone, it doomed it in another; and
one of the fairest fruits of primeval Christianity
in the eyes of observers from outside,[1] was
the brotherhood manifestly established between
Christian masters and their slaves.

That the present passage speaks distinctively
of the slave, the bought, or born, or inherited,
human "chattel," must not be forgotten. But
it seems clear that not only is there a possible
application and accommodation of the principles
and precepts to the case of voluntary and con-
tracting service, but that the application to such
service is *à fortiori*. The servant, absolutely
free to contract or not, has chosen to contract,
and so far forth has accepted binding obligations;
such obligations are at least as sacred to the
Christian conscience as those due to a despotic
necessity. The master on his side has contracted,
under conditions which bring him, of his own
will, at least as truly as if he were the *buyer* of
the person who is to serve him, into "neighbourhood" with the servant. All then that is said
here of fidelity and deference on the one side
and considerateness on the other holds absolutely
true, and with added force, when we pass in
thought from slavery to free service.

---

[1] See the *Apology of Aristides*, about A.D. 130

Ver. 5. **Ye bondservants,** who have found both liberty and Lord in Christ, **obey your flesh-ward lords,** those who own you in all that is not of the Spirit in your lives **with fear and tremor,** the deep, sacred anxiety of the will to fulfil duty in every relation before God, **in your heart's simplicity,** the unaffected desire to do right for its own sake, or rather the Lord's ; **as to our** (τῷ) **Christ ; not in the**

Ver. 6. **spirit of** (κατά) **eye-slavery,** working only when watched, **as man-pleasers,** with no higher aim than to " curry " a fellow-creature's favour for your own ends, **but as Christ's bondservants,** His to own, to use, and to bless ; **doing the will of our** (τοῦ) **God,** as it is expressed in each " next thing " of the daily duty which that thought sanctifies, **from the soul,** where the spring of holy, energetic goodwill to your neighbour, (that is, now, to your master,) rises and flows always ; yes, **with goodwill**

Ver. 7. **doing bondservice,** which thus becomes free service, **as to the Lord,** *your* Lord and true Master, **and not to men,** who are never now the *ultimate* objects of your obedience. Do this with a great hope to animate you, a power undreamt of in your life till you found

Ver. 8. Christ ; **knowing,** as a sure fact revealed, **that each one, whatever good thing he may do, shall get that thing from the Lord,** in the sense of getting the supreme reward which sovereign Love gives to serving love, in its " Well done, good and faithful ; enter into the joy of thy Lord." Yes, this shall be the blissful lot of each disciple, so serving HIM, **whether bondservant or freeman.**

Ver. 9. **And you lords,** owners, holders, employers, re-member *your* duties before you think of your rights ;

act upon your obligations to your servants, remembering their perfect spiritual equality with you ; do the same things towards them, consult their good as you expect them to consult yours ; dropping the threatening too lightly used, the harsh opposite to the brotherhood Christ has taught you ; knowing, with the certainty of revelation, that the Lord of them and of you alike [1] is in heaven, presiding and observant, and respect of persons, the partiality which yields one iota of justice to place or power, does not exist (οὐκ ἔστι) with Him.

So the Gospel leaves its message of absolutely *equal obligation*, in Jesus Christ, upon the slave and upon the slave-owner. The principle will do its work. There is no word of Revolution. There will therefore be no Reign of Terror. But silently and permanently will emerge a *Liberté, Fraternité, Egalité*, which has its deep secret in mutual human dutifulness rooted in the Truth of Christ.

---

[1] Read, αὐτῶν καὶ ὑμῶν.

THE CHRISTIAN HOME ; CONCLUSION.
THE SPIRITUAL CONFLICT

PRINCIPALITIES and powers,
  Mustering their unseen array,
Wait for thy unguarded hours;
  Watch and pray!
                    MISS C. ELLIOTT

CHAPTER XVII

THE CHRISTIAN HOME; CONCLUSION
THE SPIRITUAL CONFLICT

EPHESIANS vi. 10–20

WE have now seen the interior of Christian home-life, as it was lived in the first century, and as it is lived (with differences, in regard of the last of its relations, due only to its own pure principles working themselves out) in the nineteenth. Such homes, such households, God be thanked, are scattered over our own dear Land in numberless points of brightness, radiating good around them. They are to be found in every Gospel-lighted region of Europe, in the Western World, in the young countries of the Southern Ocean. They begin to mark with spots of beauty the darkness of the non-Christian peoples ; there is many a home now, true to the Ephesian model, in the cities and villages of China, in all the provinces of India, by the rivers and the lakes of what was lately unknown Africa, and in the islets of the Pacific. And every one of them is a precious contribution to the true evangelization of the world, and also, all the while, to its true temporal happiness and order.

"Home, sweet Home!" It is the "garden enclosed" of the Gospel; its nursery, from which blessing is planted out, even into the utmost wilderness of mankind.

I cannot forbear here the quotation of a poem, well known in Germany, where the true Home is set before us in lines which are a fit sequel to the Apostle's precepts. It is Spitta's hymn, "The Christian Household."[1]

> Oh, happy house! where Thou art lov'd the best,
>   Dear Friend and Saviour of our race,
> Where never comes such welcom'd, honour'd Guest,
>   Where none can ever fill Thy place;
> Where every heart goes forth to meet Thee,
>   Where every ear attends Thy word,
> Where every lip with blessing greets Thee,
>   Where all are waiting on their Lord.
>
> Oh, happy house! where two are one in heart,
>   In holy faith and hope are one,

---

[1] *O selig Haus, wo man dich aufgenommen.* The original is in Spitta's *Psalter und Harfe.* I quote the excellent translation given in *Hymns from the Land of Luther.*

Whom death can only for a little part,
  Not end the union here begun;
Who share together one salvation,
  Who would be with Thee, Lord, always,
In gladness, or in tribulation,
  In happy or in evil days.

Oh, happy house! where little ones are given
  Early to Thee, in faith and prayer,—
To Thee, their Friend, who from the heights of heaven
  Guard'st them with more than mother's care.
Oh, happy house! where little voices
  Their glad hosannas love to raise,
And childhood's lisping tongue rejoices
  To bring new songs of love and praise.

Oh, happy house! and happy servitude!
  Where all alike one Master own;
Where daily duty, in Thy strength pursued,
  Is never hard nor toilsome known;
Where each one serves Thee, meek and lowly,
  Whatever Thine appointment be,
Till common tasks seem great and holy,
  When they are done as unto Thee.

Oh, happy house! where Thou are not forgot
  When joy is flowing full and free;
Oh, happy house! where every wound is brought.
  Physician, Comforter, to Thee;
Until, at last, earth's day's-work ended,
  All meet Thee in that home above,
From whence Thou camest, where Thou art ascended,
  The heaven of glory and of love!

From this beautiful scene the Apostle leads us

now direct to a field of battle, overhung with clouds. "Arms and the man he sings"; and the man urgently needs both the arms, and the skill and strength to wield them. For he is beset by the hosts of evil, under their dreadful king. It will be all he can do to hold his ground, in unshaken fidelity to his divine Commander.

We approach thus the memorable paragraph which deals in the first place, explicitly and fully, with the fact of organized assaults on the Christian company by unseen personal adversaries, banded together, and trying every avenue of temptation; and then with the parts and details of a panoply which is to enable the beleaguered saints to meet them, and to overcome. Taken in itself, the passage is one of extreme interest and significance. But we first ask ourselves why, being what it is, does it occur just here? Why so immediately pass from the tranquil duties of home to the very thick of the struggle with assailing spirits?

The answer is, in part, if I am right, that a marked pause of thought takes place at the close of the previous paragraph. The Apostle is conscious of the close of his message, and draws his whole mind, as it approaches, to a closing topic which will leave his readers intensely alive to the solemn urgency of their position. He has been telling them, from the beginning onward, of the secrets of eternal grace and love, of the wonder of their salvation from spiritual death, of their peace and life through faith, of their sealing by the Blessed Spirit, of their union with Christ their Head, of His blissful indwelling in their hearts, and then of the resultant life of humility, purity, love, truth, and every gracious duty of social holiness. In closing, they must not forget that this beautiful life is all the while to be lived upon hostile ground. It is the life of a camp in the enemy's territory, to be held till the supreme Commander advances to the eternal relief and triumph. Within, all is to be mutual loyalty and love, a scene of noble order and fellowship. But the ramparts are not for one moment to be left unwatched, nor is the saint ever for a moment to live and move unarmed.

So this last passage gathers up the whole previous matter of the Epistle in the sense of an urgent reminder of the infinitely serious conditions under which the bright secrets of grace are to be lived out. The Christian is not only a servant but a soldier; he belongs not only to a home but to a citadel. And to recollect

the formidable surroundings is of course vitally
necessary if the life lived amidst them is not to
be swept away in ruin.

Meanwhile this new paragraph, though separated by a solemn pause from the description
of the Christian Home, is not by any means
isolated from it, as if there were no fitness
in the succession. For does not common experience bear out the remark that the evil powers
often win their worst advantages against us
Christians on the quiet and common ground
of life? Where we are least upon our guard
they are most upon their watch. It is above
all for "our unguarded hours" that they are
"waiting." And it is often exactly in the
unanxious freedom of home that spiritual un-
guardedness comes on, and developes into
habit. Just at home, alas, it is only too easy
for the Christian to be inconsiderate in deed
and word, to be quick or sullen in temper,
to indulge self in small but dangerous ways,
while yet a tolerable face of consistency is
maintained in more public and exterior matters.
So not for nothing does St Paul speak last
of life at home just before passing to this
great paragraph about the armed watchman of
the Lord.

Ver. 10. In conclusion,[1] strengthen yourselves always[2] in the Lord, your one possible Sphere and Magazine of inexhaustible resource, to be drawn upon by obedient trust, and in the energy of His might, sure so to be put forth on your behalf; a "strength made perfect in the weakness" (2 Cor. xii. 9) which gives it room by Ver. 11. its reliance. Clothe yourselves with the panoply, the armour *cap-à-pie*, of our (τοῦ) God; personally accepting and appropriating the defence which is already yours in Him[3]; with a view to your being able, as you thus shall be, aye, even you, to stand against the stratagems, the subtle "methods" (μεθοδείας), the calculated crafts and combinations, of the devil, the *diabolos*, the dread "Accuser" of the followers of his great Adversary, Christ,[4]

---

[1] Τὸ λοιπόν: "From henceforth," R.V. margin (cp. 2 Tim. iv. 8). But this does not so well suit the general tone of the Epistle, which has made no allusion to spiritual *weakness* as the special fault which "henceforth" the readers should amend.—The words ἀδελφοί μου should be omitted from the text.

[2] The verb is in the present tense and suggests a continuous "strengthening."

[3] For the thought of thus "making it our own" by consciously using the promises, cp. Rom. xiii. 12, 14; 1 Thess. v. 8. We are to "possess our possessions" (Obad. 18) with the promptitude and certainty of the simplest recollection and acceptance.—For passages closely akin to this cp. Rom. and 1 Thess., quoted just above, (both written earlier than this Epistle.) And see the grand verses Isa. lix. 16, 17, and a fine apocryphal passage, Wisdom v. 17, etc., which perhaps is the echo of the words of Isaiah. In these latter passages *the Lord* is the Person who arms Himself with a "panoply."

[4] See above on ii. 2 for considerations on the revealed personality of the διάβολος, "*the Accuser.*"—The Greek word is the regular equivalent in the LXX. of the Hebrew *Sâtân*, "*the*

always lying in wait for their unreadiness and failure.

Ver. 12. Because our wrestling, the hand-and-limb encounter of our Christian life, is not against flesh and
blood,[1] that is, against merely human opponents; no,
for even when we *have* to meet hostility or actual
cruelty from men, there are deeper and darker powers
behind them[2]; but against the principalities,[3] against
the authorities, against the world-rulers of this darkness,[4]
beings permitted a mysterious empire over the human
"world" in its "darkness" of ignorance and sin[5];

Adversary." For illustration of the significance of the word
διάβολος, see e.g. the opening chapters of Job.

[1] Lit. "blood and flesh"; but usage in English reverses
the order. For the phrase, cp. Matt. xvi. 17, 1 Cor. xv. 50,
Gal. i. 16, Heb. ii. 14. It will be seen that the meaning is not
(as sometimes in our popular parlance) *our own feelings*, as
when we say, "it was hard for flesh and blood to bear"; but,
mortal men, supposed to be enemies and opponents. "We
have to encounter not men but spirits."

[2] "See the language of Rev. ii. 10, and Abp Trench's note
upon it (*Epistles to the Seven Churches*, p. 104). . . . The
Apostle not merely takes for granted the objective existence of
a world of evil spirits; he carefully distinguishes it from the
world of humanity." (Note in the *Cambridge Bible*.)

[3] See above, on i. 21, iii. 10.—"The reference here . . . obviously
is to personal *evil* spirits as members and leaders of an . . .
organization under its head. . . . Cp. Matt. xxv. 41, 2 Cor. xii. 7.
Note also the '*Legion*' of evil spirits (Mark v. 9, 15 . . .), compared with the 'more than twelve *legions*' of angels' (Matt.
xxvi. 53)." (Note in the *Cambridge Bible*.)

[4] Omit the words τοῦ αἰῶνος from the text.

[5] "For allusions to the mysterious 'authority' of the Evil Power
over the human 'world,' in its ethical aspect at least, cp.
Luke iv. 6; John xiv. 30, xvi. 11; 2 Cor. iv. 4; 1 John v. 18."
(Note in the *Cambridge Bible*.)

against the spiritual hosts of wickedness in the heavenly places; the powers which carry on their dark campaign in the vast unseen, as it were the "birds of *the sky*" (Matt. vi. 28), hovering over the landscape of humanity.[1]

Such are the beleaguering forces, represented in their chiefs, which surround the children of God; at Ephesus then, in our modern life to-day. Who shall solve the riddle of their existence, and of its permission? Is it not a deeper thing than created intelligence can deal with? But are we not surrounded, in nature as well as in the spiritual world, with problems innumerable "going off into mystery"[2] where no thought can really follow, but which nevertheless are problems raised by *facts*? Our wisdom is to grasp the facts, and to meet them along lines of certainty, and to leave the ultimate enigma safe in the hands which alone can hold it, while meantime they are holding us. If these revelations of an invisible host around us, bent upon our calamity, do nothing else for us, they may at least render the inestimable service of driving us home, as for our very life, to personal dealings with our Personal

---

[1] I thus attempt an explanation of a phrase which is still mysterious when all is said.

[2] *Omnia abeunt in mysterium*, writes Bacon.

Deliverer. He can indeed face for us the dreadful personalities marshalled in the shadows that surround our life.

And now, to Him the Apostle bids us come. For is it not to Him? We shall read, in the splendid picture, of this thing and of that as our protection. But reduced to its essence, as Jerome remarked long ago,[1] the "panoply" means—Jesus Christ. The soldier, in other words, appears before us made strong for a victory which is otherwise impossible—by his relation to his Lord. He is safe, he is successful, because he is spiritually right with Christ in God-given "truth" and "righteousness"; because he is sure of Christ beneath his feet as "the equipment of the Gospel of peace" for his own soul; because he finds Christ the mighty buckler against the fiery volley when he uses Him in "faith"; because he "covers his head in the day of battle" with Christ as his assured "Salvation"; because Christ speaks through "the Word of God," and so makes Himself His servant's sword to cut the "accuser" down;

---

[1] In his commentary here: "From what we read in the passage following, and from the things said in all the Scriptures concerning the Lord our Saviour, it most clearly results that by 'all the arms of God' . . . the Saviour is to be understood."

because " prayer in the Spirit " grasps Him,
and holds Him fast.[1] Yes, here, to the last
hour of our conflict and our siege, and here
only, lies our victory. It is HE, not it. It is
the all-sufficient LORD, " objected to the fiend,"
while the believer stands safe behind HIM.

> Not me the dark foe fears at all,
> But hid in Thee I take the field;
> Now at my feet the mighty fall,
> For Thou hast bid them yield.

Ver. 13. On this account, take up, as laid before you on
the ground by Him who wrought the weapons, by Him
who *is* the victory, aye, "take up," in a strong appropriating act,[2] the panoply of our (τοῦ) God, that you may be

---

[1] It will be observed that I explain "truth" and "righteousness" (ver. 14) as referring to the believer's sincerity and fidelity
in dealing with his Lord, and not as referring to the *Lord's*
"truth" in His promises and His "righteousness" in justification.
Not without hesitation I do so; for certainly it would be perfectly
in St Paul's manner to mean justification here by "righteousness."
And we can never too clearly remember that the armour is the
armour "*of God*"; it is not human character merely but divine
grace. But *I think* that the language of Isa. lix. 16, 17, suggests
the view advocated here. Meanwhile the inmost thought all
through is that the man *really uses his Lord.*

[2] May we, without incongruity, illustrate the thought from
Virgil? In the eighth Æneid, Venus brings the invulnerable
armour to her son Æneas, perfect and prepared: then

> "He, glorying in the beauteous prize,
> From point to point quick darts his eyes
> With ever-new delight.
> Now, wondering, 'twixt his hands he turns
> The helm that like a meteor burns,

22

able, as you shall be, **to withstand** these onsets, so formidable but then so vain, **in the evil day,** the crisis (as each crisis comes on) of temptation or of terror, **and having accomplished all things** which your Captain asks of you, thus armed with Himself, **to stand,** unmoved at your post, unshaken in your loyalty, ready to the last to

Ver. 14. "tread down your enemies" in Him. **Stand therefore,** with a new conscious act[1] of spiritual resolve, **girding your loins round in** a belt of **truth,** that is to say, calm and strong in the reality and simplicity, through grace, of your relations with your King; **and clothing yourselves with the cuirass of righteousness,** that is to say, with holy loyalty, the work of God within you, to His

Ver. 15. all-beloved Will and Law; **and shoeing your feet,** the feet which have *to stand,* "firm on the rock, and strong in Christ,"[2] **in, with, the equipment of the Gospel of His** (τῆς) **peace,** "peace with God through our Lord Jesus Christ," and the resultant "peace of God" in heart and thought, embraced and enjoyed for yourselves, as your feet thus feel certainty and security beneath them.

> The sword that rules the war,
> The breastplate shooting bloody rays,
> As dusky clouds in sunlight blaze
> Refulgent from afar,
> The polished greaves of molten gold,
> The spear, the shield with fold on fold,
> A prodigy of art untold."
>
> (CONINGTON'S Version.)

Shall our "wonder," "delight," and *use,* be less?

[1] Observe the aorists in this whole context.

[2] The thought here is not of running the errands of the Master. but of holding the fort for Him.

For there is no "equipment" for the Holy War more
needful, and more effectual, than the possession by the
Ver. 16. warrior of that holy Peace. And then, against
all things, to meet every shifting assault,[1] stand, taking
up the great shield[2] of your faith, your reliance altogether
on your Lord, that look wholly outward, Godward,
which is the essence of faith, and which gives it the
saving power it has ; on which (ἐν ᾧ) you shall (remember the positive promise) be able to quench all the
missiles of the Evil One, those (τά) burning, "kindled"
(πεπυρωμένα) missiles of his,[3] which can enflame the
heart with anger, or with lust, "set on fire of hell."
Ver. 17. And accept, for behold it is offered to your
very hands, the helmet of God's (τοῦ) Salvation (σωτήριον),
even Him who is our Deliverance in Person, and whose
presence and promise "cover the head" indeed as the
soldier *faces* the battle; and the sword of the Spirit,
wrought and edged by the Holy One Himself, the sword
which is God's utterance, His spoken Truth, to be your
one sure weapon of offence against the enemy, as you,
like your Prince before you, meet him with "It is
written," "It is written again."[4]

---

[1] So I would explain ἐπὶ πᾶσιν: although the rendering "*over*
all things," as a shield is the *outwork* of the armour, is of course
grammatically possible.

[2] Θυρεόν: "the *door*-shield," the largest sort of shield, about
2½ by 4 feet in size.

[3] The metaphor is taken from the fire-arrows of ancient warfare.
Sometimes the "arrow" carried a bulb filled with burning matter.
Sometimes the point was merely wrapped in burning tow.

[4] "Doubtless the reference [of 'God's utterance'] is not to
be limited to the very words of Scripture. . . . But the evidence

So the soldier is to dress, and to stand, and to handle shield and sword against the world-rulers of this darkness and their leader. Meanwhile he is enabled, and he is commanded, to keep in ceaseless communication with his own blessed Commander—a communication which no siege can interrupt; the "heliography," the "wireless telegraphy," of heaven:

Ver. 18. By means of all prayer,[1] and petition, using every variety of worshipping approach to God (προσευχή)

of Scripture itself, as it indicates historically the principles and practice of the Lord and the Apostles in regard of the Written Word, is altogether in favour of interpreting the phrase here, as to its main and permanent meaning, of the believing use, in spiritual conflict, of the Scriptures; the Written Word, revealing the Living Word. It is true that when this Epistle was written the Spirit, whose work in producing Scripture was still in progress, was also speaking direct to the Church in other modes. . . . But that this was a great *passing* phase in the Church's experience is indicated by 1 Cor. xiii. 8, and by the broad facts of history. . . . Above all observe that the Lord Himself, in His Temptation, the history of which should be compared carefully with this whole passage, uses exclusively verbal citations, written 'utterances,' from the Scriptures, as His sword; and this, immediately after His Baptism and the Descent of the *Holy Spirit*. . . . No suggestion could be more pregnant than this as to the abiding position of the Written Word under the Dispensation of the Spirit." (Note in the *Cambridge Bible*.)

[1] "So Christian was forced to put up his sword, and betake himself to another weapon, called All-prayer; so he cried, in my hearing, 'O Lord, I beseech Thee, deliver my soul.'" (*Pilgrim's Progress*.)

and of definite request from Him (δέησις), **praying on every occasion,** at each emerging crisis (καιρός) of need and trial, from greatest to least ; **in the Spirit,** in contact with the Lord and Inspirer of supplication "according to the will of God" (Rom. viii. 27); **and, to this very end, that** you may be "in the Spirit" indeed, **keeping wakeful** in the exercise of all, full, unstinted, **persistence and petition,** "praying and not fainting"; besetting the throne of grace as those who mean indeed "not to let Him go except He bless."

And here comes in the holy *collectivism* of the Gospel. These warriors, sore bestead, would have urgent needs of their own to pray over, as the hosts of evil would seek to isolate them and bear them down. But through prayer they were also to maintain touch and continuity not with their Lord only but with "their brethren which were in the world" (1 Pet. v. 9), and so to help both themselves, through the magnetic chain of remembered oneness in Christ, and them. Their "petitions" were to go up perseveringly—

Ver. 19. **Concerning all the saints,** in Asia, in Italy, in the new Christendom at large, **and** now, amongst others, (for the Apostle is himself insatiable of intercessory prayer,) **on behalf of me;** that **word,** matter and faculty in the deliverance of the message, **may be given me,** by the inspiring and enabling Lord, as shewn **in opening of** my mouth in freedom, παῤῥησία, *unreserved* proclamation of Christ, aye, even in the capital city of the world, to make known the Secret of the Gospel, the glory of its world-wide scope and its eternal issues, so long hidden, now Ver. 20. at length revealed[1]—that Gospel on behalf of which I am on embassy, as from sovereign Court and Power—in a chain, strange decoration for an envoy! Yes, pray on for me, for this gift of opportunity and speech, that in it, "in" the field, "in" the theme, of this blessed Secret, I may, as with a "new departure" of vigour and effect,[2] speak with freedom, even as it is my duty to express my tidings.

So the long passage of deepest and gravest truth comes home at last—to the writer himself; but all for the sake of his work, which is the work of his Lord. He signals to his fellow-soldiers among "the dark mountains" to cry for him to Heaven, that he in his turn may sound louder and further, from his post of duty and danger, the silver trumpet call of "the unsearchable riches of Christ."

---

[1] See the previous occurrences of the word μυστήριον in this Epistle: i. 9; iii. 3, 4, 9; v. 32.

[2] Observe the aorist, παῤῥησιάσωμαι.

SALUTATION : BENEDICTION

'Εὰν εἰρήνη ᾖ, καὶ ἀγάπη ἔσται· ἐὰν ἀγάπη, καὶ εἰρήνη ἔσται.

CHRYSOSTOM, on ver. 23.

QUI veut connoître s'il aime vraiment Jésus-Christ *d'un amour pur*, qu'il examine, 1. s'il estime ce que Jésus-Christ estime, les biens immortels et incorruptibles, et si en le servant il ne cherche point les biens périssables; 2. s'il haït ce que Jésus-Christ haït, la corruption de son propre cœur, et l'injustice du peché. *Amen.* Qu'il soit ainsi, Seigneur Jésus ; mais aimez-moy, afin que je Vous aime, et que Vôtre grâce produise en moy l'amour qu'elle veut couronner.

QUESNEL, on ver. 24.

CHAPTER XVIII

SALUTATION : BENEDICTION

EPHESIANS vi. 21-24

NOTHING now remains but the last
messages of greeting and blessing.   He
has to commend to the disciples a faithful friend,
as his messenger and representative.   He has to
invoke all spiritual good upon the Asians, and
upon all true lovers of the Lord.

There is thus no great peroration to crown
our wonderful Epistle, such, for example, as that
glowing close of the Epistle to the Romans where
the Apostle seems to be stirred by the review
of his own sublime message into a rhapsody of
adoring blessing to the Only Wise.   That forms
indeed a beautiful conclusion to an apostolic
Letter of the first order.   But so also does this.
Nothing is more like the Gospel, as we have
observed so often in this exposition, than its
benignant power of coming down with all its

335

wealth of eternal truths to the common ground
of human life, to walk in peace and blessing
amidst the affections and the connexions which
it not only does not disturb but glorifies. So
here, from the truths of the Eternal Purpose, and
the Great Salvation, and the Headship, and the
Celestial Bridal, and from the scene of conflict
and triumph where the saints, strong in God,
stand " with the dust of principalities and powers
beneath their feet," it is with a step perfectly
Christian that St Paul comes to a dear personal
name, and to a few messages of holy love.

Ver. 21. **But that you too, as well as my other friends,
may know the things about me, my position and surroundings, how I fare,**[1] **all shall be communicated to you by
Tychicus,**[2] **your countryman, our (ὁ) beloved brother and
faithful working helper**[3] **in the Lord,** in our common union

---

[1] Lit. "what I am doing"; it is an idiom.—In the next clause
I paraphrase the active verb into the passive, etc., to keep the
order of the words.

[2] Cp. Acts xx. 4, Col. iv. 7, 2 Tim. iv. 12, Tit. iii. 12. He was
an Asian, and probably an Ephesian. Evidently he was a man
who won the Apostle's highest confidence, and kept it to the
last.—Lightfoot (on Col. iv. 7, and in the Introduction to his
Philippians) shews that the name Tychicus, though not common,
does occur in Asian inscriptions.—Observe that this is the one
personal name (besides his own, and of course the Lord's)
mentioned by St Paul in this Epistle.

[3] I attempt to convey the full meaning of διάκονος, with its ideas
of activity and subordination, by the words "working helper."

Ver. 22. with Him ; whom I am sending[1] to you for this precise purpose, that of informing you at first hand ; that you may know our circumstances, " the things surrounding " us, the Christian circle at Rome, and that he may encourage your hearts, by thus putting you and us into fresh spiritual contact ; telling you how " the same afflictions are being carried to their goal " (1 Pet. v. 9) in your brethren in the great City. For what " encouragement " goes deeper and leads higher than such news of grace, carried from heart to heart, from Church to Church ?

And now, the sweet, glad benedictions remain to be spoken.

Ver. 23. Peace, the Lord's full gift, the peace of His reconciliation (Rom. v. 1), amply enjoyed, and the peace of His inward calm, filling the soul, and the peace of mutual accord, blending all souls together, be to the brethren, as the Holy Spirit brings them ever closer to " the Lord of Peace Himself," and so to each other in Him ; and love, the divine gift in all its aspects, poured from the very Being of Him who is Love ; more consciousness of His eternal love to them, more fulness of responding love to Him, more joy in one another's holy

---

It seems unlikely that the word here is an official title ; Tychicus was too considerable a person, one would think, to be a διάκονος in that sense.

[1] Ἔπεμψα : an " epistolary aorist," giving the writer's thought as it will appear when the letter is received. Our idiom is otherwise.

happiness; with faith, which also "is the gift of God" (see above, ii. 8). For faith, direct reliance on the faithful Promiser, will at once safeguard the sense of love, guiding it along His sure line, in all its emotion and exercise, and also evermore keep it pure and warm, fed with ceaseless blessings reaped by faith. So may the precious gifts come ever "to the brethren," from God our Father, our Father in His Well-Beloved, and from our Lord Jesus Christ, One with Him, One with us; Giver, and Channel, and Gift at once.

That ever-blessed Name, in its sweet majesty, must sound yet once more before the pen is put aside. It is as if the Apostle, thus speaking of Him, with His Father, had a last fair vision opened to him of what He is as Centre of the circle of spiritual love, as Cause of the bliss of all who have found place in that circle, and are linked in love to Him who makes it what it is. The Epistle has been greatly occupied with kindred truths. We hardly need to recall again how Christ and His People in their living union have shone before us all along. But this last sentence shall speak yet again of that union, and in an aspect at once the simplest and the tenderest of all, from the believer's side. For this last moment, no "mystery" shall be mentioned; the one word shall be love. The happy Church is beheld as just the company of souls who, in the pure immortal sense of loving, LOVE HIM "who loved them and gave Himself for them." We have been told already, in previous passages, much indeed about the secrets that lie behind and above—the Purpose, the Grace, the quickening Power, the Sealing, the Presence. But here is the stream from those sacred recesses, running out glad and clear under the sunshine of salvation. Do these souls *love* the Lord Jesus Christ? Is He their joy and crown? Do they rejoice in His glory? Do they delight in His Name? Do they cherish His will? Do they look for His appearing? Is He to them indeed as Bridegroom to Bride, so that they would fain see Him "making haste upon the mountains of separation"? But above all, is He, this wonderful Being, in their life here and now, *dear* to them? Is He cherished, as the "Object of their first desire," so that His holy Presence sways their inmost man, "in incorruptibility," in the sense of all that is spiritual and divinely pure? Then there is nothing but benediction for those so related in love to such an Object.

Ver. 24. **Grace,** "*the* grace," ἡ χάρις, *His* grace, Himself in living action for their blessing, **be with all those who love our Lord Jesus Christ in incorruptibility. Amen.**

So let the Epistle and our Commentary close together, with that note, " most sweet, yet most profound," Love to Jesus Christ our Lord.

" Jesus loves me, and I love Jesus ; what more do I want?" So said a veteran student[1] of the religions of our race, rich with great treasures of human learning, richer with the grace of God, as he sank to rest, at Cannes, in April, 1899.

What more do we want? Nothing, O blessed Lord. For this means the possession of Thyself.

---

[1] Sir M. Monier Williams, Boden Professor of Sanskrit at Oxford.

NOTES

HANDFULS ON PURPOSE

Series I to X by JAMES SMITH
Series XI and XII by ROBERT LEE

A SERIES OF HELPFUL VOLUMES FOR
BIBLE STUDENTS AND BUSY WORKERS

Containing an Immense Fund of
ORIGINAL AND SUGGESTIVE MATTER
EXTENDED STUDIES IN VARIOUS BOOKS
BIBLE READINGS, GOSPEL OUTLINES
THOUGHTS, ILLUSTRATIONS, HINTS

Guide to the Series

I. Genesis: Matthew
II. Exodus: Matthew: Mark
III. Leviticus: Numbers: Mark: Luke
IV. Deuteronomy: Joshua: Judges: Luke
V. Ruth to 1 Kings: Luke
VI. 2 Kings to Esther: John
VII. Job: Psalms: John
VIII. Psalms: Proverbs: Canticles: Acts
IX. Isaiah to Daniel: Romans
X. Hosea to Malachi: Corinthians to Titus
XI. Philemon to Peter
XII. John's Epistle to Revelation
XIII. Complete Index to the Series

Demy Octavo, Cloth Bound, 7/- net per vol., 7/6 by post
The Complete Set of Thirteen Vols., carriage paid for £4 10/-

PICKERING & INGLIS LTD